For my understanding and supportive wife, Nancy Jean, my long-suffering Fourth Estate friends, Dave Jones, Mel Finch, Glenn Keever, John Raynor, and Ambrose Dudley, and for Raleigh Times associate, Ann Berry, who stood by at the birth of many of these columns.

Guy Munger, editor

Cover design by Dot Stell
Cover photo by Robert Willett

*Special thanks to The News and Observer
and The Raleigh Times production department*

Copyright 1989 by The News and Observer Publishing Co.
Library of Congress Catalog Number 89-085105

ISBN 0-935400-16-8

Also by A.C. Snow:

*A Dust of Snow*

*Snow Flurries*

# Comfort Me With Apples

A collection of columns

## by A.C. Snow

The News and Observer
The Raleigh Times

Raleigh, N.C.

*Stay me with flagons; comfort me with apples; for I am sick of love.*

— Song of Solomon.

# The Secret Life of A.C. Snow

I was going to tell you about A.C. Snow's hum-drum life: born on a Comanche reservation, kidnapped by renegades while in swaddling buckskin. At age 11, working as a longshoreman on the Lisbon docks, able to drive a barge spike through a deck timber with a bare fist and recite the "Odyssey" in the original dialect.

Sailing the seven seas on a guano freighter, boxing professionally under the name of Bonecrusher Risko and spending 14 inspiring months on a Tibetan mountaintop with Ms. Gina Lollobrigida, studying the Copernican theory.

Instead, I decided to stick with the truth.

Have you ever met a 60-year-old-plus sports department groupie? A.C., known to me as "Snowball," is one.

It started when over 25 years ago I recruited A.C. to help me cover an Atlantic Coast Conference basketball tournament in Reynolds Coliseum.

He'd been hanging around the sports department a lot and said he wanted to write some sports sometimes, figuring, I guess, if they get bored with James Joyce, J.D. Salinger and A.C. Snow, people could read sports writers — a sort of slumming.

The sports department viewed him as something of an interloper, a spear carrier trying to take over the opera or at best a square peg struggling to get into a round hole.

He didn't look like he had an athletic background. The heaviest thing he probably ever lifted was a collection of the essays of Ralph Waldo Emerson. If he ever took a P.E. elective in college, it must've been Advanced Horseshoes Pitching or Fundamentals of Winning at Marbles.

And, unbenownst then, he bled blue. As in Blu-u-ue POW-er. A University of North Carolina man from the roots of his unruly, cow-licked dark hair (now turned silver) to the flanges of his flat feet.

But A.C. did a good job in that ACC tournament. He wrote six stories on Carolina after the Tar Heels' game — and that was on a loss.

At that time, A.C. had not yet assumed his editor's position with The Raleigh Times and birthed his popular Sno' Foolin' column. But there was no mistaking his gifts.

He went on to greater heights than any sports writing ambitions would have likely taken him, becoming the envy of the boys in the "toy department" with his cornucopia of composition, sprung full bloom from his talent and imagination.

The longer he went, the more agile he became, his work sometimes as gentle as Juliet's kiss, as colorful as a rainbow, as strong as a bulldog's bite.

He stirred up people, he inspired people, he made people think and act, but mostly he made people feel good.

As editor, he had the ability to be the calm eye in the center of the constant office hurricane. The man had presence, a memory for faces and names, a common touch, and a heart as wide open as a mission door.

As a columnist, his writings about places and people brought you closer to reality and realism than any made-for-TV-documentary. He made you cry. He made you laugh.

We're doing this in the past tense, because this will be A.C.'s last book. He's going to hang it up pretty soon. But quit writing? Not until life's great autumnal equinox. You can cash a check on that.

Nor will he stop loving his Tar Heels. You won't have to read about it in the paper to know when Carolina loses. No matter where he is, his jaw slightly prognathous, his impish, rubbery face in that hang-dog look, he will gaze reproachfully at heaven and mutter something only coherent to himself.

The old quote goes something like this: "For when The One Great Scorer comes to mark your name, He writes — not that you won or lost — but how you played the Game."

A.C. Snow has played his game to the best of his ample ability, even if it wasn't in sports writing. In fact, one year he even won first place in sports writing in the N.C. Press Association contest.

So dig in, enjoy these "100 best" columns he has collected. Some are wild enough to have come out of a Comanche reservation.

— BRUCE PHILLIPS

*(Bruce Phillips is former sports editor of The Raleigh Times and is now a sports columnist of The News and Observer.)*

# Contents

| | |
|---|---|
| 'Nobody Slept With Mama' | 10 |
| A Death in the Family | 12 |
| A Mother at the Vietnam Wall | 14 |
| A Pig, a Spider, a Ticking Clock | 16 |
| The Lunch Pail Guys | 18 |
| Of Bright Bulbs and Bad Beds | 20 |
| Mixing Religion With Firewood | 22 |
| Inheritance: a Rusty Lantern | 24 |
| Back to the Norman Sisters | 26 |
| With a Bang or a Whimper? | 28 |
| The Chicken of Depression | 30 |
| Stand Up, Speak Up, Shut Up! | 32 |
| 'Lie' and 'Lay' Upon a Mattress | 34 |
| Satisfying the Customers | 36 |
| Everybody's Famous for 15 Minutes | 38 |
| Pussy Willows, Plea Bargaining | 40 |
| Genies at the Golf Course | 42 |
| The Death of the Hired Man | 44 |
| Clean Chicken, Human Comedy | 46 |
| And They Call This a 'Sport' | 48 |
| A Pretty Girl Is Still a Melody | 50 |
| 'The Last Temptation' and Religion | 52 |
| By Their Garbage Ye Know Them | 54 |
| When the Heart Is a Lonely Hunter | 56 |
| Ethics and a Pound of Godiva | 58 |
| Alma Mater, Bones for Breakfast | 60 |
| Let the Boy Make Pudding | 62 |
| A Long Time Between Revivals | 64 |
| In the Innermost Self | 66 |
| Violence and Felicity's Egg | 68 |
| Plumber Had Water on His Knee | 70 |
| A Tear for the Boys in Teague | 72 |
| All the World's a Stage | 74 |
| Once Upon a Time, 30 Years Ago | 76 |
| The Death of a Lawn Mower | 78 |
| In Oregon, a Pound Cake Browning | 80 |
| Beach Better Than Rice Diet | 82 |

| | |
|---|---|
| *Now It's OK for Men to Cry* | *84* |
| *Succulent Sonkers and No PTA* | *86* |
| *Wandering Saints in the Snow* | *88* |
| *A Big 'Oklahoma Hello'* | *90* |
| *Small Towns and Savory Souffles* | *92* |
| *Same Rooster, Different Hen* | *94* |
| *The Last Plane to Rapture* | *96* |
| *A Truck Driver's 'Type A' Day* | *98* |
| *How Do I Love Thee? Let's Count* | *100* |
| *A Matter of Grace Under Pressure* | *102* |
| *Fathers Change Life's Fuses* | *104* |
| *'Place Garbage in Plastic Bags'* | *106* |
| *Proper Etiquette While Naked* | *108* |
| *Don't Poison the Peacock* | *110* |
| *Love, Baseball and Buckroe Beach* | *112* |
| *They Do Come Home Again* | *114* |
| *'Do You Serve Colored Here?'* | *116* |
| *A Stud Somewhere in Chicago* | *118* |
| *Behind the State-UNC Rivalry* | *120* |
| *Go With Them Through the Dark* | *122* |
| *Tough for a '10' in January* | *124* |
| *Salmon Thursday, Quayle Friday* | *126* |
| *'Humpty Dumpty Was Pushed!'* | *128* |
| *Talking Frogs, Freeze-Dried Freds* | *130* |
| *Blest Be the Tie That Bends* | *132* |
| *Returning to the Old Well* | *134* |
| *Heaven and the 'Splitting Headache'* | *136* |
| *Encounter With a 'Moveable Fuss'* | *138* |
| *'Togetherness' at the Birdfeeder* | *140* |
| *Not a Trip to the Sperm Bank* | *142* |
| *Never Say It With a Chain Saw* | *144* |
| *'No Males on the Hall!'* | *146* |
| *With Beans in Their Ears* | *148* |
| *'What Will We Get for Rhoda?'* | *150* |
| *Their Typos Live After Them* | *152* |
| *Hail the Prince in Tennis Shoes* | *154* |
| *Thou Shalt Not Chew Gum* | *156* |
| *Don't Bring a Hoe in the House* | *158* |
| *Sins of the Flesh — and Runts* | *160* |
| *Under 'C' for Contraceptives* | *162* |
| *Was It a Hand on His Thigh?* | *164* |
| *Maybe as Much as Magic Johnson* | *166* |
| *You Can Go Home Again* | *168* |
| *Is God Really a Tar Heel?* | *170* |

| | |
|---|---|
| *Read My Lips! Buy Hearing Aids* | *172* |
| *Beware the Ides of Spring Break* | *174* |
| *How Long Is a Little While?* | *176* |
| *Wedding Band in the Men's Room* | *178* |
| *Mama's in the Bathtub With Daddy* | *180* |
| *Passing Grade on Parenting* | *182* |
| *Burning Flags and Apple Pie* | *184* |
| *A Bird and Pee Wee Reese* | *186* |
| *Coach Woody Hayes' Funeral* | *188* |
| *Counting Robins and Sex at Sea* | *190* |
| *A Wedding at Ballard's Bridge* | *192* |
| *Prayer Before the Kick-Off* | *194* |
| *The Neighborhood Boy* | *196* |
| *Heartbreak and Hallelujah Time* | *198* |
| *About Death and Dancing* | *200* |
| *Lead On, O Kinky Turtle* | *202* |
| *Free Advice From an Attorney* | *204* |
| *A Time When the Lilac Dies* | *206* |
| *An Encounter With Miss Brill* | *208* |

# 'Nobody Slept With Mama'

It seems appropriate that I have just finished reading Bones McKinney's book "Bones" here at Father's Day. Bones writes about how things were when he was both preaching and coaching basketball at Wake Forest to support a wife and six children. He must have been a fantastic father.

The kids had a habit of coming to their parents' bedroom at night, climbing into their king-size bed to talk. Then they usually would fall asleep and Bones would have to tote them off to their own beds.

Once, before leaving on a recruiting trip, he held a family get-together and admonished the kids, "Now, Mama can't carry all six of you to bed every night, so *nobody* sleeps with Mama while I'm gone."

Bones returned to town on a plane that also carried some celebrity or other.

"There were about a thousand people at the airport, including Edna and all the kids. I got off the plane as quickly as I could to avoid the crowd. Here comes Kenneth running up to me, shouting, 'Daddy! Daddy! nobody slept with Mama while you were gone!'"

A year or so ago, a mother we know was going through a very traumatic time over her children.

She and her husband had been going to a therapist, trying to learn how to best deal with the seemingly myriad problems.

"You know what he told us?" she said, incredulously, almost tearfully, "He said all parents must face the reality that they must look after their children until they are at least 30 years old. I don't know if I can hold out that long."

Her lament echoes columnist Richard Cohen's recent comment: "You buy a house and sell it. You buy a car and sell it. For many people, a child is the first thing — the only thing — you cannot sell, exchange, walk away from or divorce. A child is forever."

Neither of my children will be with me on Dad's Day. But both gave me unique gifts. One is not bringing my granddog for a visit. The other is not going to Greece.

The younger called from London the day before she and two Raleigh friends, Kate Brown and Ellen De Rosset, set out to backpack across Europe for three weeks. To my wife's great relief, she said they had decided not to go to Greece after all.

Now I do not mind her going to Greece. But if she goes to Greece, I have to put up with a wife who walks the floor all night. To her, going to Greece is like sailing alone down the River Styx never to be heard from again.

Greece is not the problem really. It's Italy. The girls had planned to EurRail down to Brindisi where they would catch a boat to Greece.

Everywhere we go, our well-traveled friends have warned over and over, "Oh, surely you aren't letting that child go to Greece from Italy."

The alternative is to do like Hannibal, cross the Alps on elephants, which does not appeal to my daughter and her friends.

My wife has been down on Italy since her visit to Venice where a purse snatcher made off with her friend's handbag, money and passport. Other friends have recounted similar or worse experiences, but none worse than what happens every day in New York.

Even the congenial woman who helps us with wedding gifts at Hudson-Belk's and who has lived in Europe warned my wife that "Southern Italy is very bad. There are many thieves who would steal your daughter's moneybelt. And never, never let her go to Brindisi where the men are very bad to pinch the young girls."

"Tunisia is a lot worse than Italy for girl pinching," said a friend whose son and daughter visited Tunis three summers ago.

"A woman without a veil in Tunis is considered fair game for the men," he continued. "My son's being along didn't make much difference. The men would just walk up to him and say, 'Meester, how much you want for your seester?'

"But every girl should come home from Europe with an adventure — and maybe a pinch or two," he chuckled. "My daughter was pinched several times and proposed to twice. Weeks later, she received a letter from one guy who enclosed a picture of him sitting in the top of a tree. The letter ended with, 'If you do not wish to marry me, will you please find a friend who will.' "

With no granddog coming and my wife euphoric about the canceled trip to Greece, a rather nice Father's Day was shaping up for me.

But then Katherine called from Paris to say, "Since we're not going to Greece, we've decided to go to the Berlin Wall."

"Why she'll have to travel all the way across East Germany!" my wife wailed to a friend a few hours later..

"Oh, don't worry," said Cornelius. "The worst that can happen is that the Communists may stop the train and shoot a couple of passengers. But they never pick on college kids."

There goes Father's Day. At least I can report to my daughter that nobody slept with mama while she was gone. Mama never went to bed.

*June 15, 1989*

# A Death in the Family

She came to us almost 15 years ago, a black fluff of puppy, a baby's pacifier clamped tightly between her tiny white teeth and protruding idiotically from the recesses of the small face dominated by bright shoe-button eyes.

She was the last and littlest of the litter. And the Burlington breeder from whom we purchased her had allowed the dog to sleep with her and had introduced it to the pacifier as a panacea for loneliness when the rest of the litter was sold.

The children named her Amazing Grace. Why, I cannot remember. But she lived up to her name, maintaining a day-by-day grace through which she dispensed quantum quantities of love, asking only to be loved a little in return. Amazing? In many ways she was.

She was particularly intelligent, a Morehead Scholar of dogdom. Once, when visiting our neighbors the Greens, she ignored an order from Ed to "Lay down, Gracie!"

"You know better than that," his wife cautioned. "Tell her to lie down." He did, and the dog promptly complied. She was her mother's child.

She had no enemies, save the gray squirrels that infest our woodland and audaciously invade our lawn.

They delighted in teasing the dog, who would plummet pell-mell down the driveway in furious pursuit of the nearest tormentor. Without fail, the wily squirrel would make a sudden right or left turn without signaling, sending the poodle somersaulting down the hill, resembling a black hairpiece caught up in a sudden whirlwind.

While the squirrel chattered triumphantly from the safety of a tree, Gracie would pick herself up, dust off her dignity and march stiff-legged back to the house to be let in and applauded. She never caught a squirrel in all of her 14 years.

But even in her last days, almost blind, totally deaf, and in great pain, she would stand on the back step and bark at the squirrels she knew were out there somewhere.

And although she weighed only four pounds, no dog, regardless of size, that trespassed on her turf, failed to take flight once she barked her determination to defend her family at all cost.

She was no stranger to pain and misfortune. At age 2, a St. Bernard stepped on her foot and she wore a cast for three weeks, during which time she learned to go to the bathroom on three legs, a practice she clung to all her life.

She never spent the night in a kennel. She detested dog food, which had to be laced with selections from her master's table. She was particularly partial to broccoli, green beans and strawberry ice cream.

With all the human suffering around us, I feel a little guilty about lamenting the loss of an animal. But I write this as a kind of catharsis for me and all of you who have loved and lost a pet, be it a cat, a dog, or even a parakeet.

Personally, I can't understand how people can get emotionally involved with a bird or a goldfish. But they do. A friend told me recently that his neighbor went into deep depression over the death of her parakeet. He had not taken her seriously until the grieving woman's husband approached him at church and said, "Don't say anything to Dianne about her bird dying. She's taking it real hard."

As always, we get out of a relationship what we put into it, whether it's with person or beast. But I think in our case, and probably in most cases, a dog usually gives far, far more than it receives.

On a golden October day, we buried her beneath a big oak, on the wooded slope behind the house, where the children used to take her when they built their "forts."

My wife had wrapped her in a baby blanket appropriately stenciled, "Love knows no season."

With our daughters away at college, we and the Greens, those of us who loved her most, attended to the painful funeral arrangements. Ed Green came down and helped dig the grave. Actually, he did most of the work.

And as we hacked away at the drought-baked soil, cutting through the stubborn tree roots, I remembered something reporter Treva Jones had said to me a few days earlier.

She and her husband Bill were suffering through a similar task, burying their beloved beagle, Duchess. As Bill rested a moment from his labor, Treva smiled through her tears and said, "Honey, thank God she wasn't a St. Bernard."

After we had finished, Ruth Arden brought four red roses and placed them on the little grave that we had over-planted with wild ferns. Then, quietly bearing our common grief, we walked up the hill and went our separate ways and never looked back.

Remember E.B. White's marvelous story, "Charlotte's Web," in which the compassionate spider, in tribute to her friend Wilbur, wove into the fabric of her web the words "Some Pig!"

I am looking for such a spider that will spin a web for me over Gracie's grave, a web that will catch the morning sun, and shimmer across the shadows of the quiet nook where our friend sleeps. That web will read: "Some Dog!"

*November 1, 1986*

# A Mother at the Vietnam Wall

In the lovely spring afternoon, with Washington's cherry blossoms on the wane, my wife and I took the long walk along Constitution Avenue to the Vietnam Monument.

There is no other Washington landmark quite like this one. It has the trappings of the typical tourist attraction, with the swarming school children, the contingent of vacationing senior citizens. There are the clicking cameras and the posing against the wall.

Yet there is a strange sense of hushed reverence, almost an urge to whisper, as if the actual bodies of these young men and women are lying in state here under the bright blue sky and the warm sun and within the protecting aura of the nearby memorial to Lincoln, the Great Emancipator.

We walked along the somber black wall of polished marble with its roll of thousands who had died in what many consider America's most futile wasting of its young. We paused as a teary-eyed teenager stretched on tiptoe to touch a name near the top of the wall.

Her young friends, part of a touring school group, snapped her picture as she wept.

"Did you lose a relative in Vietnam?" I asked.

"Not really. Mom dated him in high school," she said, herself a celebrity of sorts in the symbolic presence of heroes who had not been celebrities in life but who had achieved it collectively in death.

Farther along the wall we encountered the real thing. A woman who looked to be in her late 60s, gray curls peeking from beneath an American Legion type hat, leaned against the wall, her face buried between her arms, her body shaking with sobs.

This was the mother's first visit to the Wall. It had been arranged by members of the Jewish War Veterans Post 791, some of whom accompanied her on the trip. "He had finished one tour of duty and he had volunteered for another," she said, as she turned from the wall. "He was such a good son." Her husband, she explained, was too ill to make the trip.

They had brought a scrapbook of clippings about the boy's life. Included was his last letter, in which he told about a friend being killed in battle.

"They sent his mother a telegram." he wrote. "I hope my mother never receives one of those."

Ah, the telegram, that little yellow messenger of death down through the wars. I think of Homer Macauley, the 14-year-old delivery boy in William Saroyan's "The Human Comedy."

Every time Homer has to deliver one of the dreaded telegrams, he dies a little because his own beloved brother, Marcus, is away at war.

One day Homer goes to his job to find Mr. Grogan, the old telegraph operator, slumped over his desk, dead of a heart attack. The Teletype is clacking out a telegram.

Homer reads it. It is addressed to Mrs. Kate Macauley and begins, "The Department of War regrets to inform you that your son Marcus..."

Homer's first angry reaction is "I don't know who to hate."

In our own family when a cousin my age was killed in the Battle of the Bulge in the waning days of World War II, my aunt never quite forgave the world or anyone in it.

My mother told me that for years when Aunt Savannah came to visit she never failed to remind her, accusingly, "You still have your baby son. I lost mine." The eternal "Why" was always there.

Later, Mr. Spangler, manager of the telegraph office, tries to console Homer by telling him that love is immortal, that his brother Marcus will still be there in Ithaca in spirit, in the town, in the people. Homer resists. No, that isn't enough, he says.

"I want to hear his voice. I want to hear him laughing. I want to have fights with him even — the way we used to. Now where will I find him? If I look everywhere I won't find him. The whole world is different now."

We walked down to the Lincoln Memorial. While my wife climbed the long flight of steps for a closer confrontation with history, I sat on the curb, thinking about the mother with her pitiful scrapbook. A scrapbook and memories, all that is left of a son.

As we left 15 minutes later, we saw the mother, supported on either side by men from the JWV post, walking slowly away from the wall, her head bowed, her eyes red from weeping.

On this Mother's Day eve, I see in this grieving mother at the wall all mothers who have loved and lost. Some have lost in far less sacrificial ways. It is a part of the alternating agony and ecstasy that all mothers reap from their children.

*May 7, 1988*

# A Pig, a Spider, a Ticking Clock

Summer had turned in her time card when, headed homeward from an out-of-town trip, we were driving along U.S. 70 near the Angus Barn. A couple of birds were winging their way across the highway. I heard the barely audible thump, hoping my wife, who was driving, had not.

"Oh, I hit the poor bird," she wailed in dismay.

"You couldn't help it," I comforted her. But her silence the rest of the way indicated that this tiny tragedy on a bright summer day preyed heavily on her mind.

I had forgotten the incident until, next morning as we headed out to church, my wife pointed to the car's grill where the feathered remains of the bird were impaled.

I removed the bird, distressed to discover it was a cardinal. Somehow, I had hoped it might be a sparrow. Sparrows seem so expendable.

"It's a mama cardinal," I called to my wife, as I carried the dead bird to the woods.

It was easy to imagine that the cardinal couple, celebrating some special occasion, had been headed not to the Angus Barn for some prime rib, but somewhere beyond to a tree with the last delicious wild berries of the season, or to some rich refuse pile where worms abound. And I imagine she was one of those non-liberated females who followed unquestioningly wherever the male led.

I hoped there were no little ones left at home for single parenting. Perhaps there weren't, it being so late in the season. Perhaps the couple had been enjoying the empty nest syndrome.

That end-of-summer experience came back to me this week when I noticed a mourning dove lying on the street near the house. There was something symbolic in the death of the bird of peace in a violent world.

That we in our family mark the deaths of birds, with perhaps the exception of sparrows, can be traced as much as anything to writer E.B. White's genius. He was a master at giving animals a personality, character, and, most important, a soul.

In "Charlotte's Web," White created a kind, compassionate and philosophical spider who kept prolonging the life of Wilbur, an otherwise ordinary pig destined to be slaughtered.

The caring Charlotte worked night after night, weaving into her web such laudatory messages as "Some Pig" and "Terrific" to impress Farmer Zuckerman. A farmer is not going to slaughter a famous pig, the beneficiary of miracles.

Since our children read "Charlotte's Web," nobody has killed a spider in our house. Spiders are escorted out on a piece of paper.

And when someone steps out on a dewy spring morning and beholds the intricate silver skein of a splendid spider web gleaming in the grass or from an eave, she inevitably calls, "Come see what Charlotte has done!"

In White's "Death of a Pig," we again explore the universality of death that transcends the bridge between human and animal life.

White has spent sleepless hours, nursing his ailing pig, once dousing it with castor oil, all the while realizing the pig is dying.

He is faced with the amateur farmer's frustration and embarrassment at not being able to raise a pig, a failure not taken lightly among his rural New England neighbors. More importantly, the pig's death imposes on him the realization that he cares deeply for the lovable creature:

"He came out of the house to die. When I went down, before going to bed, he lay stretched in the yard a few feet from the door. I knelt, saw that he was dead, and left him there: his face had a mild look, expressive neither of deep peace nor of deep suffering although I think he had suffered a good deal. I went back to the house and to bed, and cried internally — deep hemorrhagic tears..."

In "Charlotte's Web," E.B. White contrasts Wilbur's terror of his impending death and Charlotte's quiet, peaceful resignation to hers. Readers, juvenile or adult, cannot help but absorb the subtle sermon on the inevitability of death and the need to accept it.

Like many of us over 50, White brooded on the condition of the world, its coarseness and lack of sensitivity. Still, he was an optimist to the end.

In a letter to a friend a decade or so ago, he wrote, "Hope is the thing that is left to us, in a bad time. I shall get up Sunday morning and wind the clock, as a contribution to order and steadfastness."

His writing contributed greatly to that hope and steadfastness that keeps us all going. White taught us all, children and adults alike, that in order even to begin to comprehend the complexity of life and the mystery of death, we need to be sensitive to each other and to all living creatures about us.

We have a clock to wind at our house, too. As a back-seat passenger in a crowded car, I lugged it all the way from Canada in my lap many years ago.

Its steady tick-tock in the stillness of night has been a reassuring sound over the years. Now its ticking is a reminder of our loss. E.B. White died peacefully in his sleep this week at his farmhouse near the Maine shore.

Not to grieve, though. White would not have wanted that. He left us his great legacy, his books. They should be required texts for reading, for writing, and for living.

*October 5, 1985*

# The Lunch Pail Guys

Really, the only positive thing to come out of this year's Super Bowl was Giants coach Bill Parcells' comment about the "lunch pail guys."

The weather watchers, for days droning direly on and on about a "severe winter storm," had promised we would wake up on Super Bowl Sunday with three or four inches of snow on the ground.

Sunday dawned sunny and as warm as April with the birds holding choir practice in the magnolias. Having geared ourselves to a "snow-day" schedule, we indulged ourselves with a late sleep-in, leisurely breakfast and First Presbyterian Church on Channel 5.

Suddenly, somewhere between the infant baptism and "Lead On O King Eternal," Channel 5, without apology, explanation or a "Go to hell, Harry!" abruptly switched to a sports jock babbling on and on about the Super Bowl.

Incensed, I switched off the TV and marched to the typewriter where I vented my ire:

"When God comes, it had better be at halftime, or nobody will pay attention. Even then He will have to wait on "This Bud's for you" commercials.

"If there is sudden death overtime, even God can be put on hold.

"A voice on Judgment Day will say, 'We now interrupt Eternity in order to bring you 'The Path to the Super Bowl!' "

What Bill Parcells said was that he had a lunch-pail at quarterback and that you need some lunch-pail guys on a team if you expect to win.

Lunch-pail guys. Now there's a term for you. But you have to be younger than most people are today to grasp the work-ethic significance of it. Parcells was a lunch-pail guy growing up, working in construction — roofing houses.

"I used to carry the shingles up. And if anybody dropped anything off the scaffold, I was the guy who had to go down to get it."

In college, he worked at a meat packing plant. "I used to push those dead hogs along. The big thing was to count how many hogs you pushed through by the end of the day. I'd push 1,300."

I thought about Parcells and the lunch-pail guys when Raleigh awakened next morning to a half-inch of snow and ice. At breakfast my wife switched on the radio. The half-inch had stopped the world and everybody was getting off.

"Stay home!" the early-morning man pleaded, his voice cracking with crisis. "The Highway Patrol says don't drive unless it is a case of absolute emergency!"

My wife looked at me across the breakfast table, apprehension in her eyes.

"I have to go to work," I said. "The Highway Patrol doesn't pay my salary." I reminded her of Paragraph 1 on Page 8 of the company policy manual: "Absence from work due to weather conditions is an unauthorized absence."

"But you can stay home," I said. "They'll cancel classes at State. Besides, the kids won't show up."

"Oh, no," she said, "we have a motto out there, 'We never close.' And woe to the woman who doesn't show."

I crept cautiously down the hill into U.S. 70 and headed into town. Looking up and down the empty thoroughfare, I realized that not many people in town had a policy manual that read like ours. Even those hard-nosed, Yankee Rambos who sneer at the way the natives deal with snow were noticeably absent, emasculated by a half-inch of Southern snow.

I made it into the office without a slip or slide, to be greeted by Alton Thorpe at the security desk.

"Now don't you guys panic, and go up there and write a headline, ' Killer Storm Paralyzes Raleigh!' " he said, slapping his leg gleefully.

"We don't have to, the electronic media have beaten us to it," I replied, catching the elevator to the second floor.

I went over to the composing room to pull for revision an editorial we had written praising the accuracy of the folks at the weather bureau. Our fickle weather pattern had done it to them again.

In the composing room, Carl Campbell, a quiet, soft-spoken, pipe-smoking fellow, grinned knowingly when I told him how the world had put itself on hold outside because of half an inch of snow and ice.

Carl, who grew up a gallused farm-child in the Great Depression, is a lunch-pail fellow who carried his ham biscuit to school in a lunch-pail, perhaps lard-pail, came home in the afternoon and split a half-cord of wood before dark.

Lard-pail guys are an even tougher crew. Looking out the window at the thawing street, we agreed that what's left of the vanishing breed of lunch-pail people seems to be either playing football for the New York Giants or working for firms with policy manuals that read, "Absence from work due to weather conditions is an unauthorized absence."

*February 7, 1987*

# Of Bright Bulbs and Bad Beds

In a column I wrote from Atlantic Beach last August, I mentioned that the first thing I do when I check into a beach condo is check the wattage of the bulbs in the lamps.

A younger and somewhat more athletic friend, with an inclination to brag, later scoffed: "The first thing *I* check is the condition of the mattress."

I check light bulbs because I am a compulsive reader. And I have found that most condo owners are not. Otherwise they would not equip their lamps with 60-watt bulbs and place them around the room away from the couch, forcing you to move either the lamp or the couch for good reading.

While I check the light bulbs, my wife checks the contents of the kitchen. We usually dine out on vacation, but we enjoy breakfast, and occasionally lunch, with a view of the restless ocean.

You can't beat an early morning cup of coffee with the sea breeze caressing your face, and a view of the beach with the gulls — or girls — gliding past.

It takes no more than 30 seconds for my wife to determine if the condo owners appreciate perked coffee or if they are the kind to buy frozen waffles rather than make the tasty golden ones from scratch.

But back to beds. You don't have to be on your honeymoon to appreciate a good one. Who wants to doze fitfully all night on a sad, sagging mattress that is going to send you whimpering with pain to the orthopedic surgeon or chiropractor the moment you get home?

Speaking of mattresses, at a recent newspaper convention at Kiawah Island near Charleston, we encountered one of the most maligned mattresses since the infamous one in "The Princess and the Pea.".

At Kiawah, we were assigned a lovely one-bedroom villa. Nestled in lush seclusion in that paradise-like resort, we reveled in the quiet, the occasional visits by the doe and two fawns that grazed at our door. From our porch we watched flamingos fishing from the lagoon where an occasional alligator snoozed on the bank in the hot sun.

After checking in, I amused myself by reading the "Guest Book" the owners had left on the coffee table. A note on the cover solicited guests' impressions of Kiawah and the villa.

Most had responded with effusive praise of the climate, the closeness to nature, certain good restaurants in Charleston, the long, lovely bike trails. But over the villa's three-year life span, the guest book had been generously dotted with criticism of its only bed.

Several of the bed's earlier occupants identified themselves as honeymooners. Strangely enough, they were either too shy or too ecstaticto complain about its squeaking. The laments came primarily from other guests.

A fellow from Buffalo, N.Y., on June 1 had written, "Had a wonderful time. But *please* fix the bed!" A Tar Heel and his wife vacationing June 29 voiced the same concern: "Just having legal sex. Mr. Ditch was correct. The bed still needs fixing."

The most recent entry, by a Dr. Merrill Climo from Annandale, Va., consisted of rhymed rhetoric extolling the delights of the villa and the island. But it concluded with the familiar complaint:

*The only downside of our trip*
*(twas all too soon we'd learn),*
*was noisy creaking of the bed*
*at even the slightest turn.*
*It woke us up throughout the night,*
*at just the slightest toss.*
*And merely shifting pose or limb*
*insured a sleeping loss.*
*Recorded first in '83*
*(if Guest Book you have read)*
*'Twould seem to be the decent thing,*
*to fix the g.. d... bed!*

One of my favorite bed stories comes from friend John Jordan of Raleigh. John can match blue-blooded ancestors with anybody. But one of his favorite family characters was a great-uncle who used to go to Norfolk occasionally to visit and drink with an old friend in a hotel there.

On one occasion, Uncle Saint George Tucker Jordan drank too much, set the hotel's bed on fire and was arrested for drunk and disorderly and bed burning.

In court, the distinguished old gentleman told the judge, "Your honor, as to the first charge of drunk and disorderly, I plead guilty. But as to the second charge, I plead not guilty. The damn bed was on fire when I got in it."

I am not here to debate the comparative merits of a good light bulb versus a good bed. But at the rates charged these days, vacationers have a right to expect both — in whatever order of priority their lifestyle or mood of the moment dictates.

*August 24, 1988*

# Mixing Religion With Firewood

One of the things my 10-year-old nephew got for Christmas was a "Dirty Dunk," which, not as ominous as it sounds, is a laundry basket with a basketball goal through which you toss your dirty clothes. Three points for dirty jockey shorts from across the room, two for a pair of socks nearer the goal.

Here at the office I have a Dirty Dunk. It is the desk drawer into which I pitch odds and ends of notes, clippings and correspondence for future reference. Once or twice a year I purge the drawer. Today is throw-away time.

"Did you hug God today?" asks a Syracuse, N.Y., stranger in a letter postmarked Christmas Eve that included his address and home telephone number. There is no obligation to respond, since whom we hug is a private matter unless, like Gary Hart, we're running for president.

I am amazed at the things that rile folks. A retired colonel in Raleigh has sent me a copy of an irate letter he wrote to the Nabisco Company, taking the firm to task for running a picture of Jane Fonda on his box of shredded wheat.

"Surely you must be aware of her activities during the Vietnam conflict," he writes. "She proved to be one of the most anti-American individuals in our history. She has never shown any remorse, nor has she ever apologized for her actions....Anyone who served in the armed forces will find it unappetizing to have this before us at breakfast. I for one will certainly check your products from this day on!"

Poor guy. I can imagine how a retired colonel must feel about Jane Fonda, who opposed everything he holds sacred. It would be like the Rev. W.W. Finlator going into breakfast one morning and finding Jesse Helms leering from the back of his Fiber One box.

A letter sent before Christmas asks me to adopt a killer whale. "A gift for the person who has everything," the letter begins, suggesting that for a $20 tax deductible donation I will enjoy a framable parchment certificate complete with the whale's name and photo, all in the interests of further research on the lifestyle of Puget Sound's 77 killer whales.

Anybody with two children and a granddog doesn't need to make any additional emotional attachments, least of all to a killer whale.

In an essay I saved on word usage, columnist Jack Smith talks about his favorite words.

I never gave much thought to my favorite word. I kind of like Jack's favorite: serendipity, coined by Horace Walpole, who wrote a fairy tale about three princes adventuring abroad in search of one thing and finding another. Serendipity is the ability to discover an unexpected treasure while looking for something else.

Now that I think of it, I guess my favorite word might be one that a good and wise woman taught me many years ago.

From time to time when my spirits were low and my wallet empty, the mail would bring a letter from Grammie Robinson with a small check, and the brief note: "A little nepenthe for you."

Nepenthe is from the Greek, when the ancients used a poultice to induce forgetfulness of pain or sorrow. An unanticipated poultice of a $10 or $20 bill used to do that for me.

From the drawer comes a scrawled note from a nursing home resident I have never met. Out of her loneliness she writes from time to time.

"Why don't you answer me?" she storms. "You are not any better than I am. You're probably not even as good!"

Bravo for her spunky spirit. She is one of those who will not go gently into that good night.

I am a firewood person, so I cannot let go of a classic piece of writing by former Sen. Eugene McCarthy depicting his relationship with the fellow from whom he buys firewood.

The old-timer told McCarthy that one has to make careful choices in firewood. Woods, he said, are like women — "some give heat and some give light." And he recommended oak and hickory for warmth, locust and pine for sound and color and cherry and apple for odor.

McCarthy and his woodman went their separate ways when the latter one day left a printed card "advising me to have faith in the Lord and in my fellow men (including wood sellers) and advised me to keep smiling."

McCarthy's advice to his fireplace friends is apt: "Buy only oak, be careful of philosophical wood sellers and shun those who offer religion, especially with mixed wood."

The significance of all this? Nothing other than that the desk drawer reflects the paint pot of life into which every man and woman and child splash their own colors.

They include a Raleigh motorist who owns the bumper sticker that reads, "Who the hell cares who's on board?"

*January 16, 1988*

# Inheritance: a Rusty Lantern

I recently stopped in at an attorney's office to update my will. There's nothing quite like the business of "Being of sound mind, I do bequeath" to make you face up to the frightening fact that you are mortal.

But you have to watch those lawyers. They are tricky. Here Ted comes up with a question like, "Is there anything personal you want to leave to anyone?"

The first thing that flitted through my mind was a 50-year-old lantern rusting away in my basement furnace room. A lantern none of my heirs gives a hoot about.

My thoughts next drifted back across the years to a time when restaurateur Red Balentine used to run that buttermilk custard pie commercial on the radio.

In the commercial, Red would describe the scene: "Grandma, seeing that she had come near the end, called all the grandchildren together and, starting with the oldest, began distributing her worldly goods.

" 'Now, Johnny, you can have the piece of land along the highway. Margaret, you get the tract in the meadow. And Tom, the 40 acres of rich bottomland goes to you.'

"But when she finally come to Old Red, I said, 'Hold it, Grandma. You give the rest of the children all that land. That's not for me. All I want is the recipe for your buttermilk custard pie.' "

Red, now retired, was a smart man. He sold enough buttermilk custard pie in his time to pay for a whole farm. I ate my share before cholesterol counts came into vogue.

As people grow older, they have a bad habit of attaching undue importance to the trinkets that mean little or nothing to anyone but themselves.

A friend recently recalled the time his spinster aunt walked him through her house, pointing out what was to go to whom.

"And Buddy, " she said, "I want you to have the antique churn your grandmother used all those years to make butter. It's one of my favorite things."

"I didn't give a tinker's dam for that churn," my friend chuckled. "All I wanted to say was, 'But Aunt Joyce, who's gonna get your 300 shares of RJR stock?' "

Another Raleighite recalls the time he sat in on the reading of his father-in-law's will. An entire paragraph was devoted to the disposition of a debating medal he had won in 1911 as a student at Wake Forest College.

The will specifically stated the medal was to go to the oldest child who would display it prominently in her home. When she died, it was to pass on to the next oldest child and on down, from generation to generation.

"The man had been a very successful attorney. But this little medal was his most prized possession," my friend said. "It represented a major accomplishment at a time in his life when he had not known many triumphs."

Wills can be devastating documents, sometimes reaching from the grave to reward or punish.

I recently read about a Kentucky farmer who had died in 1840 and left his worldly possessions to his second wife.

But the will clearly stated that if the wife remarried, the inheritance would be taken from her and distributed among the farmer's 12 children. The old man wanted to deny the widow the pleasures of a second marriage.

The will also made sure that a free-loading half-brother vacated the premises immediately. It stated that Thomas "should take the young filly as his own property and get another home."

The young filly in this case was not the widow but a piece of horseflesh. It was clear that Thomas was not the kind of fellow who could be trusted alone with an attractive, grieving widow. He had to take his filly and go.

As for the lantern in my basement, it is a memento of my 14th year, the year my Dad died and my Mother sent me to work for an older brother on his new farm in the adjoining county. For me — confused, homesick and lazy — it was a summer to remember.

In many respects, it was the year I started being a man, the year I learned about hard work. And thanks to a couple of buxom girls on the next farm, it was the summer I began thinking that maybe there was more to girls than "sugar and spice and everything nice."

The old lantern calls me back to that summer, the long, lonely nights when it kept me company at the tobacco barn as I fired the wood furnaces that cured the golden leaf. In the dark night, deep in the woods, everything that moved was a bear or a wildcat, or worse.

This old artifact has no significance to anyone but me. I finally realize that you can't bequeath your nostalgia, even to those who need nostalgia and have little of their own.

So years from now, someone will come upon the old lantern at a yard sale and say, "Well, what in the world is that?"

"Just an old farm lantern," someone else will answer, not realizing that the rusty relic once cast a bright light for a boy of 14 as he stumbled along the dark path of his youth.

# Back to the Norman Sisters

Spring in the foothills was never lovelier than it is now. Against the backdrop of blue mountains and soft shades of a tenderly greening world, the dogwood gleams in white masses. There is an elixir in the air that makes you wonder what folks are doing in Paradise that is better than being mortally alive in April.

We all went up to the Lantern for Saturday morning breakfast of country ham and homemade biscuits.

As we were leaving, I learned that the chatter from an adjoining dining room belonged to the Dobson Democratic Women. Through an open door, I spotted one of the Norman sisters. My niece and I interrupted the proceedings long enough to say hello.

"Oh, my dears," she said. "It just so happens we're receiving this afternoon. You must come. We have fresh flowers and strawberries and cream."

I did not linger long with the Democratic women. I could not help thinking of the ironies of life. As a kid growing up here, the youngest son of only half a dozen Republicans in the county, I would never have been caught at or allowed in a Democratic women's group.

There is no malice, political or otherwise, in the Norman sisters. For you readers who have not met them, they are three elderly retired teachers, daughters of a prominent family of attorneys, and the remaining vestiges of the Old South charm and grace we Southerners dream about but seldom encounter.

My niece, Jo, and I called in the afternoon.,

"Oh, you must have some more sherry," one of the sisters insisted.

"Remember, I come from a family of tee-totalers," I teased as she insisted on refilling my glass.

"So do we," she confided. "We never touched it until many years ago when one of the deacons in the First Baptist Church made some blackberry wine and sent some around to us. And I said, 'Sisters, since the deacon made it do you *really* see any harm in drinking it?' They thought not. And we've been drinking it ever since."

Betty is the witty one. She told about the time her friend Martha was giving a reception honoring the new Episcopal bishop at Southern Pines. As Martha was dressing, she noticed that her gown was cut a bit low for the eyes of a bishop so she plucked a big, red camellia from a vase on the dressing table and pinned it to her dress to conceal her cleavage.

Descending the stairs, she extended her hand to the guest of honor and cooed, "Oh, bishop, do see what I have grown."

Noticing the bishop's bulging eyes, she glanced down to discover that, alas, she had lost the protecting camellia several steps further up the stairs.

My younger daughter Katherine has had a love affair with the Old South since childhood when she first read Margaret Mitchell's "Gone With the Wind."

She has corresponded with Olivia DeHavilland, the Melanie of the movie version of the classic. In the sixth grade, she wrote a surprisingly good sequel to the novel — Ashley hangs himself from one of the trees at Twelve Oaks and Rhett frankly does give a damn and comes back to Scarlett after all.

In the flyleaf of the book I gave her many years ago, I reminded her that the land she loves is mostly myth. But I want to bring her here to the Norman sisters, to let her know that the Old South may be dead but that grace, and charm and quality need not be.

Those qualities will endure wherever they are nurtured. They need not be regional. Nor supercilious nor pretentious.

After two hours of stimulating conversation — "Papa always told us to learn at least three new things every day, a line or two of poetry, a bit of geography or something wonderful about our friends and neighbors" — we finally left the Norman sisters.

I brought with me a jar of bread and butter pickles inscribed to my wife and daughters. I also brought the bittersweet reminder of a more gracious time and three delightful women, the likes of which I fear my children will never know and enjoy.

*April 28, 1988*

# With a Bang or a Whimper?

I never make New Year's resolutions because, like most people, I will break them before the month is out. If to mine own self I can't be true, how can I be but false to my fellow man? Nix on resolutions.

Every new year signifies a beginning and an ending. Whether 1988 ends with a bang or a whimper, as the poet said about how the world would end, depends pretty much on the cards fate deals us.

I encountered a beginning two days before Christmas Eve when a reporter came in out of the cold to tell me she had seen in the courthouse a young couple waiting to be married by the magistrate.

So what else is new? They do it all the time.

"But the bride was so pretty, and she had on a long white dress and wore a wedding veil," she said. "You don't see that every day at the courthouse."

She was right. Looking out at the cloudy, drizzly day, I thought of how long it had been since I covered a wedding. I decided to stretch my legs by strolling over to the courthouse, where I found the couple waiting patiently in the second floor magistrate's office.

A long white dress and netted veil does not a storybook wedding make, except perhaps in the hearts of the bride and groom. Not when the wedding party has to sit through several small claims cases, including one brought by a feed store against a woman who had bought $800.46 worth of seed and fertilizer and had paid only $25 on the account during the past 10 months.

Finally, the nervous young groom, a soldier on leave from Fort Monmouth, N.J., was asked to step forward. The magistrate, about as romantic as a parking meter, fired off a few curt questions.

"Y'all wait here. I'll be back in about 10 minutes," he said gruffly as he stalked from the courtroom.

I wished the about-to-be-newlyweds well, left the cheerless room and walked back into the chilly afternoon, wishing it would snow or that the clock on the mall would chime, anything to make the ceremony more memorable than vows repeated between legal hasslings over unpaid fertilizer bills.

Back I went to a newsroom that was almost empty because of the holidays. On such days it is usually better to ignore other people's ringing phones because in most cases you don't have the answers to the callers' questions.

After all, how could I tell a State fan with any authority that Dick Sheridan would or wouldn't go to the University of Georgia? Or reassure some frustrated cook by telling her that the apple pie recipe in the Food Section really does call for a half cup of water instead of one and one-half cups.

But when the phone for the Public Record department kept ringing I finally answered it, to silence its shrill as much as anything.

A young woman wanted to know if her divorce would appear that day in The Public Record. I told her the Public Record editor was out for the holidays.

"Could you please find out?" the caller persisted. "It is very, very important."

In a moment of holiday compassion, I acquiesced, promising to call back if I could track down the information.

An hour later, I reluctantly called to convey what I thought was the sad, depressing news that yes, the termination notice of what started out as a lifetime contract of happiness would be published in that day's paper.

"I can't thank you enough," the woman bubbled as I broke the news to her. "Merry Christmas to you!"

"You sound happy," I said, caught off guard by her euphoria.

"Happy? You've made my day. Bless you!" she said. It was as if the doors of a prison had swung wide. Perhaps, for her, they had. Now, back in circulation, she sounded alive, eager. For her, an ending *and* a beginning.

And on the eve of Christmas Eve, two Circulation Department employees came upstairs to share a letter that had come in the morning mail.

A quarter was taped below a message written on lined notebook paper. The signature was barely legible, as if signed under duress.

"Dear News and Observer," it read, "I stole a newspaper from the machine. I'm sorry so I'll give you 25 cents. You may ask how I got it. Well, I used a Chunkee Cheese token and got out the paper." The P.S. at the bottom read, "I'm really sorry."

Was this some youngster who on Christmas Eve truly felt that an omniscient Santa might shortchange him next morning?

I think not. I think he is the son of conscientious parents who sat the young man down forthwith and instructed him to write the letter of apology and pay the quarter out of his own allowance. A new beginning, a fresh slate that may change the boy's direction in life.

T.S. Eliot said the world would end not with a bang but a whimper. I suppose the same could be said of a year. For you I hope there is more bang than whimper in the year that dawns tomorrow.

*December 31, 1988*

# The Chicken of Depression

There is a "Far Side" cartoon taped to a wall in our sports department. It shows some poor guy sitting on the side of his bed, staring at the window where a droopy-looking chicken is perched.

The caption reads, "The Bluebird of Happiness long absent from his life, Ned is visited by the Chicken of Depression."

I thought of that cartoon one morning not long ago when I called my sister in the foothills. Normally a bright, optimistic sort with a strong religious faith that has transported her through one crisis after another, she sounded lower than a snake's belly.

"I am sitting here drinking coffee, feeling sorry for myself," she said. "And don't give me a lecture. I refuse to feel guilty for feeling sorry for myself once a year."

Age was the source of her discontent.

"You're not going to like getting old," Zetta warned me, the kid brother.

"But you are having a good time," I insisted. "You have friends, your church. You travel now and then."

"But I have been thinking about what it will be like when I can't drive and go places on my own and have to depend on my children. I'm telling you, there really isn't much fun to getting old."

"Well, I'd like to be able to give it a shot anyway," I said, laughing. "I'd like to at least live long enough to try it."

Age can be frightening indeed when you pass a certain milepost in your life. The secret is to pretend the number on the milepost is something it isn't. Everyone should trick his mind into believing the myth that he is at least 20 years younger than he actually is.

I have just read an article that says most of us live by myths. We rely on them to make ourselves more heroic than we are. When we come home from an encounter with the boss, we exaggerate our role: "And I told him in no uncertain terms that...."

Without realizing it, we walk around in roles far more romantic than the seemingly mundane ones life has thrust upon us. There is always a King Arthur standing beside you at the stoplight. You just don't know it.

The wife who brings you an aspirin and a glass of water when you have the flu is, in her subconscious, a combination of Florence Nightingale and Joan of Arc. You'd never guess that the bald-headed guy with the paunch and the six-pack of Bud next to you in the supermarket checkout is at heart Sylvester Stallone.

How could we live without the myth that our children can't possibly survive without us? Or, as is the case with editors, that what we write carries great weight among the masses?

A friend of mine imagines he is irresistible to women, knowing all the time he has about as much sex appeal as a cabbage. Another keeps bragging that he is going to have mirrors installed on his bedroom ceiling. Myths make life bearable.

I imagine my sister made the same mistake Snow White's wicked stepmother made. She walked by her mirror one morning and absent-mindedly asked it that same foolish question: "Mirror, mirror on the wall, who is the fairest of them all?"

And when the cruel mirror answered, "Two thirds of the women in Surry County," out flew the Bluebird of Happiness and in marched the Chicken of Depression.

Moral: After 50, don't talk to mirrors.

The Rev. Rick Brand, in a recent mini-sermon at our church, invited us to remember who and how we were 20 years ago. One of life's challenges, he said, is to live so you like yourself 20 years later a lot better than you do now.

He warned against letting the high standards, the morals and the dreams that sustained us in our youth burn out in later years. To illustrate his point, he told us about a certain dog.

The dog was hot on the trail of a deer, pursuing it with great speed and diligence — until the deer's trail crossed the trail of a fox.

Beginning to tire, the dog thought, "Oh well, the fox is slower" and turned to chase the fox. But then the fox's trail crossed the scent of a rabbit. The dog, pretty well exhausted, decided that after all, the rabbit was more his style and at least attainable, so he chased off after the rabbit.

When the dog's master, hearing the distant barking, finally found the dog, it had treed a trembling mouse.

I like the story. And it applies here. Most of us, when we are far along in the race and suddenly realize we have treed a mouse, tend to become depressed. But to keep from letting the Chicken of Depression roost permanently in our souls, we need to remind ourselves that at least we didn't set out on the trail of a mouse as some do.

And that it may not be too late to double back and pick up the track of the rabbit, the fox or, in rare cases, even the deer.

*June 4, 1988*

# Stand Up, Speak Up, Shut Up!

Over Saturday breakfast at Fat Daddy's with our friends the Rossers, the subject got around to making speeches.

My wife teaches speech at N.C. State. Lou teaches English there, and Tom is a lawyer. All are used to performing before an audience. None completely understands the trauma I undergo in making speeches. All had advice.

"Be well prepared," my wife said.

"Just concentrate on some individual in the audience," offered Lou.

"Take a tranquilizer before you go," advised Tom.

I liked Tom's advice best — quick, painless. But every time I take a lawyer's advice, I remember the story about the two guys who got lost in a hot air balloon. They floated down over a fellow mowing his lawn and yelled, "Where are we?"

"You're in a hot air balloon," the man yelled back.

"He must be a lawyer," one of the balloonists complained. "He told us the answer and it ain't worth a damn."

To me, brevity is the soul of any speech.

N.C. State University Dean Bill Toole recalls being invited several years ago to deliver a speech at a major educational function in Kansas. He agreed to deliver a half-hour lecture.

"Oh, no," his host insisted. "We'd like you to speak for at least an hour."

With misgivings, Bill went home and labored for hours over 60 minutes of wit and wisdom. To gauge its length and power, he asked his obliging wife, Katie, to sit for a dress rehearsal of the address.

At the hour's end, he said, "Well, honey, what do you think?"

"Oh, Bill," she said brightly, "They'll have tears in their eyes."

"Really?" responded the surprised but pleased dean. "I don't think it's really that moving."

"Oh, yes," she insisted. "There'll be tears. Tears of joy. When you finish they'll all be crying, 'Free! Free! Free at last!' "

My worst fear — besides the nightmare I once experienced of reaching inside my coat pocket for my speech and discovering I had left it at home on the kitchen table — is that I will bore my audience.

That should be a primary concern to any speaker.

"If necessary, I think I would strip naked to keep from boring my audience," an accomplished speaker once said to me.

"Now that would surely bore them to death," quipped his wife.

Along with brevity, a light lacing of levity can enhance any speech, even the most scholarly.

Last Sunday, my wife and daughter persuaded me to accompany them to the sunrise service on the Capitol grounds. On daylight saving, that meant getting up at 5 a.m.

The day was chilly and the sun did not rise "a ribbon at a time" as Emily Dickinson says it does. It sneaked up behind a heavy cloud cover.

As I staggered through the dawn across Capitol Square I remembered what a good, church-going friend said recently.

"God doesn't want to hear a thing I have to say before 8 o'clock," she said. I agree. One sunrise service is enough.

But the day was saved by an inspiring program, including a fine sermonette by the Rev. Vernon Tyson, who wisely used a couple of light anecdotes to convey his message of resurrection and hope.

He told of the domineering wife who for most their time together had made her husband's life about as miserable as it could be.

When the poor fellow finally died, she did what many wives with bad consciences do. She had a huge marker erected at the husband's grave. It was inscribed, "Rest in peace until I come."

I trace my lingering trauma with stage fright to an unnerving experience in the third grade.

As the best reader in my class, I was selected to read the Scriptures at the Boonville School assembly, a weekly gathering of the whole student body, grades 1-12.

When I walked on stage and looked out at the vast audience, my knees started doing the Charleston. The pages of the Bible shook like leaves in a March wind. My mouth turned dry. The words wouldn't come. But the tears did. I fled.

But experts say that stage fright is natural. And indeed, even ministers with years in the pulpit tell me they wake up with butterflies in their stomach on Sunday mornings.

God did not give many writers the tongues of angels. I have heard Robert Frost and Carl Sandburg read their priceless poetry and shuddered at the rape of it. Art Buchwald, who gets $10,000 for standing up and reading one of his pieces, should get a bonus for not reading what he writes.

So when you see one of us in a public forum plodding through our pieces, keep in mind the words of the man who had been tarred and feathered and now was being ridden out of town on a rail: "If it weren't for the honor of the thing, I'd just as soon walk."

*April 9, 1988*

# 'Lie' and 'Lay' Upon a Mattress

Before every holiday, the conversation among my buddies at work gets around to plans for observing the day of leisure.

When I take a holiday, I usually spurn the crowded highways and stay home, devoting my time to a list of accumulated chores around the house. Nonetheless, I can't help feeling envious of those who plan exotic outings to the beach or mountains.

But I am always thankful for my good friend Dave Jones who, when asked how he plans to make merry over the holiday, has the courage to reply cheerfully, "Oh, I plan to stay home and rearrange my sock drawer."

I thought about Dave when I spent a muggy Monday digging up a stopped-up storm drain, all the while longing to be inside re-arranging my sock drawer. While digging, I recalled how I spent my previous Labor Day holiday.

We had gone mattress hunting, seeking a replacement for the twin bed my daughter had kidnapped and lugged off to her college apartment.

The cost of mattresses and springs being what it is, one should shop around for price and quality. So we took all the newspaper ads as we went from store to store.

My wife was leaning toward a Beautyrest.

"The one in the downstairs bedroom is so very comfortable. I'd like one just like it for mother's room," she said, anticipating a visit from my mother-in-law.

So we went to a store and lay down on all the Beautyrests in sight. There is something rather ridiculous, if not obscene, about taking off your shoes and rolling around on a mattress with the general public milling about. But that's the way it has to be done.

"A little like The Three Bears, eh?" I said to the mattress salesman, trying to cover my embarrassment as we moved from the hard to the medium to the soft mattresses. Either he had his nose out of joint or had never read "The Three Bears." He only scowled.

At the second store, we were met by an effervescent, enthusiastic young salesman who could have sold ice-cubes to Eskimos. He gestured toward one of his top-of-the-line mattresses.

"Lay down on it and see how it feels."

I quickly glanced at my English teacher wife, knowing the salesman had tramped on her pet peeve. I hoped she had not heard. I should be so lucky.

"Young man," she said, "I want you to understand that I don't mean to be critical or school-teacherish. I just want to help you. If you are going to make your living selling mattresses, you need to get something straight once and for all. You invite people to 'lie' down, not 'lay' down.

"Oh, you'll have to excuse me," the fellow grinned. "I'm a Clemson graduate. We don't get into that stuff much down there."

I interrupted my wife's complex grammar lesson, offering the Clemson man that great golden "lie, lay" rule handed down to me years ago by my journalism prof.

"It's easy," I said. "Just remember that, in the present tense, only chickens and prostitutes 'lay.' "

At the third store, we became deeply involved with Stearns and Foster. On two occasions, at conventions in New York and Denver, the mattress in our room had been so comfortable my wife had flipped up the sheets to examine the label.

"The next time we buy a mattress," she had vowed, "It will be a Stearns and Foster."

Well, the Stearns and Foster fellow not only knew the difference between lie and lay. He also knew about coils!

Wouldn't you think that the more coils the better the mattress? It's not the number of coils that counts, it's the gauge of the wiring.

We mentioned the brand name of the mattress we had lain on last.

"I think it had 15-gauge coils," I said knowingly.

"Now that's a good mattress and I mean it," our new man said. "But a little too much coil. Consumer Report recommends that mattresses have no more than 12 3/4 gauge coils."

"How much does yours have?"

"Twelve and three-fourths," he said proudly.

To tell you which mattress we finally bought would be unfair as well as free advertising. But the mattress had not been in the house for over 30 minutes before my wife decided it was the wrong one.

"It's far too firm," she sighed, like the fair damsel in "The Princess and the Pea" who felt the offending pea even through a room-high stack of mattresses.

"Perhaps for you but not necessarily for your mother," I suggested.

Now, a year later, the mattress seems fine. It is not its firmness that my visiting mother-in-law says gives her insomnia, causing her to wander about the house at dawn drinking black coffee. It's the loud snoring of the 15-year-old poodle who insists on sleeping in the room with her.

But I am glad the mattress experience is behind me. I look forward to Thanksgiving holiday when I plan to do nothing more complex and emotional than re-arranging my sock drawer.

*September 6, 1986*

# Satisfying the Customers

When Parade Magazine not long ago listed the most dangerous jobs in today's working world, I was surprised that editors and reporters weren't ranked right up there with airline pilots, who came in first.

Can you believe it? Under the white-collar job column, editors and reporters ranked 35th — last! Just opposite loom operators, whose work was relegated to last place among the most dangerous blue-collar jobs.

Obviously, the editors of Parade have never worked as newspaper reporters or editors. And probably never went near a loom operator.

True, I could never survive the terrible tension of flying one of those huge 747s with 250 souls in my hands. On the other hand, how many pilots have had a call from an East Wake passenger yelling, "Mister! I'm gonna come out to your house and beat your a-- before supper!"

It's not every time that you can soothe the savage breast by merely informing the caller that, "You'll have to hurry, we're just sitting down to dessert." Some of our patrons are without a sense of humor.

The cross-burnings and fist-fights that testy editors occasionally encountered are now rarities. They've been replaced by tongue lashings, threats and unsigned obscene letters. And an occasional march on the newspaper.

Some of you may remember the late Charlie Craven, the N&O columnist whose chief delight was putting down debutantes and N.C. State fans.

In a column about an NCSU panty raid, Charlie noted that practically all the panties thrown from the girls' dorm to the howling wolves had been made from Pillsbury flour sacks.

Before the day was out, a couple hundred State males were outside the newspaper howling for Craven's scalp, while the wily writer was safely holed up next door at Rusty's Pool Hall and Saloon having a beer with Little Man and the other characters who lived in his column.

Aggressive reporting has always involved some risk. Hiding in the shrubbery to get the goods on Gary Hart and his girlfriend was kid's stuff compared to some of our early exploits.

At a meeting of the American Society of Newspaper Editors, Walter Cronkite, a newsman long before he was anchorman, reminisced over his early days on the now defunct Houston Post.

Walter reminded us that one of the marks of a good newsman used to be "picture stealing," which is absolutely a no-no now.

"I was quite brilliant at it," he chuckled. "We didn't mind break-ins at all. In fact, it wasn't exactly breaking in since people never locked their doors then.

"One of my greatest coups was getting the picture of a young lady who had died in a particularly scandalous manner. When I got to her place nobody was at home. I entered through a side door, found the picture on the piano and got it back to the press in good shape.

"It made a great front page picture. I think I was in line for a big raise — from $15 to $15.50 a week — until it was discovered I had entered the wrong house."

The public probably will never understand the role and mission of a good newspaper. I don't think, as some tough, trench-coat types like to gloat, that its sole purpose is to "Comfort the afflicted and afflict the comfortable," although it certainly should do some of that.

As for how a newspaper operates, British journalist Allen Brian years ago provided an amusing and partly apt description.

"It is much like a brothel — short, rushed bouts of really rather enjoyable activity interspersed with long, lazy stretches of gossipy boasting, flirtation, drinking, telephoning, strolling about the corridors, sitting on the corners of desks and planning to start everything tomorrow.

"Each of the inmates has a little speciality to please the customers. The highest paid ones perform only by appointment, the poorest take on everything and anybody.

"The editors are like madams — soothing, flattering, disciplining their naughty temperamental staff but rarely obliged to satisfy the clients personally between the printed sheets."

Whoa there! Most editors, and many reporters, have had to satisfy hundreds of angry customers between the printed sheets. The First Amendment that gives us the right to "raise less corn and more hell" also gives our readers the right to raise hell right back.

And readers around here have never been too timid to exercise that right. With vigor. Especially if, as lately, they wear — and see — Wolfpack red.

Parade Magazine ought to know better. They surely know that newspapering is one operation you can never put on automatic pilot, sit back, relax and count the clouds.

*February 3, 1989*

# Everybody's Famous for 15 Minutes

Anybody who has lived in Raleigh long knows about what is probably the oldest and best-known sewing machine repair shop in town — Archie Johnson and Sons on Lake Wheeler Road. The late Mr. Johnson Sr. used to buy a weekly newspaper ad introducing "My Son Sam."

When Sam Johnson introduced himself to me at a wedding reception Saturday at Meredith College, I felt as if I had met an old friend. "Oh a celebrity," I said, pumping his hand.

"Not me. My brother over there, he's the celebrity," Sam said, indicating a handsome, heavy-set fellow with gray hair who was chatting with friends across the room. "He's the guy who tackled the quarterback in the William and Mary-East Carolina game."

His comment rang a bell in my brain. "I'd sure like to meet him," I said. He motioned his brother over.

James Archie Johnson Jr., a former coach at East Carolina, was 62 years old on that golden autumn afternoon in 1977 when William and Mary and the ECU Pirates were battling it out in Greenville. James Archie, because of his former association with the university, had been issued a sideline pass.

So when, late in the game with the score tied, the William and Mary player came sailing down the sideline on his way to what seemed a certain and winning touchdown, James Archie was in an excellent position to make a game-saving tackle.

That's exactly what he did, hurling his hefty 6-foot, 2-inch frame at the unsuspecting ball carrier.

"I hit him at about the 10 and I think he rolled to about the four," recalled the genial James Archie, a retired educator now living in Virginia Beach.

"What did the poor guy say to you?" I asked.

"I don't remember him saying a word. I think he was kind of dazed and confused. He just got up trotted off the field. They gave him the touchdown, you know."

At the wedding reception, I kept thinking about James Archie even after I almost got into an argument with the groom's friends from Goldsboro who told me over the punch bowl what a fine boy Julia was getting and I told them right back over the cucumber sandwiches what a fine girl Keith was getting. By the time we reached the tiny but tasty ham biscuits, we had agreed this was a marriage that would last longer than most.

Andy Warhol once said, "Everybody is famous for 15 minutes."

Have you ever asked yourself what might be the most "famous 15 minutes" of your life, those moments for which you think you will be best remembered?

Edward VIII gave up the throne of England to marry Wallis Warfield Simpson, thereby assuring himself a place in history that he would not now occupy had he given the woman the gate and gone on to become just another dull, ordinary king.

No matter what else he accomplishes, Gary Hart will be best remembered for gambling away his chance for the presidency of the United States on an ill-timed encounter with a pretty girl named Donna.

Richard Nixon's brillance, endurance and whatever other sterling characteristics he may have possessed can never pierce the murk of Watergate. And Bathsheba would have been just any lonely soldier's wife were it not for the 15 or so erotic minutes King David beheld her naked in her bath.

There is of course a difference between what we perceive to be our own grandest 15 minutes and what others might think them to be.

Every time I put my own mental "This Is Your Life" videotape on fast forward, it always pauses at the scene in which as a first grader I am starring in the role of "Peter Rabbit" on the Boonville High stage before the whole school — grades 1 through 11.

I am in Mr. McGregor's garden, and right on script, am crawling through the barrel in which I am supposed to lose my little rabbit jacket. Somehow, the jacket becomes hooked on a nail and I cannot free myself, rolling around in the barrel on the stage before a howling audience that realizes they are watching a real-life drama, complete with panic and tears.

That little boy's humiliating moment left lifetime scars and ruined whatever hopes he might have had of ever being another John Barrymore or Robert Redford.

I asked Ann Berry, my associate here at the newspaper, what she though she would be remembered for.

"Oh, no question. I'm the only gal who got a master's degree in Pubic Affairs from N.C. State University," she laughed, referring to that dreadful commencement program misprint when she received her postgraduate degree in Public Affairs from State back in the early 1970s.

Everybody is famous for 15 minutes? That's probably true. Some, like my friend James Archie Johnson, performed on a wider stage, before a larger audience and had a better press than others among us who spin out our great moments in comparative obscurity. But in obscurity or bright lights, most of us have been heroic for 15 minutes, at least in the eyes of the ones who care for us most.

*June 6, 1987*

# Pussy Willows, Plea Bargaining

Nell Styron came breezing into the office on a cold, gray February day bearing three stems of pussy willows that she placed on my desk.

"Believe it or not, they'll bloom in a few days," she said, pointing to the fat buds that had pushed through the stems' tough bark.

"But plant 'em in a damp place. Willows crave water, you know," she said.

Her breath of spring is welcome in a month so dreary you feel you sometimes have to call the doctor to jump-start your heart. But its impact was lessened by an earlier visit from a friend a bit confused by our court system.

The Raleigh businessman still vividly recalls that April afternoon almost a year ago when he walked to the parking lot a couple of blocks from his office.

He had just unlocked his car when he was shoved onto the front seat by a young man who, sliding in beside him, snarled, "Gimme everything you got!" He felt the cold steel of a knife blade against his throat.

As the assailant poured out a torrent of obscenities, the businessman fished desperately for the wallet in his hip pocket.

A passerby, noticing what was happening, shouted, "Hey! Leave that man alone!" causing the robber to seize the wallet and run.

Later that evening, police, responding to a disorderly conduct call from a local beer tavern, arrested the man for armed robbery after finding my friend's wallet in his pocket.

My friend Paul went through the usual courthouse routine: the probable cause hearing, the conferences with the assistant district attorney, the postponements.

He was not called for the December trial for the April crime. And he learned only recently that the assailant had been convicted, not of armed robbery but "common law robbery."

"I guess I'm kinda dumb," he said to me. "I thought common law robbery was the kind of thing where a man takes his live-in's purse without asking. I never thought that being forced to hand over your wallet while feeling the cold steel of a knife blade against your Adam's apple could be classed as common law robbery. Perhaps if he had cut my throat, it might have been just plain old armed robbery. I don't know."

The prosecuting attorney explained to me that she agreed to a "common law" plea because the accused *preferred* that to armed robbery on his record.

Did you get that? Now a criminal can choose what he wants to be tried for, what he wants on his criminal record.

"All I was interested in was getting him the maximum time," she explained. And she got it — 10 years. No, she hadn't had time to confer with the victim about the reduced plea.

I tried to explain to my friend that plea bargaining is a very popular practice in our courts these days, no matter what the stakes are. I reminded him of what occurred recently in the case of Maxwell Avery Wright, the 16-year-old Hillsborough youth who last summer kidnapped Sharon Lynn Stewart from the UNC campus, stabbed her to death and stuffed her body in a construction site barrel in Guilford County.

The Orange County district attorney made a bargain with the young man shortly after his arrest: Take us to the body and we won't ask for the death penalty.

It was probably the right decision, if an unorthodox one. As the district attorney said, without the agreement, the victim's body might never have been located and, in the absence of witnesses who could identify Wright as the assailant, the murderer might never have been convicted.

In a recent Mary Tyler Moore re-run, the station's sports announcer has been fired for making a pass at the station manager's wife. Somehow, the station's listeners get the idea the man has died instead.

Lou reads a card from a listener vacationing in Florida. "Sorry to hear about old Ed," he wrote.

"See, Mere," says the cynical Lou. "We're born, we live, we die. That's it. And maybe a card from Disneyworld saying, 'Sorry to hear about old Ed.' "

Wrong, Lou. There's more to life than that, especially for the young.

That's why I cannot forget the testimony of the victim's roommate who was with her when the two were accosted by Wright not far from Franklin Street. The friend testified that Miss Stewart was crying as she was led away, handcuffed, into the night and to her death.

Very soon now, spring will come again in Chapel Hill. The sun will warm the students huddled on the steps behind South Building. In the evenings, the air will be sweet with the perfume of magnolia.

The dogwood, in bridal white, will announce the new season. A mockingbird will trill its confused arias among the shrubs beside ancient Gerard Hall.

Spring will come again to most of us, but I cannot forget that it will never come again to Sharon Lynn Stewart, nor to all the other innocents who have needlessly died at violent hands.

*February 15, 1986*

# Genies at the Golf Course

When she heard that five men who for years have enjoyed lunching together decided to risk a long weekend at the beach together, a co-worker called me aside and said, "Don't do it. Don't ruin a good thing."

"Especially," she added, "since you already told me that three of them are Republicans and the other one snores."

Admittedly, it was a gamble. But we got along famously. We didn't talk politics, and we each had a private bedroom.

It was golf that provided the only note of discord.

When we drove out for breakfast that first morning, we noticed in the parking lot a family of five dragging their fishing gear out of a van. I have never seen such sad, woebegone expressions. You would have thought they were headed for a funeral instead of fishing.

"I got down on my knees this morning and thanked God that I don't have to go fishing today," said Dave.

"And I got down on mine and thanked God I don't have to play golf," I said pointedly, since after breakfast I knew we had to drive our two golfers 24 miles just to chase a ball around. They rejected a course only a mile away because they wanted to play on a course with "character." Time was when people had character. Now it seems only golf courses do.

As Mel and I dropped off the two linkhounds, I warned them to beware of genies that tend to hang around golf courses.

They had not heard the sad story about the avid golfer who hit his ball into the woods off the 13th tee. Searching for the ball, he came face to face with a big fellow who looked about seven feet tall, wearing a turban. A shattered whiskey bottle lay at his feet.

"Hello," said the stranger, handing the golfer his ball. "I am a genie. Until your wayward ball set me free, I was locked within the bottle you see there for the past 100 years. In appreciation, I am prepared to grant you any three wishes your heart desires."

Ecstatic at his good fortune, the golfer didn't hesitate.

"Sir," he said, "I have the smallest house in Hayes Barton and I am embarrassed and intimidated by my neighbors' big homes. Could I have a larger house?"

"Granted. When you go home you will find on your lot a 16-room mansion, six and a half baths, with a $5,000 chandelier in the dining room, a wrap-around driveway and a fur-lined Jacuzzi. And now, your second wish?"

"Even though I am second vice president at the savings and loan, I am having a helluva time keeping up with the Joneses. I would like to live in a style that would include a swimming pool, a medium-size yacht, and condos at Hilton Head and Beech Mountain."

"At this moment, your bank account has been increased by $3 million. And your third wish?"

"My wife, waiting for me out there on the golf course, has had to put up with a lot during our marriage. She has rarely complained. But for years she has coveted a top-of-the-line BMW. Do you think it possible..."

"Of course it is," interrupted the genie. "She can have a BMW and an Acura as well. But before I grant your third wish, may I presume to make a most unusual request of you. As you know, having been confined in a small bottle for 100 years, I have desperately missed the companionship of women. Could you possibly find it in your heart to ask your dear wife to spend 15 minutes with me?"

Somewhat stunned, but overwhelmed by compassion and the prospect of his new life and riches, the golfer said he would put the proposal to his wife. The decision would be hers.

Top-of-the-line BMWs costing what they do these days, the genie was not surprised when he soon saw the woman making her way through the bushes. As she was leaving 15 minutes later, the genie, with a wicked twinkle in his eye, asked, "Say, how old is your husband anyway?"

"Forty-two this past September," said the golfer's wife. "Why do you ask?"

"Well, don't you think that 42 is a little old for a man to still believe in genies?"

Golfers are not the only people who still believe in genies. To some extent, we all do.

President-elect George Bush, facing a $2 trillion national debt, is desperately seeking genies. Children everywhere are dispatching wish lists to a grossly overweight, sloppily dressed genie at the North Pole.

And at this very moment, grown men and women are pushing frantically through the crowds at Crabtree and North Hills malls, signing incredible bargains with genies named Visa and Master Card.

Between now and Dec. 24, you are going to run into more genies in our shopping centers than you'll encounter in 100 years at a golf course.

But think. How many genies have you seen in January? Not one. By then they have all slipped quietly back into their bottles, while there is hell to pay at home. That's why so many men go golfing right after Christmas, looking for a course with character.

*December 3, 1988*

# The Death of the Hired Man

My friend Grady Cooper Jr. has a little black book with important telephone numbers that he sometimes shares with me. No, it is not the kind of little black book that most men have either owned or coveted since puberty.

When I was a kid, Harvey Belten, a hulking farm boy and the oldest living high school freshman, was always bragging about his "little black book" that supposedly contained names of girls who "put out." A thin volume back then.

Even the fainthearted among us who weren't quite sure what his girlfriends were "putting out" were intrigued.

Probably the most famous "little black book" I ever encountered belonged to a Raleigh detective in the late '50s.

The Wake sheriff had charged a well-known madam, affectionately known as Miss Louise, with keeping prostitutes on her farm south of Raleigh. I covered the trial in a justice of the peace's court at Fuquay.

Miss Louise testified that the two curvaceous creatures who accompanied her to court had come up from Atlanta only to help her "pick peaches," nothing more.

Pick peaches indeed! In May with the fruit barely the size of golf balls and as green as grass? And what about all those cars, day and night, streaming in and out of the dirt road leading to Miss Louise's?

The trial was marked by some of the most regal rhetoric I have ever heard. Defense attorney Bob Cotton eloquently compared the girls to Mary Magdalene. Let him who is without sin, etc.

Prosecuting attorney Bill Oliver fought fire with fire:

"Yes, these once were virtuous women . . . But don't let their eyelids drag you into eternity. . . . Don't let them fool you with false eyelids . . . Why, they look like Hollywood stars!"

Alas, you never hear such superb courtroom rhetoric these days.

For weeks preceding the trial, Raleigh was agog over the little black book the city detective had compiled in the investigation. Parked in the bushes, he copied the license number of every vehicle that had visited Miss Louise over several weeks. Some of those license numbers, we heard, belonged to some of Raleigh's most prominent movers and shakers.

I dogged the detective for days, pleading for a peek at the book. But to no avail. Its contents were never made public, much to the relief of many.

My friend's little black book contains no such sensuous secrets. It is full of bigger game, the names of responsible service people who, when called, will come fix the leaking sink, re-cane the ladder-back chair, put in an outside electrical outlet on Saturday or fetch a load of topsoil that is not all sand.

But, alas, he has no listings at all for a hired man.

Through my friend Charlotte Swart at N.C. State's School of Forestry, I have been able toemploy a healthy, husky young rural product from time to time. But the last time I called, even she could not help me.

"Sorry, A.C.," she said. "My boys have gone on to bigger and better things—tree removal. You can't afford them anymore."

A Simon Legree employer I am not. I usually find myself giving these strapping youths the easier jobs while I do the heavy work. This fall, I sacked and toted the leaves to the woods, while my student helper stood around with the blower. When an ex-paratrooper and I moved a pile of dirt, I did two wheelbarrow loads to his one.

The last N.C. State student I hired worked well enough, although he was somewhat uncommunicative. It was the day of the Carolina-Clemson game and after he'd been paid and was walking to his car, he turned and said, with apparent malice aforethought, "Oh, about the Carolina-Clemson game. I don't care who wins. I hate and despise 'em both!"

"And a pox on your house, too," I muttered at his retreating back.

It was while rereading Robert Frost's poem about the hired man who had come home to die that I finally realized with regret that the hired man has ceased to exist.

Farmers know of what I speak. And even city slickers realize that a man who will come help split wood, rake leaves, clean gutters or dig up dying shrubs is a pearl of great price.

I dream of a hired man like the one columnist James Kilpatrick once appreciated:

"Charlie could do anything. He could paint a house, frame a door, pour concrete, patch a roof. He could lay bricks, spread linoleum, run a wire, prune a tree. He could plow a garden, build a fence, ditch a road. . . . He could kill a hog, tend bees, set a trap, put poison in a groundhog hole."

But, like Frost's, Kilpatrick's hired man died. So have they all.

*January 17, 1988*

# Clean Chicken, Human Comedy

A vital part of most newspaper jobs is to read or at least scan other newspapers. Taking the pulse of other communities helps you to diagnose your own health professionally and personally check to see if you are still in touch with the little things that count in life.

I particularly like to scan the small-town journals. In those, you find what life is all about. You may not learn much about foreign policy or the whys of tragedies such as the fall of Jim Bakker from PTL's peaks, the head-on collision of Gary Hart's sex drive with his political drive, or the numbing loss of the 37 lives aboard the U.S.S. Stark.

But small-town papers are rich with little dramas of life that most of us observe but rarely record in print.

For example, you have heard of someone who would steal anything that isn't tied down. That literally was the case up in Brevard, according to Stella Trapp in her column in The Transylvania Times.

Stella reported as a matter of record that while Ruth Hunter Philbrick and her husband were vacationing in Florida somebody stole their compost pile.

Here at home, I recently walked across the street for a cup of coffee at Hardee's on the Mall. As I sat there with a friend, an attractive young girl carrying her breakfast tray and led by a handsome black seeing eye dog, paused near our table. The dog and mistress seemed confused.

My friend got up and directed the girl and her faithful animal to a nearby table. The dog dutifully crawled under the table and lay there quietly, occasionally searching the floor eagerly for crumbs.

A few moments later the girl and the dog got up to leave. Again, they paused, as if unsure of the exit. "The door is this way," I said, pointing her toward the Mall.

"Yes, I know," she said quietly. "I was just looking for the place to put the trash."

Oh, God, I thought. If only those careless teenagers who never pick up their rooms and who litter our streets and highways with trash from Manteo to Murphy could see this young girl patiently groping for the trash can, they might find new appreciation for their sighted lives and for a litter-free view of the world.

The recent concern over clean chicken reminds me of the anecdote Dr. Albert Edwards once told about the preacher who, invited to a parishioner's house for Sunday lunch, was delighted to discover the main course was fried chicken.

Like most preachers, he doted on fried chicken. Each time he emptied his plate, the farmer's wife urged more chicken on him.

Since the platter was still piled high with golden brown chicken as he prepared to leave the table, he said to the good woman, "Madam, your chicken is splendid. Without a doubt the best I've ever eaten. Since you have so much left over could I please take some home?"

"You certainly can," said the hostess, "For some unknown reason, our chickens are dying faster than I can cook them anyway."

With my own youngsters growing up, I miss the refreshing, always spontaneous thoughts of the very young, those curious, questioning innocents who find life one exciting adventure after another.

Mary Embrey of Raleigh was driving 5-year-old Melissa to kindergarten recently when the youngster asked from the back seat, "Mama, Why does God make black weirdos?"

Caught completely off guard and momentarily wondering if she had a budding racist on her hands, Mary almost panicked but quickly recovered.

"I suppose for the same reason God makes white weirdos. Why do you ask?"

"Oh, I was just thinking about that black weirdo spider Daddy found when he was cleaning out the garage yesterday."

My neighbor, returning from a ride across Raleigh's splendid springtime, cannot erase from her mind a tragic vignette glimpsed while riding along Blenheim Street.

A dove lay dead on the shoulder of the street, apparently a victim of a passing car. The grieving mate stood steadfastly by, dangerously close, its feathers ruffled from the wind of whizzing cars. The sight frozen in my neighbor's memory and clouding her day was the classic portrait of grief of someone or something forever separated by death from its life partner.

It's spring and somehow a candle fly has invaded the house. As my wife climbs on a chair and traps it against the windowpane with a paper towel, Ogden Nash's ode to the insect comes to mind.

*The insect serves some useful end,*
*But what it is I've never kenned.*
*I do not like the ones that buzz,*
*I do not know a soul who does;*
*And as for those that crawl and creep,*
*The more they die, the less I weep.*
*Yet such is ego, low and high,*
*They'd rather be themselves than I.*

Of such is the human comedy which, as all of us know, is half-tragedy.

*May 23, 1987*

# And They Call This a 'Sport'

Sometimes when I get cabin fever in my office, I move out into the newsroom to write. I suppose I am subconsciously seeking the lost sound of voices, listening for the long-ago comforting sound of clacking typewriters, shouting city editors and whining reporters.

What was once The Raleigh Times newsroom is now the two newspapers' sports department. In the afternoon before the sports scribes arrive, the phones ring incessantly.

We who are already here try to ignore them, because most of us speak a different language and are almost totally illiterate when it comes to fielding questions from sports fans.

But on the day before the Tyson-Spinks fracas, after 19 persistent rings, I finally answered the phone, partly out of curiosity about what possibly could be so urgent so early in the afternoon.

"Could you tell me...?" the man began when I lifted the receiver.

"Probably not. Sports won't be in until 3:30. But I'll try."

"I just gotta know where or how I can watch the fight tonight." His voice carried the same urgency as a fellow who, having vanquished several Bud Lights at the local bar, had gone to the john only to find the door locked from the inside.

"Mister," I said, after advising him to call back later when the sports guys would be in, "would you mind telling me why this fight means so much to you?"

He paused, then stammered out something about a "world-class fight" and it maybe making boxing history. He ended up sounding sheepish, if not embarrassed. He thanked me, and I thanked him.

At home that night my sister called from the foothills to say that her son-in-law Charlie and grandson Chuck had flown all the way to Atlantic City to see the fight in person. Why would they want to do that, she wanted to know.

I could understand her confusion over such a waste of effort, time and money. Poor soul. Sports, even football, do not exist for her.

Four years ago, when Ronald Reagan was running for re-election, a guy who identified himself as Richard Petty called her on the phone and asked her to vote for Mr. Reagan.

"Petty?" she said, thoughtfully, frantically scanning her memory screen. "Petty? Oh, are you the fellow who has just opened up the Amoco station over near Fairview Church?"

Muhammad Ali, the crown prince of boxing, has tried to justify the fight hysteria.

"People love to be amused, love to try to understand that which they can't understand," Ali told New York Times Columnist Ira Berkow. "They love to be mystified."

Mystified? What mystery is there to a fight in which a weary 31-year-old "old man" like Spinks goes out to do battle with a sleek, powerful fighting machine 10 years younger?

At least the David-Goliath bout had the potential for upset. This one does not. Spinks had nothing going for him, not even a slingshot and two small, smooth stones.

Not even God was on his side, except maybe in the merciful way the Almighty, if He paid any attention at all, let it end in the first 91 seconds.

You realize by now I am not a boxing fan. A long time ago, during World War II, my older brother came home on leave from the Marines and during a slight misunderstanding between us, cold-cocked me with a hard right.

At the impressionable age of 17, I then and there decided boxing was not my bag, and that I should make a living doing something a little less risky, like scuba diving or maybe writing.

Such a decision has had its economic drawbacks. In what profession besides boxing can you, at age 31, collect $15 million for sticking out your jaw to be crunched?

And Tyson? That prodigy of physical violence picked up $20 million for what turned out to be child's play. That comes out to $2.5 million a punch for the eight delivered. Even so, his poor wife felt robbed, lamenting on TV that the Tysons' share of the $70 million pot was mighty small potatoes.

Pardon me while I weep. The folks in South Raleigh, whose welfare and Social Security checks will be a little late because of the Fourth of July holiday, no doubt will sympathize with Mrs. Tyson.

Not to worry, dear. You'll get by somehow. There are always food stamps and double coupons at the Sav-A-Center.

One of the so-called celebrities attending promoter Donald Trump's big prefight bash tried to explain the public's inexplicable preoccupation with the fight by saying, "People love to watch someone get beat up. Boxing touches that violent spot we all have."

For some, boxing touches that spot in us that makes us want to puke — a sporting term for throwing up.

As a spectator sport, boxing, in my mind, ranks right up there with watching someone die in the state's gas chamber. I did that once, too. And upchucked afterward.

*July 2, 1988*

# A Pretty Girl Is Still a Melody

I have never gone in for judging beauty contests. I agreed to help select this year's Miss Coats because my friend Jan Anderson talked me into it.

One of the other judges had fallen and broken her knee-cap and I was Jan's "ram in the bush" so to speak. You remember how, when God decided that Abraham shouldn't sacrifice his son Isaac after all, He provided a substitute sacrifice — a ram caught in a nearby bush.

I became Jan's "ram" because she figured I owed her one. She has agreed to sing "How Great Thou Art" at my funeral. She is a woman who likes to collect her dues in advance.

When I expressed misgivings over my abilities as a pageant judge a friend remarked, "All you have to do is like girls."

But I kept thinking about John Ciardi's little poem:

*All day I have been thinking about girls.*
*All the girls I have really thought about,*
*my daughters excepted, are grandmothers now.*

But anyway, Jan thought I'd be good at the personal interviews, which were conducted at the home of Bill and Sybil Pope.

To get there, you leave the paved highway west of Coats and wind down a graveled road. Suddenly around the bend you come to the Pope place, a veritable Tara, with its columned mansion centered in a green expanse of freshly manicured acres.

There in the comfortable den, we put the questions to the nervous contestants.

"Who are the Hornets?" asked one of the judges, a woman from Charlotte.

The contestant squirmed uncomfortably before whispering apologetically, "I'm sorry, I don't know."

"Praise God," I muttered to myself, pleased that here was someone who admitted to being more in tune with Emily Dickinson's poetry than professional basketball.

When another contestant was asked what kind of man she wanted for a husband, she replied, "He'd have to be a gentleman."

Asked to define "gentleman," she struggled mightily. Not an easy question. Every woman has a different answer. But most will agree that a gentleman is not just someone who opens car doors for women when people are watching or sends flowers to the office on birthdays or anniversaries.

Feminist activists don't cotton to beauty pageants. They see them as chauvinistic exploitation of young women. The issue is debatable. But if they're really looking for that kind of crusade, they should tackle Playboy Magazine.

On a recent beach trip with the boys at the office we found a copy of the popular publication in our rented condo. It was the Big East basketball issue featuring eight lovely coeds, naked as jaybirds, from Big East colleges and universities.

Later at a party in Raleigh, I ran into a friend who once was an executive in Hugh Hefner's corporation.

"Those girls must get paid a mint for posing nude," I suggested.

"Not at all," he said. "Only a few hundred bucks . . . maybe as little as $400. Of course the centerfold girl gets more."

"That's all? They would do *that* for so little?"

"It's the exposure they're after," he said. "Posing for Playboy can lead to other things."

I can well imagine.

Consider this scenario. A few decades from now one of those Big Eastcoeds, a grandchild on her lap, is thumbing through her scrapbook of memories. She turns a page and there she is — centerfold Miss April of 1989, wearing only a smile and a hair ribbon.

"Look, dear," she is saying. "This is your Grannie back in 1989. Ah, those were the days, my love."

That will never happen with the coeds from Coats. Color me naive, if you like. But I believe there is a wholesomeness in that little community that Playboy cannot spoil.

Where else does the local preacher open a beauty pageant with prayer? Where else do you find young people still listing their heroes or heroines as Mom or Dad?

The pageant moved swiftly and sweetly. I scored swimsuit, talent and evening dress as conscientiously as possible, careful during the swimsuit category not to be influenced by howls and whistles of appreciation from the boys in the audience.

It was a very close contest. The final decision did not quite reflect my own rankings. After the crowning, I was torn between fleeing Coats to escape being tarred and feathered or lingering to congratulate the winner and comfort the runners-up.

Obviously it was no time to tell the girls that nobody lost. But years from now, they will pause in the midst of diapering a baby or closing a big deal in the executive suite. And they'll look back with sweet nostalgia on that warm night in April when they were young and beautiful and hopeful. And happier than they then realized.

*May 12, 1989*

# 'The Last Temptation' and Religion

In the foothills, the corn is green. Politics is coming to a bubble. The revival is in progress at Fairview Baptist Church and there is consternation in Paradise.

Petitions protesting the release of "The Last Temptation of Christ" have been passed out in the local churches. That's the film that portrays Jesus as the imperfect savior, a man torn by the doubts and desires of the ordinary mortal, including fantasizing about sex with a tattooed Mary Magdalene.

Foothill folks are so astounded and disgusted by mimeographed excerpts from the script that they discuss them almost in whispers. Free speech has gone too far. This is the cry of fire in the crowded theater.

I am not deaf to my kin's lamentations. The world could do without this movie. But when they argue that the film is not the work of the devil but also of "the liberals," they go too far.

"Liberals" is a fairly new word to them. It generally denotes some kind of four-headed creatures who live in or around Raleigh and other large cities.

They include those miscreants who are tearing the Baptist church asunder by entertaining thoughts that not every word in the Bible is pure, unblemished, literal fact.

I am among the latter, and yet had absolutely nothing to do with "The Last Temptation of Christ."

I tell them that my wife, who on that very day was back home in Raleigh teaching the Sunday school lesson on Moses, had encountered conflicting evidence in her research on the business of the Golden Calf the children of Israel built while Moses was on the mountain top receiving the Ten Commandments.

One source reported that the calf probably was made of wood, encrusted with gold.

"There just wasn't enough gold for a solid gold calf," I explained. "Not unless they stole it. Remember they had been in bondage all those years."

"Wrong!," respond my relatives. "After those terrible plagues, the Egyptians were so anxious to see the children of Israel go, they showered them with gold and trinkets."

Outnumbered and intimidated by a barrage of quotes from the Scriptures, I backed off and tried to ease the tension by telling them about an incident a friend once related to me.

His father had lived in Nashville, Tenn., where, at a downtown intersection, two Baptist churches stood opposite each other.

A motorist stopping at a service station at the same intersection asked about two Baptist churches being so near each other.

"Oh, they had a big argument and one church split off from the other. You know how the Baptists do that."

"What were they arguing over?

"Well, as I understand it, one faction believed that Pharaoh's daughter found Moses in the bulrushes. The other faction believed that Pharaoh's daughter *said* she found Moses in the bulrushes."

Stony silence greeted my little story, and the point I was trying to make was wasted on the desert air of firm conviction and unshakable faith in the inerrancy of the Scriptures.

To me, it is the basic teachings in the Good Book that count. Also, the language of the King James version is beautiful almost beyond belief. So why fight over minor variances in interpretation?

Rev. Michael Laidlaw, an inspiring young man who has been preaching at our church this summer, in a careless moment, recently strayed from the complex seminary definition of religion. He defined it as "one part fact, one part exaggeration and eight parts imagination."

And how many parts pure emotionalism?

One of my relatives rejoiced that two local youngsters, ages 6 and 8, had been "saved" during the revival.

"Saved from what?" I blurted, without thinking. How could a 6-year-old's conscience be so ridden by "sin" that he should go toddling down the center aisle to be saved?

I assured my kin that they could not possibly win their battle against "The Last Temptation" by signing petitions. The lust for bucks usually wins. A few days later the release of the film proved me right.

That evening, at dusk, I walked alone down a winding road where row upon row of corn as high as an elephant's eye marched on either side. I coveted the outward peace and the blessed silence of this place.

And, for a moment, I envied also the hard rock of my folks' faith, the cemented mind-set that ultimately triumphs over every worldly assault on their religion.

"The Last Temptation" will make a few million dollars and then rot in Hollywood's film library. The land and the faith of the people who live on it will long survive.

*August 20, 1988*

# By Their Garbage Ye Know Them

As soon as the Supreme Court ruled that it is not illegal to go through other people's garbage, I started for my neighbors' trash cans.

I should think that reading other people's garbage would be far more interesting and accurate than reading palms or tea leaves, even if sorting through old coffee grounds, lettuce leaves and used Bounty towels makes the undertaking a bit messy.

A justice who disagreed with the court's majority opinion aptly noted that someone's garbage can be very revealing. "A single bag of trash," he said, "testifies eloquently to the eating, reading and recreational habits of the person who produced it."

Indeed it does! By our garbage we are known. A trash can's contents might tell you which of your neighbors is on the pill or which one's children have driven her to Valium.

Discarded All-Bran cereal boxes can witness to one neighbor's digestive problem. Another's Lean Cuisine wrappers testify to an on-going battle against calories or cholesterol. From his garbage, you may learn that one neighbor drinks too much. Or that another is in trouble with Internal Revenue.

I know some of my neighbors very well. They are like family. But will I every really know what makes them tick until I peruse their garbage? Will its contents confirm what I think I know about their personalities and lifestyles? Or are there sinister secrets lurking there among the discarded cobs of Silver Queen or between the layers of Penthouse or Ladies Home Journal?

Before you go off half-cocked and start poking into other people's garbage, keep in mind the question of etiquette.

Does one ask his neighbor's permission to rummage through his trash? Or do you do it secretively while they are at the beach or at work?

And how do you explain yourself if you get caught?

"Oh, excuse me, Frank, my wife has misplaced her pound cake recipe, and I thought that maybe somehow it ended up in your garbage."

Still, I tend to frown upon forewarning. Advanced notice can't help but result in censored garbage. If there is anything duller than censored garbage, I can't think of it.

Furthermore, serving notice surely will make your neighbor feel self-conscious every time he totes out the garbage. On the way to the trash can, he cannot help asking himself, "Is there anything in this garbage that the Snows might disapprove of?"

At our house, what goes into the garbage is an ongoing controversy between me and my wife.

She never throws anything away. Without me, an interloper would know absolutely nothing about my household by reading our garbage. At least I help the browser a little by trashing things like 20-year-old tax forms, expired coupons for Pizza Hut specials and endless invitations to win a free Crockpot by attending a land sale at Lake Gaston.

Even so, I am the logical target every time my wife misplaces something. She automatically assumes I have transported the missing item to the trash can.

"Have you seen the invitation to Evelyn Scruggs' wedding?" There is indictment, arraignment and conviction in the tone of voice.

"I didn't know we were going to the Scruggs wedding. You know we have the Snow reunion that same weekend. And you know I'm in charge this year and you know I need to go up on Saturday to set up the tables, buy the drinks and reserve the ice."

"We can do all that Sunday morning if we leave early enough. I promise to get up at 6 a.m., and we can be in Yadkinville by half past nine. You've known the bride's family for 30 years. And, besides, I want to go."

I fished the wedding invitation from a shelf above the telephone. And we went to the wedding. We did it her way, and it worked.

Many years ago, when my friend Kidd "You'll Be Glad You Did" Brewer lived in the glass house atop the hill overlooking Crabtree Valley, he was repeatedly harassed by people dumping garbage on the winding road leading to his house.

One day, Kidd got down on his knees and sifted through the pile of trash until he came up with several letters, all addressed to a young couple who lived nearby.

Kidd, normally a likable soul, was hot as a hornet. He bagged the garbage, drove to the lane to the couple's house and rang their door bell.

When the young husband answered, Kidd said sweetly, "I believe this is yours," dumped the bag of reeking refuse on the living room carpet, turned and left.

The couple took Kidd to court. But after Kidd apologized, a sympathetic judge, Pretlow Winborne, dismissed the charge. But to many of us, that was Kidd Brewer's finest hour.

I lost my nerve as I approached my neighbor's trash can. But I did find lying on the ground a discarded flier from attorney Sam Johnson down the street urging us to buy brooms he was selling for the Lions Club.

Why had we not received one of the fliers? Was Sam in a funk with me over something? You never know about lawyers.

Lest my neighbors worry, let it be known that I would no more rummage through their garbage can than I would climb a tree outside their bedroom window at night. Why should I? I can get more trash than I want by flipping on the TV.

Also, let it be known that the Supreme Court only gave police permission to raid other people's garbage. The rest of us still go at our own risk.

*June 11, 1988*

# When the Heart Is a Lonely Hunter

In a mini-sermon last summer, Dr. Albert Edwards of First Presbyterian Church suggested that we sometime write down at the end of a day all the things we had learned during that day. He said we would be amazed by the length of the list.

"I have often wondered," he said, "how in the world the midshipmen at the Naval Academy get their hats back after throwing them into the air at graduation. Do they go around for an hour or more asking each other, 'Have you got my hat?'

"But then one day, a woman who has a son at the Academy answered my question. She said most of the hats are claimed as souvenirs by kids who are also after the coins the midshipmen traditionally slip under the hatband before heaving the hats into the air."

His comments stirred the reporter's inherent curiosity and craving for confirmation. I called the Naval Academy to see if this was fact or fiction.

"It's mostly true," said the fellow in the information office. "Except I haven't heard about the money.

"The hats are indeed discarded, since the graduates are issued new headgear with their new insignia of rank. And yes, a lot of kids claim them. But so do some of the graduates' relatives."

The minister's suggestion has not been lost on me. I have a new appreciation for the things I learn every day.

I have learned that when the postman brings, as he did last week, a window-envelope reading in big black type, "Pay to A.C. Snow, One Million Dollars," you don't buy a BMW or tell the boss where to get off. You throw it in the trash — unopened.

I have learned that a wood fire on the hearth can be effective psychotherapy, even though the cost of the wood isn't covered by Blue Cross. And I have learned that oak and hickory are the best of all woods for that purpose.

I remember a wonderful column by Eugene McCarthy, the former Minnesota senator, quoting the wisdom of the man from whom he had been buying wood for years.

The wood seller emphasized that you have to make choices among woods, which, he said, "are like women — some give heat and some give light." He recommended oak and hickory for warmth, locust and pine for sound and color, poplar for light, cherry and apple for odor.

The senator eventually lost his good woodman to religion. "As he became more religious, the quality of his wood declined," said McCarthy. "And the last wood bought from him smoldered in my fireplace. I read the card he had left. It encouraged me to have faith in the Lord and in my fellow men (including wood sellers) and advised me to 'Keep Smiling.' "

Since then, McCarthy has warned fellow Minnesotans to buy only oak and to be careful of philosophical wood sellers, shunning those who offered religion, especially with mixed wood.

And I have learned anew how cruel and painful are life's inequities, how hollow the phrase "all men are created equal." I experienced a new lesson in that while buying at McCrory's downtown the wind-up toys my children have expected in their Christmas stockings since they were 3 years old.

Waiting in line ahead of me at the checkout counter was a very old and wrinkled black man, tottering on a cane. He obviously was in near-terror at the prospect of paying for the two flashlight batteries he held in his hands.

In his other gnarled hand, he tightly grasped a small, old-fashioned snap pocket purse like the one my dad used to carry.

Caught up in the noisy, crowded chaos of Christmas, the old man's chin trembled with anxiety. My efforts to reassure and help only confused him further.

Finally he mustered the courage to approach the cashier, who took the batteries and quoted the price, something over a dollar. The man's long, bony fingers poked around in the tiny purse and came out with two wrinkled dollar bills. I saw that he had one left, and felt guilty that I had spent $2 each for wind-up toys for two college girls.

While most of my Christmases past have faded, memories of a few come alive every December. There was the year when members of my large family had finally scattered, each to his own destiny, and my mother and I were alone at home.

It had snowed all day, but the night was clear and fiercely cold. The stars sparkled like brilliant diamonds against the black velvet of night. The hard-crusted snow, filmed with ice, glowed like quicksilver. The loneliness was as penetrating as pain.

But across the frozen fields, along the winding road, gleamed the headlights of a car, slowly approaching. A favorite brother had dared the snow and ice to come from Winston-Salem to spend Christmas Eve with us, had come home to find what he, too, had missed — the glow of family, the warmth of belonging.

Within the wilderness of our secret selves, the heart is indeed a lonely hunter, ever reaching for something the mind does not know quite how to identify.

We do not have to be "Christian" to sense that intensified searching at this time of year. We only have to be human, and alive, and receptive. When we finally feel that mystic magic, in our hearts we throw our hats in the air.

Merry Christmas.

*December 20, 1986*

# Ethics and a Pound of Godiva

A Raleigh woman, grateful for the quality of an article one of our summer interns had written about her, had sent a box of Godiva chocolates to the newspaper. And as I walked through the newsroom late in the afternoon, I heard the Scene editor instructing the fledgling journalists in the basics of newsroom ethics.

"As you know, we're not allowed to accept gifts," Bob was explaining. "At least not gifts worth more than $10."

"The last time I checked, a pound of Godiva was about $20 bucks," I volunteered in passing. The trio discussed options.

"We could send it to an old ladies' home," one intern suggested.

"Or return it to the sender. But that might hurt her feelings."

"Or if we split it three ways, it would come under the $10 max," the Solomon of the interns proposed.

"Well, if we don't do something soon, the damn stuff's gonna melt in this heat," concluded the more practical and hungriest.

I don't know what happened to the Godiva. But I remembered this little scenario through these long hot days when once again ethics — from the pitcher's mound to the Oval Office — is taking quite a beating.

Minnesota Twins pitcher Joe Niekro was booted from Monday night's game with the California Angels for throwing balls that, as someone said, "danced like Baryshnikov."

When the suspicious ump marched to the mound and ordered Niekro to empty his pockets, out fell a tell-tale emery board.

Not guilty, wailed the pitcher, fearing he would be punished for doctoring the ball. He just likes to keep his nails nice for his pitching appearances.

On the six o'clock news, a prostitute admits on camera to having sex with more than 200 men since she discovered she has AIDS.

Big-time TV evangelists rip off destitute widows' welfare checks to gold-plate their toilets.

High government officials admit, without apology, to lying and deception and become national heroes in the minds of many Americans.

Against this background, quibbling about whether to accept a pound of chocolates from someone who liked what had been written about her seems silly, doesn't it?

It is not that our profession, like Caesar's wife, is above suspicion. It's just that because of the nature of its business, it must always try to be. It is a profession whose credibility can be damaged if not destroyed by favors or gifts from people whose activities are the public's business.

Reporters are taught to beware not just of "Greeks bearing gifts" but of any offers of gifts or favors that might influence how they write their stories or editorials. That wariness becomes a part of our conscience — sometimes to the extreme.

Former Mayor Jyles Coggins wandered into the office last week and unburdened himself of an accumulation of gripes — about me, my profession and some public servants whose names I won't reveal, to protect the innocent — and Mr. Coggins.

Always colorful, and as blunt as a rusty ax, the former mayor hasn't changed. For example, he said of one current public servant, "He is so dumb he can screw up a one-car funeral." Coming from a man who owns a cemetery, his analysis was not without credibility.

We spoke of many things: Raleigh's growth, politics, and the skyrocketing value of good land. His reference to the latter reminded me, a novice gardener, of my disastrous but expensive efforts to buy rich topsoil.

Without thinking, I asked, "Mr. Mayor, do you know where I can get some decent topsoil. I am tired of paying $70 for truck loads of sand and rock full of ragweed seed."

Now this is a question I ask wherever I go, even at church and parties. I am the Diogenes of dirt, ever looking for the honest topsoil merchant.

But when Mr. Coggins replied, "Why, you're welcome to get what you want over behind my cemetery," a five-alarm siren went off in my brain.

Now I don't think for a moment Mr. Coggins wanted anything out of me or the newspaper. He would have guffawed, if not sneered, at the suggestion that either his or my soul could be traded for a half-load of topsoil, especially from a cemetery. But there is no way I can accept dirt from Mr. Coggins' graveyard, even though I own a couple of spaces in it.

One night recently on my walk around the block, I passed a towering magnolia where two little boys, about 5 or 6, love to perch in the late afternoon, free of the bonds of earth and parents and little girls.

As the boys were descending the tree, I heard one say, "I have done something you wanted to do. Now you gotta do what I want to do."

Ah, a budding sense of justice and fair play. I wondered: Will it survive the many tough tests ahead? Will this boy also some day sneak a piece of emery board into his jeans pocket on the way to the pitcher's mound, or perhaps, in the bigger leagues, carry a cake to Khomeini? Or will he find Godiva chocolate too rich for his conscience?

A lot depends on the examples set by his parents, his teachers and his fellow countrymen - including his President.

*August 8, 1987*

# Alma Mater, Bones for Breakfast

Having sausage and eggs, "fresh-squoze" orange juice and Bones McKinney for breakfast isn't so bad. Especially if it is served up around 9 a.m. at the Carolina Inn on the campus of your alma mater on a sunny wintry day.

But if you go back to your alma mater — wherever it is — looking for what you left there, expect to be disappointed. It's no different from going back to the old homeplace where you grew up. I've done both, time and time again — with the same results.

At Chapel Hill for a North Carolina Press Association meeting, I persuaded the AP's Ambrose Dudley to walk with me across the old campus to my dorm.

"Whatta you wanna do that for?" he groused, but went. Ambrose is a son of the University of Kentucky, and he is suspicious of anything that looks baby blue. He doesn't really believe God is a Tar Heel.

Walking past the arboretum, he spotted some baby blue crocuses bravely blooming through a crust of snow.

"Now just look at that," he criticized. "Where else would you find a bunch of weird crocuses blooming in January except at Carolina?" Pushing on, I apologized for the crocuses' poor timing and reminded him that Chapel Hill will do almost anything for attention.

"Whatta you wanna go back to your old room for anyway?" Ambrose persisted.

"I don't know," I explained lamely. "I just like to go back and see who is occupying that same little bit of space that once was my whole world."

This time, I took the stairs two at a time as I did those decades ago — less vigorously, yes, but still two at a time. The strong odor of cooking greeted us. Someone was burning his french fries.

Walking down the hall toward my old room — 201 — I heard the sound of heavy breathing. As I walked past an open door, I saw a boy and a girl locked in a passionate kiss, their hands roving over each other's body like the arms of an aroused octopus. Higher education is higher than it was when I lived in Lewis.

I did not linger long. The door of 201 was locked. Outward investigation revealed that a girl named Katherine lived within. She obviously is a popular young lady, for many messages had been left on her door.

But you can go home again — in memory. Bones McKinney, preacher, ex-basketball coach and a North Carolina landmark, proved that the next morning as he led us on a laughter-filled frolic into yesteryear and the days when he coached the Wake Forest Demon Deacons.

He recalled what it was like playing at Reynolds Coliseum when

Everett Case was king of the mountain and State usually won.

"They just didn't lose in Raleigh," said Bones. "Most of the ACC referees lived in the basement of Reynolds and had a real affection for the Wolfpack."

One night the officiating was really bad and Bones was stomping and yelling and throwing towels along the sidelines. Finally, one of the officials raced over and snapped, "Shut up and sit down, Bones! You're just mad 'cause we're winning!"

As a Baptist preacher, Bones was one of the few people who ever managed to serve both God and sports — with equal enthusiasm. But it wasn't easy.

He not only coached basketball. On weekends, he motored out into the boondocks to preach the gospel from rural pulpits that paid $35 per sermon. When a coach had five kids, back before Nike shoe contracts for coaches were invented, you had to be innovative and versatile.

Bones did not lack for critics — at home or abroad. He remembers coming home one night after a basketball game and being asked by his 5-year-old, "Who won, Daddy?"

"They did," sighed Bones.

"Daddy, you ain't much of a coach, are you?" the boy said resignedly.

"Son, don't say 'ain't!'" Bones snapped.

And then there were the fans, always the fans, including the N.C. State follower who, seated near the players' bench, once yelled, "Bones, you're just stupid!"

"And you're drunk!" the frustrated coach yelled back.

"Yea, but I'll be sober tomorrow," retorted the Wolfpacker.

What worries me is whether our children will have any nostalgia to draw on when they are older. Life moves so swiftly now along its plastic path, there seems little that will endure as nostalgia.

Some time ago, Irving Howe in New York Magazine touched on that very thing, pointing out that today's young people are obsessed with reminiscing over their parents' and grandparents' reminiscences, having none of their own worth remembering.

"They aren't nostalgic for anything they themselves have experienced with either joy or anguish," Howe said. "They're nostalgic for the nostalgia of other people."

At least the nostalgia I found in my old dorm and in the stroll across the campus of the oldest state university was the stuff I had helped create, out of my own youth, out of my own longings and my own remembering.

*February 6, 1988*

# Let the Boy Make Pudding

It was late in the afternoon when the handsome red cardinal came to my neighbor's window feeder for his bedtime snack. The few remaining sunflower seeds were his nightcap, his bowl of cereal, his Breyer's butter pecan.

When the female alighted beside him, he paused in cracking a seed's tough shell. He cocked his head inquisitively, almost proffering her the broken seed in his beak. Changing his mind, he gulped down the morsel.

"You notice, he's suddenly getting the urge to play the perfect gentleman," my neighbor remarked cynically. She has a thing about male chauvinism. She remembers how all winter the male has chased the female from the feeder.

"Yeah, it's spring and he's making promises," I commented.

"What kind of promises?" Ruth Arden wondered.

"Probably, a respectable bungalow in a Chinese holly in North Raleigh. And to love and cherish. And to help raise the kids." I said.

"Raising the children should be enough in itself," I added, remembering a bird scientist's report that a baby robin can eat up to 14 yards of earthworms on its last day in the nest.

"And what do you suppose he gets in return for those promises?" I laughed, as the two cardinals flew off into the dusk.

"What men usually get in exchange for promises," my neighbor replied bitterly.

There is a tide in the affairs of men these days that seems to be going against them. Who can, with authority, account for the prevailing feeling that the male is on the defensive?

Like Southerners paying for social sins of their ancestors, today's males are paying for the sins of their fathers — cruel, insensitive sins visited upon women down through the centuries.

But some males are fighting back. In Tennessee, a fellow has sued the county school board for allowing a textbook that he feels offends the God-given concept of the roles of the male and the female.

In one of the Holt Basic Reading series, the first-grade story goes like this: "Pat has a big book. Pat reads the big book. Jim reads the big book. Pat reads to Jim. Jim cooks."

What offends the Tennessean is not that Jim, the boy, is around when he and the girl, Pat, cook raisin pudding, ham and tomato on toast. It is the fact that Jim cooks first.

That, according to the Tennessee fundamentalist, constitutes teaching secular humanism and confusing the God-intended role of the sexes.

While doing some spring cleaning recently, my wife came across a much-worn, dog-eared children's book that both my children read when they were toddlers and both still occasionally recite.

The story, also published by Holt, in 1966, is called "Daddy Is Home." It pictures two children, arms outstretched, racing toward the father who is just returning from work. The mother, smiling her approval, remains discreetly in the shadows.

The few pages of text read: "Daddy is home! Daddy is home! Look, Mother, Daddy's home. 'Hello, Daddy!' everyone says."

I remember still those afternoons when I would pull into the driveway, see a small face pressed against the windowpane, and hear, ere I entered the door, the happy cry, "Daddy's home! Daddy's home!" a common greeting in most households when kids are young.

Even now I sometimes return from out of town to be greeted by grown children's teasing call: "Look, Mother! Daddy's home!" And we have a good laugh about it.

I imagine this is the sort of thing that has happened in most homes. Daddy has long been the family hero, even though Mom worked just as hard at the office or in the classroom or at home. Good moms taught their youngsters to love and respect Dad, whether he deserved it or not.

I don't know if that has been the case with Mr. and Mrs. Cardinal. Perhaps not. Perhaps he is a stinker, merely out of instinct. But the female is greatly to blame for the male's elevated concept of himself and for much of his selfishness.

I have no problem with Jim's cooking first. If, as a kid, I had cooked first, or at all, my culinary repertoire would be more appealing than hard-boiled eggs and over-done rice.

But don't lay a guilt trip on all men for the way they are — or were. Were it not for the over-indulging women in their lives, they might have been and still could be better.

So, Dad, it's never too late. Teach your kids to say "Look, Children! Mama's home! Mama's home!" And let your Little League boy miss practice one day to stay home and make a raisin pudding.

*March 29, 1986*

# A Long Time Between Revivals

It was the first time I had been to a "revival" in so many decades I can't remember the last time. So, as I sat in the small rural church in the foothills with my sister, my mind raced back to my youth when the summer revival was as much a part of growing up as going barefoot on the first of May, swimming in the creek and doing hard, physical labor.

Back then, revival usually lasted a week and featured a preacher from some other church to give members a change of face and tone and temperament. Most were Bible-thumpers, preaching eternal hellfire to a congregation of farmers, their wives and youngsters.

It wasn't that we yearned so much for Heaven as it was that, when the preacher got steamed up, we so feared Hell.

Things have changed in my sister's church. They have replaced an older minister with one of youth and vigor. And Stewart Mauck, the visiting preacher from the nearby village of Siloam, was no over-the-hill Bible thumper.

He looked so boyish, I remarked to my sister that he and Lee Johnson, the regular pastor, both lean and tanned and dressed in their summer cords, looked more like a couple of tennis pros playing hooky from the country club than serious fishers of men.

To be perfectly candid, I did not expect much. I was pleasantly surprised.

He took his text from Matthew 19, the parable of the rich young man who asked how he could have eternal life and was told by Jesus to go and sell all he had and give to the poor.

He walked away sorrowfully for he could not make that sacrifice. The passage contains the familiar admonition that it is "easier for a camel to go through the eye of a needle than for a rich man to enter into the kingdom of God."

"Now I suppose you folks out there think I am going to preach against the rich man," the minister began.

We certainly did. I could see the congregation settling back comfortably in their pews. Few considered themselves rich enough to be the target of this particular sermon. As we all know, the most wonderful sermons are those aimed at the guy in the next pew or those sinners who didn't make it to church at all.

"One evening recently, I pulled up behind a car, a new Mercedes-Benz," the minister continued. "And I noticed that it bore one of those personalized license plates that read, '4REGO'— for our ego. And I thought of how we all have those particular things whose only purpose is to feed our egos."

He went on from there, noting that the rich man's money is only a symbol of the many material gods we put ahead of the one God: love for our homes, cars, boats, clothes. Putting these first is just as bad as the rich man putting his wealth first.

He spoke briefly and well to an audience transfixed. The sound of his voice was broken only by an occasional booming "Amen!" from a gentleman a few pews away from me.

When it came, the altar call was low key, but the voice carried a sense of urgency. It was a far cry from the fire and brimstone altar calls of my youth, with an Elmer Gantry type threatening, "Tomorrow may be too late and you will burn forever in Hell if you pass Him by one more time."

There was none of that here. We sang the familiar Baptist hymn of invitation:

*Oh, do not let the world depart,*
*And close thine eyes against the light,*
*Oh, sinner, harden not your heart,*
*Be saved, oh, tonight.*

I found myself inwardly pulling for the minister, much as I would for a UNC football team on the two yard line on fourth down, hoping he had scored, hoping that converts would flow down the aisle as they do at the Billy Graham crusades. Not one went. This is a small church and the field of sinners has been gleaned, over and over.

But I learned from my sister that there had been one conversion earlier in the week.

"We had prayed for it for years," she said, pointing out that the convert was almost 24. Not many sinners last that many summer revivals before answering the call. I had held out until I was 16.

"His mother shouted out with joy," my sister added.

"Why? Was he a rounder? A hell-raiser?" I asked.

"Absolutely not," my sister said, a little indignantly. "In fact, he's a very good boy; he just hadn't become a Christian."

After the service, we walked to the nearby recreation building for refreshments. A table was spread with an abundance of excellent food from country kitchens. I sampled chicken stew, piping hot, delicious, brought by my sister's friend Irene. I listened to the drone of conversation, detecting a closeness and sense of community not found in many large, city churches.

I went out into the starry, spring night, refreshed and relaxed. It had been a long time between revivals. Perhaps too long.

*May 31, 1986*

# In the Innermost Self

In each of us, there is a craving for some private part of our lives to be off-limits to others, whether it's our emotions, our money or our trivia.

Many years ago, I started a personal savings account at the old Branch Banking and Trust Company next door to the newspaper office.

From each paycheck, I squirreled away a few bucks for a rainy day. Over the years, the account grew to around $3,000. A couple of other husbands here at the office were doing the same thing.

These accounts were private affairs, because we then banked with bankbooks. Banks never sent statements on savings accounts. But one day, without advance notice to its depositors, the bank changed its policy and mailed statements — to our home addresses.

I came home to find my wife in high spirits. "The most wonderful thing has happened!" she said. "Did you know we had $3,000 at Branch Bank and Trust?"

I confessed to the secret account, feeling not only a sense of personal loss but also a sense of guilt, somewhat like I imagine a husband with a secret lover must feel when he has been found out.

Many of us who write transfer this same squirreling-away phenomenon to our work. We file away ideas and information in our heads until, through age or mental infirmity, the brain's storage capacity diminishes.

Then we store those little nuggets elsewhere, in my case in the right-hand drawer of my desk. They age there until the right occasion for their use arrives.

From time to time, usually in the spring, the drawer overflows and it is necessary to sort and destroy, with reluctance.

Here is an up-beat note from Ms. Dorene Palermo:

"People from New York City have a hard time accepting that anything outside the 'Big Apple' exists. To actually discover it not only exists but comes very close to being the "promised land' would scare them to death.

"My husband is a 'natural born' Northerner and I have lived here 15 years and love it more every day. I rue the time when business reasons cause me to have to move."

Bob Bryan of Raleigh, one of Gen. George Patton's soldiers during World War II, responds to a column that mentioned in passing my dislike for Patton, the "slapping" general.

"Patton wasn't liked generally by infantrymen," Bryan wrote. "On one occasion he was known to have stated to an entire division that he would prefer to see 25 infantry men killed than to see on e tank knocked out. Tactically, he was probably correct because the tank might save more than 25. But you can see how popular he was with such statements."

Bryan was in LeHavre, France, waiting to board a homeward-bound ship, when the word came that Patton had been killed in a traffic accident. "I saw one of the biggest celebrations I have ever seen, with men, some from his own division, dancing all over the place. I tend to believe Patton was a great armor general but should never have been allowed to command infantry."

A Midwesterner now happily settled in Cary writes, "Getting used to some Southern sayings took some doing. One that really threw us was 'I'll carry you there.' Others were 'crack the window' and 'mash the gas pedal.' "

Among the newspaper clippings is an anecdote from the late Sen. Sam Ervin about a man named Joshua on trial for bootlegging in mountainous Wilkes County.

"Are you the Joshua who made the sun stand still in Jericho?" wisecracked the judge.

"No, sir," the man replied, "I'm the Joshua who made the moonshine still in Wilkes County."

Here is an old column by Sam Ragan dealing with an intriguing matter, what librarians find in books returned to their libraries, especially the kind of bookmarks left in the volumes.

He remembers the strangest marker of all, one found in a book returned to Raleigh's Olivia Raney library: a fried egg.

The drawer is a potpourri of bits and pieces of others' lives and thoughts. The heart indeed is a lonely hunter. But at times it cries out to be heard, and its owner shares, to a limited degree, what is stored there. We are the fortunate heirs who sift and select and savor, and when possible, share with you.

Everyone has an "Off Limits" sign posted within. Oh, sure, he lets a few privileged people past the gate. But even they cannot plunder the most private preserve of the heart with immunity. If you are lucky enough to be let into the innermost vault of someone's emotional bank, take off your hobnailed boots and step softly, on tiptoe.

*March 8, 1986.*

# Violence and Felicity's Egg

Every year about this time I find myself wishing I had entered the bad Hemingway short-story writing contest out in California. But I never do.

I would like to win the first prize expense-paid trip to Florence, Italy, and sit at a table in the original Harry's Bar, where Ernest Hemingway often took himself and his characters for a drink. Also, writing badly in the Hemingway style can be a challenge as well as fun.

Los Angeles Times columnist Jack Smith was one of the seven judges chosen to pick the best bad Hemingway from the 30 finalists already culled from 2,600 entries. The judges were unanimous in their choice of the entry of Mark Silber, a New York ad executive.

In Silber's story, a man has come to Kilimanjaro with a woman to gather ideas for a series of haiku he is writing. He is on the mountain, dying of dysentery complicated by writer's block.

"Now he would never write the things he had saved to write until he learned to spell them. For instance, 'accommodation.' One c, two m's or the other way around. He wasn't sure. Or 'chrysanthemum.' On rugged Kilimanjaro there was not even a dictionary." "He could taste Death in the wind. He could hear it tiptoe around the camp site. He could see it climbing a tree, hiding in a garbage can, tripping over a root. Clumsy Death..."

So much for the Hemingway contest. But I suppose I must have been searching for a little bit of Hemingway, bad or good, a few weeks ago when I plowed through 45 manuscripts entered in this year's Raleigh Fine Arts Society short-story contest held in the Wake schools.

I found plenty of violence but little Hemingway, although I occasionally encountered sparks of creative talent. But in story after story, I kept stepping over dead bodies: stabbed, shot, hanged. I was surprised at the matter-of-factness of the violence that threaded through these young writers' manuscripts. So much gore, so little sensitivity.

Some of the plots read as if they came right off the TV screen. Others, I guessed, were the stuff of real life, domestic wars, deceit and deception by friends, disillusionment, a haunting fear of death by auto.

A few years ago, when my own high school daughter entered the contest, she came home complaining about the ground rules established by her teacher.

"She says that nobody can die or get murdered in our stories," Katherine complained. "I don't think that's fair."

Smart teacher, I thought. Now, instead of relying on a character's untimely death to carry her story, my daughter would have to concentrate on characterization, which in the long run is the strength of the short story.

Characterization requires detail, the tedious long-suffering devotion to detail missing from so many high school — and college and later — manuscripts.

I'll trade six bodies shot through or bayoneted or hanged from the hot-water pipes in the basement for one good, strong paragraph on how a man cries or what a toddler feels when for the first time his mother leaves him at the schoolhouse door.

Teachers are like miners of old, panning the classroom shallows day after day, ever hoping to catch a glint of gold amid the mud and gravel, a clear-cut, straightforward Hemingway line, a gentle touch of Frost perhaps, or the hint of a young, budding E.B. White.

All the murder and mayhem a writer can muster can't hold a candle to the clear, sweet prose of a White letter to a class of New England sixth-graders who had sent him their essays to read.

"To thank you and your teacher Mrs. Ellis, I am sending you what I think is one of the most beautiful and miraculous things in the world — an egg. I have a goose named Felicity and she lays about forty eggs every spring. It takes her almost three months to accomplish this. Each egg is a perfect thing. I am mailing you one of Felicity's eggs. The insides have been removed — blown out — so the egg should last forever.

"Thank you for sending me your essays about being somebody. I was pleased that so many of you felt the beauty and goodness of the world. If we feel that when we are young, then there is great hope for us when we grow older."

I'm not blaming today's young writers for reflecting the violent themes of the world in which they live. But there is no reason either to ignore altogether those miniature dramas that gave us Felicity's egg or the greater, personal confrontation with death on Hemingway's Kilimanjaro.

*April 5, 1986*

# Plumber Had Water on His Knee

Frustration, unlike fog, doesn't come in on little cat's feet. It comes in calamitous quantity, sometimes packaged in weeks instead of days.

My week began with another spat with my old nemesis — things mechanical. This time it was the coffee machine. I dropped 25 cents into the slot and punched "decaffeinated, extra light."

Nothing happened. I tried again, with a different quarter. Same results. Pretty soon the machine and I were engaged in name-calling and fisticuffs.

"It takes 30 cents. They raised the price yesterday," a fellow behind me said.

"Without a public hearing? Without anything being in the newspapers!" I cried.

I felt better when I arrived home to find the plumber there. A plumber who makes house calls underscores the wisdom of the poet who said a thing of beauty is a joy forever.

Any tradesman in the house making repairs is a thing of beauty. For the time is not far away when you will have to take your sink or your commode to the shop for repairs. Some of us can remember when doctors made house calls, too.

Our plumber is a nice fellow. We got him from the Coopers who got him from a friend of theirs. He even comes at night when necessary. Don't ask me for his name.

Spreading the names of good repairmen is a sure way to end up without one when they're needed. A friend once told me he'd sooner give out the telephone number of his mistress than share the identity of his trusted, available plumber.

I suppose my plumber's rates are as reasonable as most. But I was glad I was sitting down when he presented his bill. As I wrote the check I told him I wished I had studied plumbing instead of journalism.

He said he wished I had, too, so I would know how lucky I was to sit all day in a clean office playing around with words instead of getting down on my knees and unstopping dirty sinks. Or worse.

I felt bad about my wisecrack, especially since he had come straight from the doctor's office to fix our sink. When I had called him at home the night before, he wasn't sure he could come so soon. "I have water on my knee," he said.

"I have water all over the floor of the downstairs bathroom," I pleaded. He promised he'd be there the next afternoon, after he had seen his doctor.

"Don't fret," he said, as he accepted my check. "That's almost to the dollar what my doctor charged me today."

"I wish your doctor had charged you less. It would have been easier on me," I said

When I think of plumbers and doctors in the same breath I think of the delightful story about the plumber who was called to the doctor's house to remedy some plumbing crisis.

"Good lord, man!" gasped the physician, looking at the plumber's bill. "Why, that's more than a doctor charges!"

"I know," smiled the plumber. "That's why I switched to plumbing."

One thing that makes repair and doctor bills so painful is that usually they suddenly dash to bits the hope of acquiring some of our pet desires.

A friend recalls when he received an unexpectedly high electrician's bill.

"When I got his bill, I knew I'd be pushing the old Snapper for another year at least," he sighed.

And a woman I know confessed that once, after her doctor precribed 75-cent pills for a chronic ailment, she squealed aloud at the prescription counter, "Oh, dear, there go my alligator shoes!"

Quite often errors in billing will rouse the consumer's ire, as some of our newspaper subscribers know. But usually folks are willing to make adjustments. That was true in the case of the split rail fence for which I was billed almost $100 more than anticipated.

"When I ordered the fence, the fellow said it would cost $6 per section to install it. And I ordered five sections," I explained to the fence department. "That comes to $30 for labor in my mind, but then I've never been good at math."

"Didn't he tell you there was a minimum labor charge of $60?" the fence lady asked.

"He did not. Otherwise I might have ordered 10 sections instead of five just to use up the $60 worth of labor I paid for," I joked.

"And there was an extra $48 labor charge for taking down the old fence," she said.

"Hold on here! I had taken all of it down except the posts. Surely they didn't charge $48 to remove six rotten fence posts, in addition to the $60 installation charge that should have been only $30."

"OK. You can deduct the $48 charge for pulling up the posts," the fence lady said agreeably.

People who fix things are to be greatly admired, be they plumbers, mechanics, or doctors. My craft's importance seems to pale in comparison. When I mentioned this once to a mechanic working on my car, he tried to make me feel better by saying, "Mechanics can move cars. . . . Words can move nations."

But when it comes to moments of emergency such as unstopping the bathroom sink or removing water from the tub, words fail me.

*May 17, 1986*

# A Tear for the Boys in Teague

I wouldn't say the punishment dished out to the bad boys in Teague Dorm at the University of North Carolina at Chapel Hill is exactly cruel and inhuman. But it sure is different.

You remember the terrible Teagues. A Teague dorm man, dressed in drag, was crowned UNC's 1983 Homecoming Queen. Teague paid for the plane that buzzed Kenan Stadium pulling a banner reading: "Your momma sleeps in Teague."

Their luck ran out last spring when some Teagues got drunk and called a black female housing official a racial name that went out of style about 30 years ago.

University officials finally lowered the boom: They made Teague coed, moving 91 women into that former macho bastion of 200 men.

Boy, do they know how to torture guys! That's sort of like Br'er Fox throwing Br'er Rabbit into a formerly all-male brier patch suddenly inhabited by several dozen female rabbits.

When it comes to sex education, our universities usually are well ahead of the times. The advanced lab courses began with the institution of coed dorms in the 1970s when universities abandoned a role once known as "in loco parentis."

For those of you who never studied Latin and don't know that all Gaul is divided into three parts, "in loco parentis" means "in place of parents." In the old days, colleges and universities tried to fill the role of parents for students away from home.

They had rules. And curfews. And even panty raids — for which the raiders could be expelled. When's the last time we had a campus panty raid?

I first realized things were out of hand when a young lady I know went off to UNC-CH and was assigned to room with a big-city girl from Texas. Everything went well until the sophisticated young Texan's boyfriend started dropping around at night.

Before long, when the small-town Carolina girl would come in from the library, she'd frequently find her dorm room locked and her bucket of toiletries and nightgown parked just outside the locked door. So it was down the hall to spend the night with a chum who didn't have a lover sleeping in.

Even at once-conservative N.C. State University, it's open season for sex. A couple of years ago, a student I knew told her adviser that she wasn't getting any sleep because her roommate's boyfriend was homesteading in her room.

She said she had complained to the authorities and was told she could move into another room.

"Why should I have to move?" she wanted to know. "Why not my roommate?"

Her adviser tried to find out. Ask a foolish question, get a foolish answer: Young men have a right to visit in women's dorm rooms until 1 a.m.

Now who's gonna enforce the rule. Who has the gall to knock on a door at 1 a.m. and ask a young man to get out of a girl's warm bed on a cold night and go sack out in his own room?

So last spring, when the Wake County schools adopted a realistic sex education program to prepare kids for high school or college sex, I said: Praise Allah!

Not everybody cheered. My phone rang a lot.

One irate mother called to say, "When I mentioned to a friend — a grown woman with children — that they were talking about sodomy in the sixth grade, she was confused. She didn't even know what it was. She thought it was something you took for indigestion. Or some kind of turf builder."

She wanted me to do something. I did. I called Central Office. "Tell me about those dirty movies you're showing."

"Come see for yourself," they said.

They even served popcorn. The movie was low-key, informative, in good taste, almost boring. It certainly wasn't as titillating as movies many sixth-graders see at home on HBO or the VCR or when their mothers drop them off at local theaters.

This upbeat, happy-ending film said nothing about sodomy. Resisting tremendous peer pressure, the girl did not give in to the boy, and he still loved her anyway. They both decided to wait awhile.

As sixth-graders in Surry County, none of us had ever heard of sodomy or much else relating to sex. But that year many of us got our first glimpse of the condom. (It was not called that, of course.)

One of the town boys kept one in his wallet and at recess we would go out behind the Agriculture Building to look at it. He said he knew someone at the drugstore, but we doubted it. It surely must have been snitched because nobody in the sixth grade would ever have had nerve enough to go in and buy one.

Anyway, we had no idea how much the thing cost. And if we had mustered the nerve or money to ask for "rubbers," which was what they were then called, the druggist would have humiliated us by saying something like, "Why son, we don't carry canning supplies here. Try Reid's Department Store."

But all that's history. The university is finally getting tough. If you don't believe it, ask the boys in Teague Dorm.

*September 10, 1988*

# All the World's a Stage

It is hot and humid. And lunchtime. And down on the Mall Across from the Wachovia Bank, a shirt-sleeved street preacher is laying it on heavy, sweat streaming from his face and his sun-baked arms.

"Ye sinners! Ye fornicators! Ye adulterers!" he hollers, his voice echoing for blocks around. "The last days are here! Repent! Repent now before it's too late."

The street preachers mean well. They, too, have a place in God's plan. But when I see one, I cannot help but remember the incident of the poor farmer who one day looked up at the sky and saw clouds that seemed to form the letters GP.

Thinking it meant "Go Preach," he went into the house, grabbed his Bible, drove into town and started preaching fire and brimstone on street corners.

Alas, by the time he realized that the sign in the sky had merely meant "Go Plow," he had lost the farm and most of his friends.

Under the awning at Hudson Belk, lunch-timers are lining up to pay $7.50 for a blood test that will tell them their cholesterol level. Cholesterol is the "in" health worry this year.

Folks now brag about their low cholesterol readings the way they used to lie about their golf game or their children's SAT scores.

Just inside the store, a pretty young thing is trying to seduce passing males into buying a particular brand of perfume for men.

"What does 'Obsession' do for a man?" I asked as she blocked my path to the escalator and extended a small vial of free perfume.

"It makes you smell good."

"Do I smell bad?"

She didn't answer.

The argument that real men don't use perfume obviously is now passe. So are the days when a perfume called "Sweat" enjoyed a brief heyday.

Surely, it must have been some high school or college coach who fathered the idea of bottling sweat and selling it for $50 an ounce to male-hungry females.

Former Wake Forest coach Bones McKinney once remarked that the worst thing about coaching basketball is having to huddle with the players during time-outs.

"Try sticking your head into a bunch of sweaty men who have been running up and down a basketball court for half an hour," he said. "They stink like polecats!"

On down to Wyatt-Quarles where I bought sunflower seeds for the spoiled birds who visit my feeder. The ungrateful wretches had turned up their beaks at the black seed I had bought and were holding out for the striped kind.

It's a shame that we have created a welfare state in birddom. A titmouse visits my feeder, splits open a seed and flies directly to her nest where she stuffs the kernel down the gaping mouth of her young. Poor things. How many suburban birds alive today have never tasted the succulence of a fat, juicy earthworm, hauled fresh from the soil by their own honest toil?

Up by the post office, a car has pulled over at the curb. A man clutching a pigeon to his chest is climbing into the back seat.

Even the dullest reporter couldn't resist this obvious news story: a pigeon being hijacked from downtown Raleigh, where pigeons are as plentiful and about as welcome as fleas.

"Where are you going with the pigeon?" I asked the young, olive-skinned man.

"He ees sick. I take heem home," he said nervously in a heavy accent, apparently thinking I was a member of the SBI or the SPCA. Meanwhile, the panting pigeon, its beady eyes blinking furiously, seemed pleased with all the attention.

I complimented the Good Samaritan, and he rode away nuzzling the pigeon affectionately. "What's he doing with that pigeon?" a stranger asked. I explained the unusual mission of mercy.

"A likely story," scoffed the skeptic. "Probably gonna eat 'im."

At Wachovia Bank, a lanky guy is teasing a bank employee.

"How come you didn't speak to me yesterday?"

"I didn't see you."

"Guess not," said the grinning fellow, who explained that he washes windows atop high-rise office buildings, sometimes 13 stories above the street.

"You ever fallen?"

"Nope, and falling is not something I'm good at. You just don't get many practice falls in my type of work."

You can tell it is the dog days of summer, newswise. A TV cameraman is taping a hot dog vendor. He zeros in for a close-up of the hot dog nestling in its bed of slaw and chili.

The odor is tantalizing. But I have not eaten a hot dog in more than 15 years, not since I paid too close attention when someone graphically described what goes into the typical frankfurter.

Shakespeare was right when he said all the world's a stage. And indeed we are the players who strut and fret our hour there and then are heard no more. The secret is to enjoy the play as much as you, catching every chuckle, every tear before the final curtain falls.

*August 6, 1988*

# Once Upon a Time, 30 Years Ago

Thirty years ago I came to The Raleigh Times as a city hall reporter.

A week or so after I arrived, an erratic but imaginative city editor by the name of Tom Wood said, "Oh, and I'd also like you to write a human interest column. We'll call it 'Sno' foolin.' "

That was the beginning of my affair with Raleigh and the people of a town that back then claimed only 60,000 souls, most of whom recognized each other on sight.

I find myself, like Thomas Wolfe, wondering where the years have gone.

"Time," he said, "is collected in great clocks, and hung in towers, in sleeping cities, time beats its tiny pulse out in small watches on a woman's wrist, time begins and ends the life of a man, and each man has his own, a different time."

It certainly was a different time and place that March morning when I drove over the rolling, clean-swept approach to the capital city from the west on U.S. 70, encountering nothing but the Ranch Motel and Preston Rhodes' Amoco between Durham and Crabtree Creek bridge.

"Old Raleigh" still lived in those high-ceilinged mansions along Blount, Person and Hillsborough streets, although even then the paint had begun to peel and the aristocracy of the Old South only rarely ventured out on trembling legs, like faded butterflies stunned by early frost.

The town was serene, happy and self-centered. While other Southern capitals clamored to be served by the new Interstate 85 snaking southward, Raleigh said no thank you. The interstate would offer easy access to hordes of dreaded Yankees who would come pouring into Raleigh and change things.

But change was inevitable. IBM slipped across the Mason-Dixon line and Raleigh hasn't been the same since, much to the chagrin of some isolationists and the delight of other Raleighites, not to mention transplanted Yankees.

Yes, they came — by the thousands. But not to burn Tara, steal the horses or rape the women as some old Raleighites feared.

Their worst crimes, it seemed, were luring away the maidservants and raising the price of real estate and visits to the hairdresser.

With mingled excitement, nostalgia and confusion, many of us have watched Raleigh and Wake change over the years. As a columnist I have sought to temper the change with attempts at humor and compassion.

You — oldtimer and newcomer alike — have responded in a most gratifying way.

Together, we have paced the hospital hall during the birth of babies. We have shared the heart-tugging experience of pushing a child out the door on his first day of school. Together, the mechanically inept among us have fumed and fretted over our children's dreaded "class projects," always due "first thing in the morning."

Together, we have loved and buried our dogs. Adjusted to the emptiness of house and heart when the kids went off to college, and experienced the same frustrations at their inability to live within their allowances or make the simplest of decisions while masquerading as self-sufficient adults.

You have cheered my wife's crusade to stamp out the misuse of "lie" and "lay." Alas, the mission seems doomed. Only recently I heard a local radio personality broadcast from Nassau that he was "laying on the beach." I do hope someone gathered the eggs after he went back to his hotel.

You have complimented me by buying my books, many of you going the extra mile by writing to say you enjoyed them or that you sent one to Granddad in Seattle or to Aunt Pearl in Maine, who, like me, loves the mountains.

I even appreciate those double-edged compliments such as the one from the Wyoming lumberjack who wrote movingly that "I like your book a lot, I keep it on the shelf in the john and read a column every morning," and the comment from Dr. Robert Ruark, my wife's beloved obstetrician, who once said to me, "I read a chapter every night and it lulls me right off to sleep."

In any city, and Raleigh is a city now, readers tend to identify with a newspaper's columnists, whether they be Dennis Rogers, A.C. Snow or others. To borrow the telephone company's overworked slogan, personal columns are a way for readers to "reach out and touch someone" in a world that seems to grow even more cold and impersonal.

In this last Saturday Times column, I want to say thanks to you readers who have enriched my own stint of three decades of writing columns.

You are what keeps a columnist columnizing.

This is by no means a swan song. "Sno' foolin' " is not leaving the neighborhood, only moving up the block — or, in this case, to the Saturday morning News and Observer. I hope you'll come along.

*November 28, 1987*

# The Death of a Lawn Mower

When it comes to lawn mowers and husbands, my wife believes in Alexander Pope's advice, "Be not the first by whom the new are tried." She has had one of each for almost three decades.

I do not totally subscribe to her argument that if you can predict how something will act and have adjusted to its idiosyncrasies, be it husband or lawn mower, you'd better let well enough alone.

There is something a bit unsettling about being compared to a lawn mower. Especially one that we have had for 28 years, that is hard to start, tends to conk out at the most inopportune time and has three wheels purloined from four other broken-down but less hardy mowers.

I put my foot down recently and announced, "I'm buying a new lawn mower."

"I won't use it," she said, just as firmly. "I like the one we have."

"That's because I mow and you don't," I retorted, which wasn't quite fair.

"You know I mow in summer," she insisted.

"Yes, I know. And you know that with the droughts we've been having, the grass grows very little in the summer."

I've been waiting for years for the old mower to die. It is a pain to push. When a wheel falls apart, my neighbor Ed Green trots down and replaces it with an old one. I leave it out in the rain. It still starts.

How could my wife like it? It almost murdered her once.

We had just moved into our house and she had left a hammer lying in the grass where she had been repairing the clothesline. I was mowing full speed through the high meadow when the mower struck the head of the hammer, splitting it into three chunks of shrapnel.

My wife was walking through the den when one of the pieces, traveling at the speed of a bullet, missed her head by only a couple of inches, imbedding itself deep into the brick fireplace. I have never quite trusted it since.

So last week, I went up the hill to see Jerry Napier, the lawn-mower man who came to our neck of the woods about the same time we did 28 years ago when Crabtree Valley was a cow pasture and the shopping center wasn't even a gleam in Seby Jones' eye.

"What have you got on sale?"

"Friend," said Jerry, "that reminds me of the time when I was shot down behind the lines in Korea and held captive by the Communists."

"Oh, Lord," I thought. "I never knew Jerry was a war hero," and braced myself for a long-winded tale better fit for an old soldiers' reunion than a lawn mower outlet.

"Yeah, it took months for us to learn to read a smattering of Chinese. We only had one book, a worn-out, tattered copy of Confucius' own words. And I remember one thing Confucius said as clear as yesterday: 'When distinguished editor walks into business place and asks what on sale, say everything in damn place on sale.'"

I stood around and watched him operate, a master salesman.

A man walked in with a little boy in tow.

"That's a fine-looking young man you have there," Jerry said to the father. "He'd make a good trade-in on a new mower."

"Push model or a self-propelled?" grinned the father, going along with the act.

"Why a fine lad like that — a self-propelled job." Fishing a penny from his pocket, Jerry handed it to the lad.

"I'm so glad you dropped by. I been having all kinds of trouble with that gum machine over there. It just quit on me. You look like a right smart young man. How about going over there and seeing if you can get it to work?"

The youngster walked over and inserted the coin. The machine spat out a couple of pieces of gum.

"Now look at that!" Jerry exclaimed. "A young genius. Why you just keep that gum, son, and I sure do appreciate your fixing that old machine for me!"

Selling is a fine art. Salesmen are born with the gift. I could not give away ice-water in Hell.

When I think of salesmen, I cannot help but dwell on the tragic hero of Arthur Miller's "Death of a Salesman," in which Willy Loman, after 36 years on the road, has lost his touch and has been put out to pasture with a wife to support and no income.

After Willy Loman's suicide, his brother-in-law Charley explains the man. "Nobody blames this man. Willy was a salesman. And for a salesman, there is no rock bottom to life. He don't put a bolt to a nut, he don't tell you the law or give you medicine.

"He's a man way out there in the blue, riding on a smile and a shoeshine. And when they start not smiling back — that's an earthquake. And then you get yourself a couple of spots on your hat, and you're finished."

But it has been my observation that when a salesman is clicking on all cylinders, he is a man apart. The world beats a path to his door, as it does to the fellow who sold me my new lawn mower, the one my wife is beginning to enjoy.

*May 21, 1988*

# In Oregon, a Pound Cake Browning

When I go home at night, weary after a day of writing and wrestling with real issues or just whether or not to have a half or whole piece of Japanese fruit pie at the Capital Room at lunch, I am rarely in a mood to take on more causes.

For therapy, I do one of two things. I change out of my suit and tie, put on a pair of shorts, and go down to my 6-by-6-foot garden to see if my tomato has grown during the day and if the bugs have devoured the new leaves on the heavenly blue morning glory struggling to climb the woodpile.

Or I go inside, sip a cool drink, sit in front of the window and watch the squirrels continue their hapless assault against my squirrel-proof bird feeder.

One day recently, my wife called me in from tomato-watching.

"There's a woman here who wants you to sign a petition," she whispered at the back door. "I told her you were in charge of petition signing in this house."

"You mean you let her in the house — in the den?"

"Well, it was hot outside. And she looks harmless enough."

My wife is like that. She gets along with strangers. Once when I misplaced her at the San Francisco airport, I found her over by the luggage carousel dictating her pound cake recipe to a stranger from Oregon.

"Strangers are the best people to know," she once said. "They make no demands; you make no commitments. You just pass in the night without touching."

Ah, yes, that's what we like to think. That's what Frank, the hero of Richard Ford's novel, "The Sportswriter," also thought. He was a self-sufficient loner, who was always getting inside people's lives and then backing out in a hurry when the going got tough.

In the book, Frank becomes a casual friend of Walter, a fellow he met in the Divorced Men's Club. Walter, whose wife ran off to Bimini with her water ski instructor, attaches far more importance to the two men's relationship.

When Walter commits suicide, he leaves Frank a note asking him to look up a child he had never seen, one conceived when he was 19 and a sophomore in college.

Angry, Frank refuses. "What happened to Walter on this earth is Walter's own lookout. I'm sorry as hell, but he had his chance like the rest of us."

The stranger in my den did indeed look harmless enough. About 30, she wore a longish dress that reminded me a little of what the flower children wore back in the '60s.

She shoved the clipboard at me.

"I don't sign petitions," I said, explaining the nature of my work. Not wanting to seem rude, I invited her to sit down and birdwatch with me. I did not offer to show her my tomato. One can go too far with strangers. After all, Southern hospitality these days can be sadly misunderstood, and, who knows, even translated into a sexual harassment suit.

"Aren't you interested in good causes?" the visitor asked, almost accusingly.

"Causes? Causes are my business," I said. "I've been up since 6 this morning caring about causes. Why, I was at work at 7 o'clock this morning writing an editorial espousing the good cause of passing a $125 million bond issue for Wake County school kids.

"And I am worn to a frazzle mentally from pushing the seemingly hopeless cause of keeping a grassy strip down the middle of the Raleigh Beltline instead of replacing it with one of those ugly concrete walls they call a New Jersey barrier. And isn't trying to get Liston Ramsey and the legislature to leave town a worthwhile cause?"

Causes? I refrained from telling her about the frequent nightmares in which I am being ridden out of town on a rail because of some good cause. How do doctors stand it — being God all day and then being called out at night to perform more miracles?

But my visitor paid little attention to my causes. We are like that. Our cause is the only cause. Everybody else's cause is some kind of silly obsession.

"Well, then I think I'd better go," the woman said.

My wife leaped to her feet, full of apologies, and urged a glass of water on her and even fixed a second cup for the road. I was afraid she was going to invite her to stay for dinner.

Like it or not, we are our brother's keeper.

Even Frank later relented, went to Florida and spent considerable time and money looking for a child, who, he finally concluded, had existed only in his dead friend's troubled mind.

So I like to think that perhaps this very day some housewife in Oregon is pulling a golden-brown pound cake out of the oven. And tonight when her guests rave about its fine texture and succulent goodness, she may smile and say, "Would you believe I got the recipe from a woman from North Carolina I met at the baggage carousel in San Francisco Airport one day in the spring of 1981?"

*July 9, 1988*

# Beach Better Than Rice Diet

As is my custom, the first thing I did when I walked into the condo at the beach last week was to check the light bulbs.

One thing I've learned about most people who own places at the beach is that they do not read. No matter how exclusive the location, how shimmering the ocean out front, how elaborate the furnishings, most condo lamps are equipped with 60-watt bulbs.

The phenomenon indicates a nation that no longer reads. Yet in just about every place I stay, there is a TV peering out at me with baleful eye from its rattan stand. And often there is a wet bar that helps the occupants pass the time and tolerate the TV fare.

So I head for the nearest grocery store and buy a couple of 100-watt bulbs so I can get on with what is one of the best parts of my vacation: reading for pleasure instead of for "professional enhancement."

The menu is varied. A bit of Lee Smith and Reynolds Price, topped off with a hefty serving of Gore Vidal's "Lincoln," with dessert provided by Sam Donaldson. Now if you want to make an enemy out of a friend who also is a Reagan Rambo, give him Sam's "Hold On, Mr. President!" for Christmas. He will never forgive you.

I gave up long ago trying to decipher the personality of the owners of the places we rent for a week or two. The clues normally are locked in the "owners' closet."

What these people are like is concealed behind the typical beach decor: paintings of gulls or lighthouses or beached sailboats on the walls, bedside lamps shaped like snails, and fish netting draped strategically here and there.

My wife can tell within 30 seconds of arrival what the woman who rules the condo year round is like by merely opening a couple of kitchen cabinet doors. If she finds a Mixmaster, a colander, muffin pans and a sharp kitchen knife, she is apt to say approvingly, "This lady can cook," even though usually at the beach we have our evening meals out.

Some condos in every complex are inhabited by year-round owners who are not subject to the "No Pets" house rules that govern the paying guests. They are allowed to keep dogs, although we had been told, much to my satisfaction, that we could not take with us our own granddog, Summer Snow, that my daughter had left for us to babysit while she visited a friend in San Antonio.

I ran into one of the "dog owner" residents in the elevator at Windward Dunes, which is presided over by Kevin Willis. Two handsome beagles, eager to put their paws on firm ground, pranced impatiently around the elevator, sniffed my leg and smiled at me. But their master could not muster a half-hearted grin or a grunted greeting.

This time, our place included a telescope in the living room. I zeroed it down to the beach, eight stories below, aiming at a provocative swimsuit, handkerchief size, stuffed with a well-endowed torso. All I drew was darkness.

My wife removed the lens cover and tilted the scope upward. "It's for studying the stars," she reminded me caustically.

The ocean is my therapist, erasing my mind of the deadlines and decisions of day-to-day life, leaving only such momentous chores as deciding whether to walk on the beach early or at mid-morning, whether to eat at the Beaufort House or the Turtle Reef, or whether to have strawberry or Oreo topping on my yogurt at the Sea Spray at Salterpath.

The ocean's moods are much like man's: joyful at times, glistening purple, blue and green. At other times pensive, sighing out its sorrows against the shore, or angry, lashing out in the night, tossing and turning in its own private agony, sometimes crying softly in the afternoon, with rain cascading silently on the sand.

Beach time is the time to catch up on correspondence. We ride down to the little post office on the causeway where Postmaster Ellis Jones, who once lived in Raleigh, is pushing cheerful good will to friend and stranger alike, along with the new, handsome wildlife stamps.

I am fascinated by his tie, adorned with thin metal replicas of all the "LOVE" stamps the Postal Service has issued.

"As you can see," he chuckled, "I'm into lightweight love, not that heavy stuff you get on 'As the World Turns.' " My wife bought the new William Faulkner stamps for a note she had written to a literary friend. I put a red fox stamp on a card to a nature-loving relative in the foothills.

Mr. Jones said he liked Faulkner, in small doses.

"No, you don't read Faulkner before breakfast," I agreed.

Leaving the beach, I felt the same sadness I always feel at the death of summer. My wife, ever the optimist, cheered me. "September," she said, "is a new beginning, just like the next chapter of a good novel you can't bear to put down."

That helped. I also remembered the newspaper article she had read the day we arrived. Travel columnist Arthur Frommer had recommended several bargain summer vacations, including a two weeks, $2,000 stay at the Duke diet center in Durham. Our time at the beach was more pleasant and less expensive. At Duke, you don't get Oreo topping on your rice.

*August 22, 1987*

# Now It's OK for Men to Cry

I had picked up the book at the downtown library and had stopped at Hardee's for a cup of coffee to take back to the office. The young girl behind the counter spotted the book.

" 'About Men,' " she said, reading the title. "You oughta be reading a book called 'About Women' 'cause for sure, you men don't know nothing 'bout us women."

"You are too young to know whether men know about women," I laughed as she handed me my coffee and urged me to "have a good day."

I did not tell her that men not only don't know much about women, they know even less about men — about themselves. But as this collection of essays from the popular New York Times column of the same name reveals, men finally are coming out of the closet.

They are being allowed to say how they feel. Occasionally they are being permitted to cry. Some are getting up the nerve to say, "Yeah, I'm afraid of the dark. I'm afraid of all the responsibility, and most of all, I'm afraid of not measuring up to the stereotype of what is a man."

In the book's foreword, columnist Russell Baker points out that from the day we were born, men have been cursed with at least three requirements: (1) utter fearlessness, (2) zest for combat and (3) indifference to pain.

I must say I have faked all three most of my life. So have most men.

In the Air Force during World War II, I quaked with fear when occasionally driven to a foxhole during rare bombings of our bases in the South Pacific. Zest for combat? I have always preferred verbal combat to fisticuffs, only in rare cases risking life or limb in violent encounters.

As for pain, I could never just bite down on a bullet and not flinch while someone cut an Apache arrow out of my back as cowboys did in the old Western movies. And I am eternally grateful for having been spared childbirth.

In these essays, men share their private thoughts and experiences on family life, infidelity, divorce, friendship, sports, love, war and marriage. Through them, readers, especially women, learn a lot about the male mystique.

Not long ago, a woman here at the office asked me what I and the three men I lunch with talk about. "What on earth do men say to each other that they don't say to their women?"

I hadn't thought much about that. So, without alerting my buddies, I took mental notes during lunch at the Capital Room.

Item: My lunch companions are excited about the new telephone that will flash the name of the person calling. They say it will help them trace the obscene calls they've been getting lately from strange women.

Item: Wives who want to walk or jog with their husbands: how to discourage them without hurting their feelings because they walk too slowly and want to stop and gossip and exchange cake recipes with their neighbors.

Item: After a pretty Capital Room model swishes by in a Ralph Lauren dress, a general discussion of women's taste in clothes and men's tastes in women.

Item: One man's wife, told by her husband he's not going to buy a house at Figure Eight Island, had said, "O.K. Buster! But it will be the first thing I do after your funeral." A statement like that, my friend says, can excuse a lot of marital sins a husband might be guilty of.

Item: A joke about "this couple on their honeymoon, who suspected their suite was being bugged..."

Light stuff, huh? Men's finest hours are rarely recorded. Their moments of true courage and endurance go unnoticed except by those closest to them.

In "About Men," one man remembers the agony of accepting the doctor's cold, hard news that his newborn son is mongoloid, the term the doctor then used.

Another describes the aching loneliness he feels after his wife leaves him. Another relates his feelings when his kid brother is murdered. One writes of what it's like to start coming apart at 50 — emotionally and physically.

I remember once when my rambunctious nephew Abraham, age 5, came clonking through the kitchen in his low-slung jeans and hard-soled leather boots and, spotting me loading the dishwasher, stopped short and said with alarm, "Uncle A.C., men don't do dishes!"

A year or two later, my daughter, returning from a visit to his house, reported that she had seen Abraham, that tough little Rambo, standing in a chair doing dishes.

So, while being a man has never been easy, it's getting better. Mens *do* do dishes and real men do eat quiche, and now and then men do cry. Baker says crying is even becoming fashionable.

*September 19, 1987*

# Succulent Sonkers and No PTA

When my wife returned from her church circle meeting recently, I inquired as to the subject of the discussion.

"The circle leader talked about Heaven," she said. "She asked us what we thought Heaven is like. She didn't get around to me, but I identified with one woman who said, 'Heaven is a place where at the end of the PTA meeting, six or eight parents don't hang around demanding to know why Johnny isn't making all A's.' "

Obviously, this perception of the Promised Land was prompted by the teacher's harrowing day at school and the pile of papers at home waiting to be marked.

There is a lot of truth in the old song that includes the refrain, "Everybody talkin' 'bout Heb'n ain't goin' there." But, come to think of it, Heaven is not a place where you camp out all night in order to get the first ticket, as students do for the State-Carolina football game.

I am reminded of the evangelist who asked everybody in his congregation who wanted to go to Heaven to please stand. Everybody stood but one fellow.

"Brother Jones, don't you want to go to Heaven?" the puzzled preacher asked.

"Oh, yes," the man replied, "I thought you were getting up a load to leave tonight."

Most of us Southerners grew up with the mental image of Heaven as a place with streets of gold, a lot of harp-playing and a gray-bearded Saint Peter welcoming everybody at the Pearly Gates. My Southern Baptist upbringing emphasized that you had to earn admission and that thieves, liars and lawyers had precious little chance.

Paradise is something different to everyone.

I love the story about an old tomcat who died, went to Heaven and was greeted by Saint Peter, who told the cat that if he needed anything, just to let him know. Tom said he wanted very little except to be left alone, free of dogs and nagging pussycats.

Saint Peter issued the same sort of welcome to a brace of mice that arrived soon after. They, too, happy to be there, wished for nothing except for occasional servings of cheese and now and then a side order of fillet of feline. They scurried happily down the golden street and turned into a mouse-hold stuccoed with cultured pearls.

But they were back a day later.

"Heaven is bigger than we thought," their spokesperson complained to Saint Peter. "And our legs are so short it is really hard for us to get around. We wonder if perhaps we could be fitted with skates."

"Of course," said Saint Peter, and sent them around to the Heavenly Toy Shop where they were issued tiny golden skates with jeweled wheels.

Sometime later, Saint Peter, making his rounds, came upon the old tomcat, sitting on a small cloud, smiling happily, his arms crossed contentedly across his stomach.

"How you doin,' Tom?" Saint Peter asked.

"Wonderfully well!" exclaimed the cat. "I'm crazy about this place, the peace, the quiet, the heavenly music. And, oh, Saint Peter, I just can't thank you enough for those delicious meals on wheels!"

My concept of Heaven changes according to time and place and circumstances. Last weekend, I felt pretty close to Paradise as I journeyed through the foothills on a perfect September day, the air laced with the brisk hint of autumn, cornflower blue skies and the sleepy sound of insects sighing farewell to summer.

We drove far back into the hills beyond Low Gap to the Annual Sonker Festival at the 187-year-old Franklin House. The huge, rambling house was the home of Jesse Franklin, governor of North Carolina in 1821.

My sister, an expert on sonkers, viewed the array of blueberry, strawberry and sweet potato pies with skepticism and dismay. They were not true sonkers, she said, because they lacked the side crusts. And the top crust of the sweet potato had not been properly laced with the special dip of vanilla, melted butter and milk as it simmered to ecstatic perfection.

Nevertheless, I enjoyed roaming the old mansion, listening to the bluegrass bands, and watching the frenzied flat-foot dancing on the front porch.

"How do you do it?" I asked an elderly mountaineer who had danced non-stop for half an hour. "You must have trained for this by working a farm all your life."

"Nope, I spent 35 years on the looms in a Mount Airy knitting mill," he said, admitting he was pushing 70. "I was so glad to get out I been dancin' ever since."

Can you imagine a newspaperman's role in Heaven should one be fortunate enough to get in? I think I would like to be a stringer for Gabriel's Daily Trumpet, not wanting fulltime work, you understand. Can't you imagine the excitement of covering a press conference called by Saint Peter to announce that the Rev. Jerry Falwell indeed had done as Jimmy Carter suggested at his recent Meredith College appearance and gone to Hell? We would have to put out a special edition.

*September 20, 1986*

# Wandering Saints in the Snow

Proud of having gotten to work through the ice and sleet Monday morning, I now faced, in the afternoon, the looming glacier of the steep hill as I turned into my street.

Waiting for a four-wheeler to pull another stranded car out of my path, I saw in the rear view mirror that a Blazer had pulled in behind me. A young man with a cheerful grin on his face jumped out and walked over to the car.

"Would you like me to pull you up the hill?" he asked. "I've got a chain."

"Thanks, but I don't think I'll need you," I said. "But hang around, just in case. And how much do you charge?"

"Charge? I don't charge anything!" he retorted, his face flushing angrily. 'I've already pulled 10 people out this afternoon."

My cynicism, while embarrassing, was not without cause. A few years ago, under similar circumstances, another young man had worked this same little piece of slippery real estate. That Greedy Samaritan later bragged to a friend how he had made $200 in one afternoon snaking out stuck motorists at $25 a car.

I remembered the man in the Blazer for days, savoring his unselfish gesture. Valor and charity are not dead, I thought. It must be true that bad weather brings out the best in us. If that is true, then Raleigh must have been a citadel of saintliness for the past few days.

Except in my case. If I never see another snowflake before I retire it will be fine with me. These past few days have been those that try men's souls, not to mention women's endurance.

On Snow Day II, I also managed to get to work, but in the afternoon, I found myself up to my axles in snow at the bottom of my hill. Stalled.

A wrecker came up U.S. 70, turned and headed back toward town. Then, spotting me stuck in the snow, the driver parked his vehicle and walked over.

"Before I push you out of the mess you're in," he said, hands on hips, surveying the scene, "I want to tell you how stupid I think you are to attempt that hill in the first place."

The putdown was all he charged for pushing me back into the highway so I could make it to a cleared Crabtree Valley parking lot where I left the car overnight. Goodness again had shown its graceful face.

On the morning of Snow Day III, neighbor Sam Johnson and I set out walking on the frozen crust to my car in the Crabtree lot. It was like dancing the light fantastic in galoshes in an ice-skating rink.

Crunching gingerly down the Glenwood Avenue median, I suddenly went down like an ambushed buffalo. Hoping nobody had observed my undignified plight, I scrambled to my feet in time to see Sam, one of

Raleigh's foremost legal eagles, hit the ice, his briefcase flying in one direction, his hat in another.

"Are you hurt?"

"Only my pride," he said, as one of his clients who had witnessed the indignity pulled alongside in a van and offered us a ride to my car.

Sam's remark about injured pride underscored again the fact that most of us are far too concerned over appearing ridiculous to others. It also reminded me of the story of the three ministers who, after skinny-dipping in a pond on a hot summer day, were headed back to the bank for their clothes when a couple of women came jogging through the woods.

Two of the men instinctively covered their nakedness with their hands while the third covered his face.

"Why in the world would you want to cover your face instead of your privates?" one of the two puzzled preachers asked their companion.

"It all depends on how one is recognized," the third minister quipped.

It is amazing how five inches of sleet can disrupt our world and temporarily change the vibrations of our lives. So much taken for granted, like sunshine, a car that will move, and footgear that doesn't feel as if it is encased in cement.

A grateful reader calls and leaves a message: "The little boy delivered The Raleigh Times last night and placed it on the front stoop. It has changed the way I feel about young people." But another calls to complain, "How come I didn't get my Times tonight?"

To the latter, I had no good answer except to say, "I guess for the same reason that we didn't get any mail for two days." It goes back to the lunchpail work ethic I mentioned in a column a couple of weeks ago.

My neighbor, the retired postman, agrees. "I can't remember ever missing a mail delivery," he said. "And I had employees who walked five miles in the snow to get to work and then went out and delivered their routes for eight hours."

For most of us, there is no real sense of victory in having prevailed over what we mistakenly regard as the worst that winter can throw at us. We never know when or from where Mother Nature will deliver her next blow: drought, tornado, a flood.

At least, thanks to our February frustration, we now know more about how to cope with nature. We know more about ourselves than we did before. And we know more about our fellow man.

*February 21, 1987*

# A Big 'Oklahoma Hello'

I was at the airport early, having read in the paper that, due to traffic delays caused by new construction, RDU users should get there an hour before take-off. I used that as an excuse to get there an hour before arrival.

I have said hellos and goodbyes at RDU for almost 30 years. But this time I was in line early for what Will Parker in the great musical by Rodgers and Hammerstein called "an Oklahoma hello!" My wife was coming home after a long, long month in Switzerland.

Being apart for a month from someone you've been married to for 27 years is no big deal in today's mobile, freewheeling society. But it is for some of us staid, self-confessed squares.

It's not that I wasn't well-cared for in my wife's absence. Friends and neighbors saw to it that I was well-fed and entertained. I was simply fed up with a month of bachelorhood, a lonely house that groans in the night and an empty pillow beside me.

My sister had come down from the foothills to keep me company, bringing for the weekend two cousins I had grown up with. For a couple of days, my place was knee deep in nostalgia. But not until after a little period of adjustment.

I came in from unloading their luggage to find the three women standing in the middle of the den, looking down at Amazing Grace, our decrepit, much-afflicted 14-year-old poodle. Gracie's many ailments include a collapsed trachea which, when she is nervous, sends her into what sounds like terminal coughing spasms.

"How does he stand it?" Dot was saying, apparently referring to me.

"He just has to have the poor thing put to sleep," said Cecile. Gracie only coughed louder.

"She only does that when she's nervous," I interrupted. "And if three strangers walked into your house and promptly started talking about putting you to sleep, wouldn't you be a tad nervous?"

Turning to my sister, I added, "And how would you feel about having Tommy put to sleep?" Tommy is her one and only beloved son.

"But Gracie is just a dog..." she began.

"Oh, how I wish that were true," I said. "Gracie has never been just a dog."

But my sister did herself proud, preparing delicious meals for me and keeping her promise to introduce the neighbors to her sweet potato "sonker," which people in these parts have never heard of, much less tasted.

It was pure coincidence that on that very day I received a call from Dick Byrd, a Greensboro public relations consultant who is doing some work for Surry Community College back home in the foothills.

"Tell me, A.C.," he said, "what is a 'sonker'? It seems they're having a 'Sonker Festival' up here in September.

"You should be at my house tonight and find out first hand," I said, explaining that a sonker is somewhat like a cobbler, only more so.

"Where does the term 'sonker' come from?" he wanted to know. "I asked one of the natives up here and she turned on her heel and walked away, apparently insulted by my inexcusable ignorance."

Since I didn't have time to relate the several myths about the origin of sonker, I promised to discuss it further when next we met.

They say that while one spouse is away, the other will play. And several friends offered to give me numbers from their non-existent "little black books." It is amazing the number of married males who would so much like for you to do what they never have the nerve to do.

But I confess I did go out with another woman, my wife's longtime friend and college chum. It doesn't sound very daring or romantic but I might as well level with you: We had permission, as it were, before our spouses left the country, her Tom to teach in England, my Nancy to study in Switzerland.

Our "date" was the first for me in a very, long time.

"Shall we be discreet?" Barbara laughed, when I called.

"Of course not," I retorted. "Any man past 40 wants to be seen by as many people as possible when he goes out with another woman."

We went to a movie and shared a box of popcorn. Before and after the movie we talked primarily about her husband and my wife and all our children.

Much to our disappointment, as we left the theater, we didn't recognize a single person in the crowd lined up for the second feature.

"You know," Barbara chuckled later, "'running around' is not nearly as exhilarating as we've been led to believe, is it?"

We are all home now, my wife, her husband. The children are gearing up for college. The dog coughs less.

Cicadas sing loudly through the humid nights their farewell chorus to summer. The wood thrush, whose splendid notes will cease at the end of the mating season, sends her swan song through the woodland.

For once, I grieve not for summer's passing, longing for the cooler days of late September. I welcome, above all, normalcy, knowing all the while that normalcy will never come again.

*August 2, 1986*

# Small Towns and Savory Souffles

A friend of mine said recently that she and her husband are thinking about moving from one of Wake's small towns into Raleigh. They want to be in the "mainstream" again.

This is a difficult choice for them as it would be for anyone who has lived in and loved small-town America. There is a charm and pace and peace that one doesn't trade easily for convenience to shopping centers, good restaurants, nightlife and culture — not to mention traffic james, acres of asphalt, billboards and the abrasiveness of rubbing shoulders with mobs of strangers.

A few weeks ago, on my way back to the foothills, I stopped in Burlington, where once I worked in what was then indeed a small town. I rang up an old friend, Dr. Paul Maness, a fine physician who somehow also has retained the heart and mind of a poet. And I also telephoned a couple of one-time bachelor buddies, Joe Davidson and Jiggs Askew. We agreed to meet at Wendy's for lunch.

No jet set this. Wendy's is one of the in-places for lunch there. We beat the crowd, and took a table in the sun, by the window. It was like a huge family reunion with everybody there knowing everybody else and half of them stopping by our table.

Jiggs introduced me to a young lawyer he was supporting for district attorney.

"How did you get this guy to support you?" I asked the young man. "I can't remember when Jiggs was ever FOR any politician," I said, indicating my cantankerous buddy from bygone days.

"Well he's promised to deliver the senior citizen vote," laughed the lawyer.

"In exchange for what?" I wondered, to which the candidate replied, "He hasn't said."

"You ain't getting nothing from me until you quit embarrassing me by jogging through town in 18-degree weather in your short-shorts," chided Jiggs. "Folks will think you're 'tetched' in the head."

There is a difference between metropolitan and small-town journalism, too.

Recently I received a note from Glenn Keever, along with a clipping from a weekly newspaper.

"I wish your reporters would learn to compose articles like this. Why can't we have this kind of reporting here in Raleigh?" he chided.

The article dealt with a sorority meeting. The writer's florid style made the routine meeting sound like the coronation of a major monarch. "The skies were blue as the new day dawned and sunlight glistened on yard and field...Inside, the fireplaces glowed, as did the sorority sisters.

"Savory souffles, casseroles, vegetables, salads and calorie-rich desserts sent aromatic smells throughout the house."

The singer who provided the program "radiated like a golden ray of sunlight that flickered on everyone present." And "the sunshine's warm embrace greeted the members and their guests as they exited.."

"We need to read more about glistening sunlight, savory souffles, flickering rays and smiles," teased Glenn. Or was he teasing?

I remember my days as a cub reporter in a small town where savory souffles and glistening sunlight were daily fare of the newspapers. Obituaries and funeral notices were better read then the front page.

We published the names of not only the pallbearers, but also the honorary pallbearers and after that, the "flower girls," those women and children who made up the retinue of wreath-bearers.

The number of floral arrangements once served as the gauge of the deceased's significance on earth. And woe unto the reporter who misspelled a single name among the 50 to 75 participants in some of the bigger funerals.

And once the "society" editor, describing a tea at the Country Club, wrote that Mrs. So and So and Mrs. Such and Such "poured at both ends."

A small town is a place where gossip beats the newspaper to your doorstep, where you can lie in bed on a Sunday morning and simultaneously hear the bells from the First Baptist, First Presbyterian and First Methodist churches, where, when the word gets out that your wife is out of town, you'll have three invitations to dinner by noon.

It's a place where a housewife, lonesome for company, can, while sweeping her front walk, encounter enough friends to arrange a bridge party, a shopping trip and a weekend excursion to the beach.

It's a place where borrowing a cup of sugar from a neighbor is a compliment and paying it back is an insult.

As I look down the road toward retirement, I keep thinking about a high acre of land we own near Fancy Gap, Va., adjacent to the Blue Ridge Parkway. The plot looks out on range after range of the Blue Ridge Mountains.

We sometimes go there in the spring or fall and sit on a blanket on "our land," listening to the spruce pines' soft sighing, watching the sun's last rays catch the brilliance of mid-October's canvas of color. In the spring we look down on banks of wild azalea and rhododendron. Silence comes in huge slices.

Could we be happy there? I think so. Who knows for sure?

"Perhaps for a week or two or even a month at a time," my wife says. "But I don't think I want to leave Raleigh permanently."

I do not envy my small-town friend her difficult decision. I would remind her that savory souffles, flickering rays and glistening sunlight are not easily come by and shouldn't be discarded lightly.

*April 26, 1986*

# Same Rooster, Different Hen

"You know, we just don't have the caliber of presidents we used to," a friend said to me recently. "Remember the great ones?"

I agreed, admitting that after more than three decades in the newspaper business, I have become a bit cynical and find my list of Great Ones getting shorter every day. I asked him to encourage me by naming a few.

"Lincoln, Roosevelt, maybe Kennedy, Washington, Jefferson." He didn't mention Calvin Coolidge. Nor did I. And I am not sure what prompts me at this late stage to reveal that I was named for that seemingly dour, unfortunate man.

It was my father's fault. A staunch Republican, he developed a bad habit of branding his children born during Republican administrations with the name of the president in office. How would you like to go through life named Warren Gamaliel Harding Snow?

By the time I, the last son, came along, my mother had had it with Republican presidents. She balked at naming the last one Calvin Coolidge. She did not balk often, but when she did, neither heaven nor hell could move her.

I remained unnamed while the great debate raged. Old Dr. Stone, who had come to the house to deliver me, stomped out angrily, shouting over his shoulder, "If you two can ever decide on a name, go up to the courthouse and tell somebody."

Several years ago, preparing for a trip to England, I went by the state vital records office for a copy of the birth certificate required for a passport.

After a long search, the young woman in vital records reported she could not find any record of my having been born. A bit stunned by the news that officially I did not exist, I asked her to search further.

Finally, she returned with a certificate in her hand.

"Do you think that you could possibly be Baby Boy Snow?" she asked. Together we pored over the certificate. My birth date was there. So were my parents' names. Baby Boy Snow was me.

The implications were staggering. Yes, she said, I could abandon the Calvin in my name. Or my entire name if I chose. I was tempted, since the first name my mother laid on me, a French name from some still undetermined source, was really more of an albatross than the second.

Apparently, though, my mother had thrown my father a crumb, agreeing to Calvin. But Coolidge? No way. Thanks, Mom.

So, at vital statistics, I momentarily toyed with the idea of starting over name-wise. I have always wanted to be Kevin.

"You can be Kevin if you want to," the vital records woman said. "But

I wouldn't advise it. You'll be letting yourself in for more red tape than you can possibly imagine."

Calvin Coolidge probably was the butt of more jokes and anecdotes than any other president. But at least Cool Cal had a dry, penetrating wit. That should count for something. It may indeed have been Mr. Coolidge's greatest asset.

In a column several months ago, Los Angeles Times columnist Jack Smith told about the time when the president was asked his opinion of a soprano's "execution" during a White House concert.

"I'm for it," Mr. Coolidge was quoted as saying.

One of my favorite anecdotes has to do with the time the Coolidges visited a poultry farm.

Mrs. Coolidge was walking ahead of the president and happened to see a rooster performing his duties. She asked her guide how many times a day the rooster rose to the occasion.

"Dozens," she was told.

"Tell that to the president," she supposedly quipped.

Apparently someone did. When the president came along and saw the same rooster still at work, he asked, "Is it always the same hen?"

Oh no, he was told. It usually was a different hen each time.

"Tell that to Mrs. Coolidge," the president snorted.

It's hard to imagine that this outwardly strait-laced pair could have had such an exchange. Myths in time tend to be accepted as truths. Still, one never knows what people are like behind the masks they turn to the public.

But we do accept as fact Dorothy Parker's famous quip. When told that President Coolidge had died, she asked, "How do they know?"

As a child, I resented my father for what he tried to do and could hardly wait to punish him by becoming a life-long Democrat. He died before I was old enough to vote.

Had he lived longer, I doubt that the man who thought Republicans and Baptists were truly God's chosen people would have ever let me go home again as a Democrat and a Presbyterian.

So I say to you men out there siring sons, be compassionate. You can't help passing on to your heirs the color of your eyes and hair, your big nose or cauliflower ears, your inherent tendency for high blood pressure or heart attacks. But for heaven's sake, let the lad choose his own politics.

*October 8, 1988*

# The Last Plane to Rapture

Last Monday, one of the boys in sports remarked, "A.C., if I'm not here in the morning, you'll know I've gone to Rapture."

He was referring to the conviction among many fundamentalists that the beginning of the end of the world was Tuesday.

The next morning, I was pleased to see Tim at his desk, handling sports as usual, getting on with the Earthly game of life rather than up there with the heavenly hosts rehashing the disastrous Oklahoma-Carolina game with the few saints wearing Carolina-blue halos.

When I congratulated him on his survival, he said, "It ain't over until sunset."

When it comes to the Rapture, I'm a lot like a Georgia woman interviewed on national television.

Asked about her views on the phenomenon, she said, "Well, the Bible always said ye shall know not the day or the hour."

"In other words, you don't think there's much to this Rapture business," the television reporter prompted.

"Now wait a minute," the woman said. "You ain't gonna get me to say nothin' like that!"

She's right. Why gamble?

I never took the Rapture very seriously because as a child growing up in the Baptist Church, I too was taught "But of that day and hour knoweth no man, no, not the angels of heaven, but my Father only."

The prospect of being carried off without advance notice worried me considerably when I was a child. But I always hoped that when the world ended, it would be during the work week when we were priming tobacco and not on a Sunday afternoon when we were playing kick-the-can or aintney-over.

Another bit of Scripture also haunted me. That was the part about "Then shall two be in the field; the one shall be taken, and the other left." As I worked side by side with my brother four years older, I frequently and selfishly prayed, "Lord, let it be Warren that is taken, and me that is left."

There was never any doubt in my mind that I wanted to go to heaven. But like most of us, I never wanted to set a departure date.

That thought was dramatically revived this past summer when, vacationing at Atlantic Beach, I accompanied my friend Bobby Ivey to the United Methodist Church as Salter Path. I had never gone to church at the beach before. It turned out to be the most exciting experience of my vacation.

United Methodist at Salter Path is a far cry from Edenton Street Methodist in Raleigh. Or First Presbyterian, which I attend.

It had been a long time since I had such a taste of "the old time religion." The music was terrific — a powerful choir backed up by a piano, organ, two guitars and drums — all highly amplified. It had us tapping our feet and many of the parishioners clapping their hands. It was the kind of music we could shag to or be saved by.

Pastor Foster Reynolds was articulate. Loud. And very mobile — especially for a man his size, moving his big frame back and forth around the pulpit. His text was on travel — about catching the plane for "that big trip we're all going on. The last trip, if you know what I mean.

"You'd better get your passport now! You won't have the usual 30 days," he stormed. And I half-way expected him to add, "And you can't depend on Jesse Helms' getting it for you at the last minute."

And he told the story about the preacher who asked those in the congregation who wanted to go to heaven to raise their hands. When all but one did, the astounded preacher shouted: "Brother, you mean to sit there and say you don't wanna go to heaven?"

"Oh no, preacher," the fellow said meekly. "I just thought you was gettin' up a load to go now."

"Well, brothers and sisters," roared Pastor Reynolds, "I want you to know I'm getting up a load for now. Today!"

When the world didn't end Tuesday, the Rapture folks extended the deadline until Wednesday at 11 a.m. At 11:05, Ambrose Dudley from the Associated Press called me at work and said with feigned astonishment, "You're still here!"

He explained it is customary for doomsday folks to set new deadlines when the first ones don't work. "When one date runs out, they just reload and wait," he said.

One Raleigh woman who, along with her husband, has suffered, sacrificed and struggled for years getting the kids through adolescence and college, married and settled down, was upset by the prediction that seven years of tribulation will follow the Rapture.

"You mean there's more to come?" she howled. "I thought I was finally through it!"

I agree with Joanna Hicks of the Sign of the Fish book store in Raleigh about knowing just when the world will end. "It's very difficult to nail God down to anything. He's the one who does the nailing."

But I keep watching the Associated Press wire to see whether there is a bulletin, expecting, and perhaps hoping, it will tell us that Jim and Tammy are missing and have gone on ahead. You know they'd want to get there early and pick out the biggest mansion, one over by the pearly gates with gold doorknobs and a kidney-shaped swimming pool.

I confess that, despite the terrible shape the world's in and the trials and tribulations of life, it's still a pretty nice place and I'm like the guy who didn't raise his hand. Of course I wanna go to heaven, but, please, could I catch the very last plane out?

*September 17, 1988*

# A Truck Driver's 'Type A' Day

I could tell by the way he walked from the dump truck, striding angrily toward my car, that he was Type A — the uptight kind doctors say are headed for a heart attack. But he looked as if he meant to cause one, not have it himself.

You've met the Type A's. You may be one yourself. Do you pace the sidewalk while waiting for your wife to put on her make-up for a movie that started 20 minutes ago?

Does your car wear a bumper sticker such as the one I saw recently on a pickup truck: "Don't Mess With Texas!"

Are you the guy I saw turn crimson with anger in the supermarket checkout because the cashier asked to see your driver's license after you had plunked a six-pack of Coors on the counter? If you are, I don't blame you.

There you stand, grossly overweight, your belly hanging over your belt, your head as bald as an onion. You're at least 55 years old and she's hassling you for an I.D. You don't have to feel sorry for leaving her in tears. But you are Type A, so watch it.

The day of my encounter with the Type A truck driver I had had a Type A day myself. But I had remained serene throughout and was headed home.

I had not reacted when, returning from lunch, I found the Dear Abby clipping some smart guy had left on my desk.

It was the one in which a woman said she had had extramarital sex with a real estate agent, a salesman, a construction worker and an editor. She found the construction worker to be the best and the editor the worst.

So much for one woman's poor taste in sex.

Nor had I complained about the telephone call from someone who muttered something about a "bottle stopper."

"I beg your pardon?" She repeated herself. Asked for still further clarification, she had yelled, "I said 'How much is a whopper?' Isn't this the Burger King?"

Nor had I lost my cool when three people in quick succession called to complain they had not received their morning paper. Four others groused about missing comic strips.

When your telephone number is only one digit different from the Circulation Department's, you expect these things.

It could have been worse. A friend who moved to Raleigh many years ago somehow ended up with the telephone number previously assigned to a local house of prostitution.

"Tell me," he said one morning over coffee, "Who the hell is Tatie

Mae? I keep getting calls late at night asking for Tatie Mae. She sure is a popular lady, whoever she is." When I told him she was the local madam, he changed his number next day.

So now I was headed home, feeling pretty good about myself, perhaps even sanctimonious, as I pulled off Downtown Boulevard and onto the little street that goes up by the old Hayes Barton swimming pool into Glenwood Avenue just below Five Points.

I was coasting gently into Glenwood when suddenly I heard brakes screeching and a horn blasting. A heavy dump truck hurtled past, only the paint on our vehicles separating us. He swerved into the other lane, moved up the street a half a block and stopped. I pulled up behind the truck.

The man was furious. As he strode up to my car, I remembered what my Dad used to say when a neighboring farmer came calling, "He walks like he has corn to sell."

"Man, whatta you think you're up to? You almost killed me!" he shouted.

"Sir, you ran a yield sign back there and almost wiped us both out," I replied calmly, remembering Mayor Avery Upchurch's crusade for more courteous drivers in Raleigh. Besides, the guy looked half my age, was twice as brawny and ill as a hornet.

"Man, you crazy! You the one run a stop sign!" he yelled.

"Look, sir, I've been driving this route for over 30 years. I had the right of way. Are you from out of town?"

"Out of town? No way. I been driving this truck through here for years. You don't know what you talking about! You wanna call the law and let him settle it?"

"Can if you want to. But you'd be terribly embarrassed."

I offered to go back with him and point out the three yield signs he had ignored. But he stomped off toward his truck, pausing from time to time to yell a few more epithets in my direction.

Later that night, I related the incident to my wife. Instead of the anticipated sympathy and shared indignation, I received another tongue-lashing.

"How many times have I pleaded with you to come to a complete stop and look to the left before you enter that intersection!" she stormed.

"But I have the right of way," I protested.

"You have the right to get killed! That's the right you have! Don't forget you have family responsibilities. You still have children in college."

So there you have it, folks. Few of us are born Type A. Life makes us that way. And so do the Type A's we meet along the way.

But be of good cheer. New medical research pooh-poohs the earlier warnings. In fact, Type A conduct is now in. It can relax you, if you don't get killed in the process.

*March 12, 1988*

# How Do I Love Thee? Let's Count

"After 16 years living in Alaska, this is just wonderful!" said the woman behind us at the Friends of the College concert. "I can't wait until next year to get season tickets!"

I could not resist turning around and saying, "Ma'am, you can have my seat next year. I'm not coming."

"You can't mean that," she said with a smile.

"We have all heard that life begins when the children leave home. For me, it will begin when my wife stops buying FOC season tickets," I said.

There is nothing wrong with Friends of the College, which probably is the best buy in the South when it comes to first-class entertainment. It's just that I am suffering from culture burnout.

Now don't cross me off as your basic uncultured clod from the hill country. I had a course in music appreciation in college. As a lad, I played piano by ear. And on my first job at the Burlington Times-News, I was music and drama critic.

Not by choice, I admit. I was drafted and sent out into the night, without overtime pay, to cover the fledgling community theater performances and the civic music association concerts.

But then I also occasionally reviewed Carolina League baseball and I fear, in retrospect, that I brought a touch of the outfield to the concert hall.

I shudder in remorse, thinking of the crudities imposed on those struggling young artists, some of whom moved on to Carnegie Hall, despite amateurish reviews by a color-blind police reporter who hardly knew a coloratura from what my friend Jiggs Askew calls a "messy-soprano."

That was small-town journalism. As a cub reporter, I did everything, including photographing autopsies for the police department. Occasionally I was assigned to "society" news, such as the inaugural reception of Gov. Kerr Scott.

The society editor, assigned to go to Raleigh for the event, paled at the prospect, wailing to Editor Howard White, "Oh, please, I can't. I'm just not up to it. Can't you send A.C.?"

He could. And did. To Raleigh I went, intimidated neither by the assignment nor Kerr Scott and his Branchhead Boys.

These were my kind of people. I had visited the Scott farm at Haw River several times. Kerr Scott put on his pants the way I did — one leg at a time. And he shoveled manure out of his stables the way we had back home — righthanded.

My account of the affair was comprehensive and colorful, leaving no detail unmentioned, not even the Madeira lace tablecloth or the tasty finger sandwiches.

Marriage is a state of give and take, of making concessions and gaining some. She goes to your family reunion. You have her folks in for Christmas and Thanksgiving. She suffers through the football game with you. You endure the chamber music concert with her.

At the Canadian Brass intermission, I approached a man who, yawning widely, kept looking impatiently at his watch.

"What are you getting out of this?" I teased.

"Tomorrow, I get to watch the Redskins and Giants — without interruption."

How do I love thee? Let me count the ways: 28 years of Friends of the College, five Madrigal Dinners, untold seasons at Raleigh Little Theatre, a couple of "A Christmas Carol" performances and several seasons on the canvas seats at NCSU's Thompson Theatre.

For several years, my wife has assembled a table for the annual Madrigal Dinner at N.C. State. She is running out of prospects, most of whom, when approached, now say defensively, "But we've already done that."

Once she tried to recruit our friends Joe and Catherine Davidson of Burlington, who had stopped in for a visit.

"What is a Madrigal Dinner?" Catherine asked.

"It's where you pay $30 a couple for the opportunity to eat a small cornish chicken with your hands, like Henry VIII, and drink soup out of a bowl," I blurted.

"But there are also authentic costumes and good entertainment, including excellent excerpts from Shakespeare," my wife said positively and hopefully.

"Shakespeare!" cried Catherine, rising from the couch. "I hate Shakespeare! Joe, get your coat, we've got to go home."

All this is not to say I don't enjoy cultural events, although I confess I am more into Burl Ives and the "Blue Tail Fly" than Leontyne Price and Tosca's "Pace, Pace."

And I am particularly proud of Friends of the College, having journalistically stood by 28 years ago when the concept was being hatched, a duckling that has matured into a sparkling swan.

And after all these years, I still marvel that five musicians from Canada can entertain and thrill a packed house at Reynolds Coliseum every bit as well as five members of anybody's basketball team.

But alas, for me, burnout is burnout.

*December 13, 1986*

# A Matter of Grace Under Pressure

It was one of last week's golden days that made you think that God had said, "This is the last one and I'll make it my best."

The sun warmed the slumbering earth. The sky was periwinkle blue, the air as crisp as a new dollar bill. The mockingbird in the ginkgo tree down by the Post Office trilled her medley as if rehearsing for the heavenly chorus.

In a mid-morning dash to the bank, I almost ran down a wino lurching toward the fountain that bubbles in the middle of the Fayetteville Street Mall.

Returning a few moments later, I saw the man, his face a stubblefield of despair, staring into the bubbling fountain. If it had been a river, he would have jumped.

Ah, the street people we have with us always. For most of the year, they blend into the background of our daily lives, as commonplace as the pigeons that flutter out of our paths on the way to lunch.

In the spring, along with the first crocus, they creep out of the shadows into the sun. They prick our conscience.

We wish they would go away. How prone we are, when grieved by the loss of a young and promising friend or some man of great merit, to look upon these and question the wisdom of the Almighty.

Then I remember an incident recounted by our preacher the Rev, Rick Brand. It had to do with his Durham friend, the Rev. David Tucker, who works almost exclusively with street people, from counseling them to feeding them at his church's soup kitchen.

It was only natural that the Rev. Mr. Tucker sometimes wearied of his work, with its constant association with the poor and the downtrodden and their seemingly insoluble problems.

So one Saturday he decided to get away for a while and to take the bus to visit a friend in a nearby town. He took a roundabout route to the bus station, hoping to avoid his charges who, he felt sure, would make some demand on him.

As he entered the station, his heart sank. There stood one of his regulars, a shiftless sort who sometimes sat outside the soup kitchen begging coins from the poor as they entered. But much to his surprise, instead of hitting him up for a handout, the wino spoke cheerfully and passed him by.

At the ticket window, the preacher found that, alas, the fare was more than he had expected. Despite his pleading and promises to bring the small difference by Monday, the agent refused to sell him the ticket.

As the disappointed minister turned to leave, he saw the wino, who apparently had overheard the conversation. The old fellow was shuffling about the terminal, passing his battered old hat among the waiting passengers.

Soon he walked over and, without a word, poured the small collection of coins into the minister's hand. There was enough to cover the cost of the ticket, plus the price of a Coke.

"This was an example of grace under pressure," Rick Brand said.

I encountered a demonstration of unexpected grace last summer in an Asheville shopping mall where I had gone with my wife and college-age daughter.

We had spent the night before at a bed and breakfast place that served piping hot and powerful black coffee. Caught up in the pleasure of a leisurely breakfast with coffee on a flower-bedecked patio that looked out over a mountain range, I indulged in too much caffeine.

I did not realize this until, at the mall, the world started spinning and waves of nausea swept over me. I staggered. My daughter Melinda put her arm around me, led me to a nearby bench and said, "You're gonna be OK, Dad. You're just having a caffeine reaction."

I was surprised and even embarrassed by this dependency on someone who all her life had been dependent on me. But her strong arm and her quiet, reassuring voice gave me a new perspective of a child growing into a young woman.

It is difficult to imagine a reservoir of grace in a wino. But we must remember, as we walk lightheartedly into spring toward the Easter awakening, that even the "least of these" were young once.

As boys of summer, they ran barefoot across the grass, chasing fireflies in the twilight, or on a sweltering day swam naked in a cow pasture creek, in close company with catfish and water moccasins.

As confused, fearful adolescents, they turned and tossed on sweaty sheets through the long hot nights of puberty. As young men of four and twenty, they also saw visions and dreamed dreams.

But somewhere, sometime — whose fault it was I do not know — something didn't click. A cog slipped in the scheme of things, and the delicate balance of chance and time and place and chemistry that determines so much of our lives was forever lost.

Long ago, someone or something snuffed out that inner light that gives each of us our cause for being. I can think of no worse fate than to face eternal winter, knowing that never again will springtime come to the soul.

With that in mind, it doesn't take much grace to strew a little compassion in the path of these.

*March 19, 1988*

# Fathers Change Life's Fuses

A paragraph in a recent Ellen Goodman column about the electronic world we live in struck a responsive chord with me.

She told how, when she was a kid and the lights went out in her house, her father would go down to the basement and replace a burned-out fuse.

"To the best of my knowledge, my father never made a household repair, with the single exception of changing a fuse. This was a task he managed to cloak in such mystery that my sister and I would gaze in admiration when he descended the cellar stairs in darkness and returned in a halo of resurrected light."

I am much like Ellen Goodman's father. I once overheard a conversation between my wife and a tradesman who had the gall to suggest, "It's so simple, your husband can install it in a few seconds."

"Don't be ridiculous," she said. "On a good day, my husband can change two lightbulbs."

One of my earliest memories of mechanical failure is, as a lad, being sent by my older brother to the barn to hitch Old Mike to the sled. When I drove by the house, sawing the gee and haw lines savagely while Old Mike bucked and kicked at the traces, my brother rushed out angrily.

After freeing Old Mike from the painful experience of the heavy trace chain banging against the most sensitive part of the mule's anatomy, my brother gave me a tongue lashing I never forgot.

It was the last time I was sent to hitch up Old Mike, who thereafter regarded me with total contempt, tossing his head angrily and baring his teeth viciously whenever I came near.

Luckily for me, and surely for them, I am the father of girls. It's been easier to measure up. Even in these egalitarian times, parenting girls normally does not involve heaving footballs, dancing around a campfire in a loincloth and Indian headband, or spending the night outdoors in leaky tents during torrential rainstorms.

One night recently I went over to Aldert Root Elementary school to address the young writers there.

Principal Carolyn Earp had prepared me for the possibility of a small audience. "There are a lot of dance recitals and T-ball games going on," she said. We both know that in competition with dance and athletics, literary affairs rank rather low on the priorities list.

We both were pleasantly surprised. The place was packed. Ah, I thought, the game has been called because of rain. Actually, it wasn't. Some dads were so dedicated they had left the ballfield where those miniature replicas of themselves either had hit a home run or struck out.

Now they had come to the school to see what their little Hemingways and Elizabeth Barrett Brownings had written. You see, all is not lost.

Some fathers measure up with fishing pole and earthworms. Tony Jordan came by this week to tell how he and his son had just visited a very private fishing hole.

"We had no sooner dropped our lines, than both of us got a bite. What a whopper! I pulled and pulled. So did Michael. My line broke but the boy kept tugging away and finally landed him. A big old bass. He had taken both our baits and still had my hook in his mouth."

Sinking hooks in the very same fish is real togetherness.

As many of us know, fatherhood comes in stages. To survive with ego intact, fathers must adjust to the changing roles they assume in the eyes and lives of their offspring.

A lot of fathers can find themselves in the interview with Beth Campbell in Studs Terkel's marvelous book, "American Dreams: Lost and Found."

Beth is remembering her father and the many sacrifices he made for the family, including maintaining a lake house the family soon outgrew and abandoned.

"I was really angry at him," she recalls in the interview. "How could you have totally denied all your own wants? You've lost it all, and no one appreciates it. He has to deny it because if he were to accept it, his whole life would seem sad.

"All the lines in my father's face, it's not just aging. He feels out of touch. When I was young, I saw him as a hero. He seemed handsome, athletic, rich. When I was young, he seemed very competent.

"When I became an adolescent, I didn't like him anymore. He seemed corny. He seemed too proud of me, always wanting to brag about me, show off his daughter. When I was in college, I felt real guilty. He paid for it. I couldn't wait to have a job, I didn't want to owe him anything . . . "

Most dads will insist their children owe them nothing, nothing except love, which they have well-earned. But many youngsters find that to be the most burdensome debt of all to pay.

Their frantic frenzy for freedom, their eagerness to please their peers, and their uncertain sorting out of emotions and values can obscure love as completely as the oyster obscures the pearl.

Years from now, many, like Beth, whose father was killed in an auto accident shortly after the interview, will look back at Dad and see the way he really was, and be sad.

Meanwhile, a dad worth his salt hangs in there to the end, sustained by a sense of humor, in much the way that a friend this week moaned, "I only hope I can afford what they are going to give me for Father's Day."

*June 14, 1986*

# 'Place Garbage in Plastic Bags'

ATLANTIC BEACH — I wondered why the beach was so empty on such a glorious day. The strand stretched lazily along the lip of the ocean. A few distant figures silhouetted against the sky looked like black specks on the great desert scenes in the movie "Lawrence of Arabia."

And then I remembered. It was Friday, almost 3 p.m., and time for the wedding! My restless 18-year-old and her friend Susan Kirby had changed their day's entire itinerary, staying at the condo to catch the wedding.

"We'll come in, shower and dress before the wedding and be ready to go out tonight to the Dock House over in Beaufort," I had heard them say that morning.

I am not into the soaps. But I understand that much of the world, at home and at work, comes to a standstill at certain times Monday through Friday for the likes of "General Hospital" and "All My Children."

On this Friday, the day of the barren beach, Crisco the cop was getting married.

"It's Frisco, not Crisco, Daddy," my daughter peevishly had corrected during the previous day's segment as I sat across the room with a bad book, occasionally picking up bits and pieces of the great unfolding drama.

So I left the quiet, beautiful beach and went in to the wedding. It was a ridiculous affair.

On Thursday, the bride-to-be had gotten cold feet about marrying a cop and "not ever knowing when he leaves the house if he will come home alive." She loved Crisco so much she canceled the wedding.

Crisco's friends, all the policemen's wives, Felicia's friends and everybody at General Hospital worked feverishly to change Felicia's mind. In a day or so, the word went out: The wedding is on!

But anytime you cancel a wedding there are problems. An hour before the ceremony, the couple was not only short the caterer, who had been canceled, along with the flowers, the chairs and, alas, also the preacher. But everything, including the parson, was procured in short order. And at last, there came the bride!

They were a handsome couple, Felicia in her lace, with something borrowed and something blue, Crisco in his police uniform, without gunbelt of course. As they strolled down the garden aisle toward the altar, the wail of police sirens filled the air.

The bride tensed, but was quickly reassured by Crisco who whispered firmly, "Honey, nothing is going to stop this wedding now!"

"Oh, isn't he sweet?" wailed our girls, eyes moistening with tears. I snickered cynically.

Crisco was right. Nothing stopped the wedding — nothing except a commercial and the clock. The segment ended just short of the voicing of the vows.

"They always break it at a dramatic point," my daughter explained. "They have to hold over something for Monday." I understand from a reliable source that the wedding indeed was culminated on Monday.

This annual week at the beach is the quiet time of my life, totally relaxing: long walks, seafood, snoozing until 9, coffee on the deck with a clear view of the blue Atlantic. But this time, I had procrastinated in choosing the light reading I usually take along.

At the last moment, I asked a well-read friend for suggestions. I was surprised when he recommended Sidney Sheldon's "The Other Side of Midnight."

"I know," he said, responding to my puzzled look. "But this is his best, probably the only good thing he has written."

"The Other Side of Midnight" was not available at the library. But the librarian suggested I take another. "This is the best," she promised, handing over "Master of the Game."

Still skeptical, I saved Sheldon until the last. I thoroughly enjoyed a couple of novels by Tar Heel authors, Lee Smith's "Black Mountain Breakdown," and Anne Tyler's "The Accidental Tourist."

Both are superbly written stories, in which the authors probe the psyches of their characters with the delicate skill of a surgeon performing brain surgery.

When I had read everything in the condo but the wallpaper and the house rules — e.g., "Please don't run on the deck." "Place all garbage in black plastic bags" — I decided to take on Mr. Sheldon.

The contrast was devastating. It was like switching from vintage wine to flat beer, beer heavily sudsed with sex.

"He took her in his arms and kissed her hungrily, feeling her warm body pressing against his." How many times have I read that cliche or its equivalent? As a literary effort, the book went downhill from there.

I can't say what influence the soaps and second-class literature will have on our young generation. Perhaps life is indeed a soap opera or a bad book in which the characters go from one shallow thought to another, from bed to bed, spouse to spouse, crisis to crisis. Perhaps the most important thing is taking her in his arms and kissing her hungrily.

But I can't help thinking that the sign at the condo reading "Place all garbage in black plastic bags" didn't apply only to watermelon rinds and egg shells.

*June 28, 1986*

# Proper Etiquette While Naked

A fellow who has been going to the doctor a lot lately lamented to me the absence of a good book on etiquette at the doctor's office.

"After all, who sees more of us than our wives or lovers?" he asked. "Only our doctors."

He has a point. Many patients have a hard time working out a comfortable relationship with their doctor. Although doctors are mortals like the rest of us, many find it difficult to relate to them as just ordinary, likable people we'd enjoy knowing better and under different circumstances.

"I never know what to call my doctor," my friend said. "What do you call yours?"

"It depends on how bad I feel when I go in," I laughed. "Some days I call him God. Because I expect miracles. No, seriously, I call him Frank — after he asked me to "

And some folks have a hang-up about socializing with their doctor. A Raleigh woman confided to me that she had to switch physicians after she and her husband started seeing him and his wife socially.

"I just couldn't have it both ways," she sighed. "He was a good doctor but he was a better friend. I had to choose."

Patients also tend to over-revere their physicians. Every time I go to the doctor, my my wife scrutinizes my outfit as if I'm going to the undertaker.

"Oh, dear, you have on a brown sock and a blue one," she says.

She never does that when I visit my barber or the plumber comes to my house. A doctor could care less about what a patient has on. Much of the time when he comes in, we have on next to nothing anyway.

But dressing properly for the doctor has been instilled in us from childhood. Three years ago, a college-age friend severely banged up in an auto accident was still in the emergency room when his distraught mother rushed in. The first thing he said to her was, "Don't worry, Mom. I have on clean underwear." His mother smiled her gratitude through her tears.

The fellow who lamented the lack of a guide on patient-doctor etiquette recounted a recent visit to his doctor.

"The nurse escorted me to one of those little cubicles, told me to strip and handed me a sheet to wrap myself in. Every 10 minutes or so she'd knock briskly. And as I would clutch the sheet around me, she'd peep in and say, Doctor will be with you shortly."

"Then the doctor finally came in and we got down to business. There I was stretched out in the most compromising position imaginable, naked from the waist down, with that same pretty nurse standing right there assisting.

"I kept wanting to say, 'Ma'am, will you please hand me my sheet?' I would have even settled for a fig leaf."

Another friend is worried about having pulled a social faux pas at Rex Hospital a couple of years ago.

For weeks he had postponed seeking treatment for an ailment that had stubbornly defied various over-the-counter balms and nostrums.

But one night around 1 a.m., the pain became so excruciating that he rolled out of bed, dressed and drove to the emergency room.

"I was in such agony, I thought nothing could be worse," he said. "I was escorted to an examining room, told to undress and lie down. A few minutes later, the nurse returned, wheeling in a tray covered with all kinds of things — scalpels, tongs, ice-picks and a five-bladed Swiss army knife.

"After she left, I lay there for what seemed like a small eternity, eyeing those gleaming instruments of torture. Then I jumped up, put on my clothes and took off. I haven't had the first pain since.

"But I do think maybe I should have waited around long enough to tell somebody I was leaving."

Then there is the business of who takes your blood when you go in for a physical or cholesterol check. Don't ask. You have no choice.

The first thing you do is glance around the lab to see if there are any new faces aboard. If there is, start praying you'll get one of the old-timers. A new face sometimes, not always, means she has only recently graduated from taking blood from an orange.

One morning, I counted my good luck when I noticed across the room a new nurse struggling to take blood from a big fellow with the biceps of a weight-lifter.

"You mean you didn't get it this time either?" he whimpered.

The lady in white tried again. No blood. Finally, she called in reinforcements.

"That's your contribution to science," I said softly as I walked by, rolling down my sleeve.

"Yeah," he growled "Thanks to the animal rights activists they aren't allowed to experiment on animals anymore. So it's back to us."

I could go on, but won't. Writing doctor-patient etiquette is risky business. All I can advise is take a bath at least a couple of days before you go and be sure to wear clean underwear.

*July 19, 1989*

# Don't Poison the Peacock

These are the lazy, hazy days of summer in the foothills where I visited recently.

The katydids sing in the shimmering heat. The fields are heavy with ripened wheat. But rains have delayed the harvest. The corn is almost as high as an elephant's eye. And some of the neighbors have died.

Out of the corner of my mind, I am hearing my sister say to a relative, "Yes, and would you believe it? Out of all those seven sisters, only one has a living husband. And they really aren't that old. Why do the men always go first?"

I could tell her. But she wouldn't believe me.

At the Lantern Restaurant, I listen to the buzz of conversation from a nearby table. One of the women apparently has excused herself to go to the restroom. In a little while, when she has not returned, another inquires, "Do you think Priscilla is OK.?"

"Oh, yes. She has migraines."

"Oh, too bad. You know, I haven't been bothered a bit by headaches since I got back from my trip to the Holy Land."

At our own table, one of the women is afflicted with a severe case of poison ivy.

"I got it pulling weeds from the iris bed. It got so bad I went to the doctor and he has given me something to take.

"I found out it is a steroid and I called him up and said I sure didn't want to get hooked on steroids like those football players, and he said, 'My goodness, Myrtle, there isn't enough steroid in those pills to hurt you.'

"But I know better. Since I've been taking the stuff I can work out in my garden all day long and, by nightfall, I still feel like jumping over the housetop."

My sister is saying how much better she is feeling since she traded her blood-pressure cuff for a used lawn mower. "People take too much medicine anyway."

Back at the table behind me, there is talk about a man who has left his wife after 35 years.

"Well, if you had to go to *your* mother-in-law's for chicken every Sunday for 35 years, you might do the same thing."

When we get home from our trek through the mountains, my sister discovers that the neighbor's peacock has passed through her flower beds, leaving a path of devastation among the impatiens and geraniums.

"I hate to do it, but I am going to have to poison that bird," she says, gazing mournfully at the mangled flowers.

"You can't do that!" I caution, thinking she is serious. If it is bad luck to kill a mockingbird, think what disasters would befall anyone who poisoned a peacock.

I have learned more about peacocks from Flannery O'Connor than I have from life. She kept 40 of them at a time. But then she was always a bit weird.

Until I read her essay, "The King of the Birds," I did not know that peacocks live to be 35 years old, that only the male puts on the big show and that he unfurls his tail when he feels like it, no matter how much you coax or coerce.

Miss O'Connor tells about the time a telephone repairman visited the farm and kept urging one of her peacocks to "Come on, bud, get the show on the road."

Just as the fellow was finally driving away in disgust, the peacock unfurled. Miss O'Connor ran after him calling, "Hey, wait! He's doing it!"

The lineman swerved his truck back around in time to catch the brilliance of the full tail, only to comment, "Never saw such long ugly legs. I bet that rascal could outrun a bus."

Beauty is in the eye of the beholder. Miss O'Connor also recounted the time that an old black woman, beholding the peacock in all its splendor, muttered in awe, "Amen! Amen!"

And the time a truck driver, arriving at the O'Connor farm with a load of hay, came upon an unfurled peacock in the middle of the road. He slammed on his brakes and shouted, "Get a load of that bastard!"

Peacocks were not on my mind when I retired that night in my sister's back bedroom. I drifted off to sleep under a blanket of cool mountain air.

Sometime around midnight, my sleep was punctuated by a piercing, blood-curdling scream just under my window. I leaped straight up in the dark, only to remember the neighbor's peacock. In the past I had heard them crying from the neighbor's pond across the fields, none had ever roosted right under my window.

For the remainder of the sleepless night, the peacock screamed every 20 minutes or so. Next morning, when I went in to breakfast tired and bleary-eyed, I said to my sister, "Go ahead, poison the damn peacock!"

The culprit was still with us, strutting arrogantly around the yard like some Aztec god decked out in a diamond-studded cloak and train.

"The least he could do is show his tail," someone said.

"He showed his tail last night," I groused.

I am not over-fond of peacocks that scream in the night. They remind me too much of legislators who dilly-dally in July.

*July 13, 1989*

# Love, Baseball and Buckroe Beach

The research paper in anatomy is due and there are books about heart surgery and the artificial heart scattered about the den floor. My high school senior is learning how the heart operates mechanically. She already knows something of how the human heart functions emotionally.

I recently attended the Broughton High Queen of Hearts dance, an extravaganza of pomp and pulchritude played out against a backdrop of "The Wizard of Oz," complete with Dorothy and Toto, the Scarecrow, the Cowardly Lion and the Tin Man, all dancing down the Yellow Brick Road.

Looking at the young lovelies in their lavish gowns, escorted by handsome youths, self-conscious and cramped into tuxedos, I thought how breakable are the hearts of the young, especially at this age.

My mind flashed back to the time when the first young man came to call on a daughter of mine. His name was Ronnie. He was five. His mother, of course, drove him to our house to pick up his date.

I remember marveling at his self-assurance as the sturdy little fellow stepped sprightly from the car, came courageously down the walk and up to the door. I have often wondered what happened to Ronnie, who that summer moved to South America, ending a painless romance that remains a pleasant photoprint of memory.

Years later, the young man who came calling on my second daughter's first "real date" was far less assured. So was his 14-year-old date. In fact, the whole household was tight as a drum over the event.

"Daddy!" the distressed daughter exclaimed when, passing through the den, she saw me sprawled on the couch reading a book. "You're not going to the door in your gardening shoes and without your tie, are you?"

I groused back to the bedroom, changed my shoes and put on a tie, adding a jacket for good measure, just in time to answer the doorbell.

There he stood, a likely looking lad of barely 16, clean of face, clear of eyes, dressed to the nines, looking as if he had been poured into his tight-fitting, faded jeans. He wore an unusually cheerful sports shirt and a pair of obviously well-loved, well-scuffed Nike sneakers. When I extended a greeting, along with my hand, his palm was wet with perspiration.

He did not linger long. As the couple backed out of the driveway, my wife glanced out the window.

"Oh dear!" she cried. "He doesn't have his lights on!" I had to restrain her from running down the street after the car.

All that seems a long time ago. I no longer remember the boy's name, only the sense of something beginning over which I would have less and less control as time went by.

During a discussion of how the heart hurts from non-physical causes one of the more senior men here in the newsroom reminisced over an early infatuation.

"When I was 16, I was in love with an 18-year-old named Almarie so much it hurt," Jim said. "She was beautiful. She got a job in a printing plant in Newport News, Va., and told me that if I would come up to see her sometime, we would go to Buckroe Beach and have a picnic.

"The very next Sunday, I caught the train to Portsmouth. It cost 45 cents and stopped in the Port Norfolk area. I then had to catch a bus (10 cents) to the ferry that went across the Elizabeth River to Norfolk. That was 5 cents. I had to pay 10 cents on the trolley car that ran to the Newport News ferry dock. That ferry cost 25 cents and I got seasick on the crossing.

"At the ferry landing in Newport News, I put 5 cents in a pay telephone to give Almarie the good news that I had arrived; and she said she had a headache and couldn't go to Buckroe that day.

"So I had to retrace my steps, to the tune of another 95 cents. I never went back to Newport News or Buckroe Beach.

"About 20 or 25 years later, my sister's husband died in Almarie's hometown. When I went down for the funeral, one of the first to come by my sister's house with condolences was Almarie (she was going to sing at the funeral).

"When she saw me, Almarie came up and hugged me, gushed all around, and said, 'Lordy, I surely do want to apologize. I'm so sorry I had that headache that day and couldn't go with you to Buckroe Beach.'

"And with the beautiful Almarie finally in my arms, all I could think about was all those nickels and dimes and quarters and trains and trolleys and ferries between Ahoskie and Newport News."

This past week, I had a call from Calvin Coolidge White, former president of a local business college, and the man who knows more trivia about our American presidents than anyone in the world. He was calling from the hospital where he had had heart surgery — "Six bypasses, A.C.! Count 'em. Six!

"Yeah, I'm over here collecting baseball bats!" he sighed.

"Baseball bats? At the hospital? What on earth for?"

"I'm gonna use 'em on all those people who told me there was nothing to heart surgery."

I plan to borrow some of Calvin Coolidge White's baseball bats to use on people who say that being young and in love doesn't hurt. It does. I remember.

*February 22, 1986*

# They Do Come Home Again

She is home for the weekend, bringing youth's light and laughter, along with the laundry basket of dirty clothes, the unfinished class assignments and her typewriter.

The telephone comes to life again. Cars and friends come and go. Departures and arrivals are as erratic and unpredictable as fall showers.

The weekend winds down to Sunday afternoon and she is bent over the typewriter in the den. It is an electronic marvel that chirps when a word is misspelled or the typist reaches the end of a line. As she hurries along copying her theme, the den sounds like a cornfield of chirping crickets.

"When is the paper due?" I ask, already suspecting the answer.

"First thing in the morning."

Nothing has changed since elementary school when we tried to build the Ocracoke Lighthouse in papier mache, since high school when the big research papers were coming due. "First thing in the morning" is the theme song of the curse of procrastination that complicates the lives of the young, and is visited upon their caring parents.

"How do you spell miscellaneous?" "Is every day one word or two?" she asks her resident dictionaries, me on the couch and her mother in the kitchen.

"What footnote style should I use?" she wants to know. Her first-day handout from her teacher doesn't say. Mother scurries about looking for the "MLA Handbook," that accepted Bible of English teachers.

"I don't think I have these footnotes quite an inch from the bottom," the student moans, examining the first typed page.

"So what! It doesn't matter. You should be graded on your creative work, not your typing," I fume, impatient with education's corseted obsession with form rather than content.

The assignment is a good one, innovative and challenging. She is comparing and contrasting the Ben in Arthur Miller's "Death of a Salesman" with the Ben in Wolfe's "Look Homeward Angel."

Now, she has mislaid the page number for footnoting a quotation. I enlist in the rescue after my wife unearths my copy of Wolfe's novel from the downstairs bedroom.

Of all the great books of the 20th century, this is the one I would most like to have written. On the yellowing flyleaf is the penciled price I paid for the book 41 years ago at a Greensboro second-hand bookshop. A steal at 45 cents.

Every man should read or reread this novel, this pulsing, pulling story of a boy groping his way toward manhood. Here is described so perfectly, so poignantly, the pain and suffering of puberty that we all have known.

I personally identify with the young Eugene Gant, the sprawling boarding house, the big, brawling family, each member wrestling with his own secret fears, his personal flaw.

I, too, was the youngest and mine was the more sensitive view of the fierce passions and competition for attention, love and purpose that seethe through most large families, cresting at times in conflict, hurt and sorrow.

Half a century later, today's young suffer the same nagging guilts and fears as the boy of Altamont, the same sensual nightmares that frighten and confuse.

There is still that awful, gnawing loneliness, the pain of puberty, the struggle to break free, to know one's self and each other. The loneliness especially echoes through Wolfe's words:

"Naked and alone we came into exile. In her dark womb we did not know our mother's face; from the prison of her flesh have we come into the unspeakable and incommunicable prison of this earth. Which of us has known his brother? Which of us has looked into his father's heart? Which of us has not remained forever prison-pent? Which of us is not forever a stranger and alone?"

I am grateful for my daughter's teacher, whose name I do not know. ("She must be good, Daddy, she taught at Harvard") for acquainting my child with the greatness of Wolfe.

But I rage against the piecemeal fast-food fashion in which it is served to a classroom massed with 450 youths, some of them hungering for the rich, rewarding and intimate exchange that good literature deserves.

No university, regardless of its claim to greatness, can ever be much more than mediocre as long as it subjects its undergraduates, many in their most receptive years, to such callous intellectual abuse.

The typist sighs dispiritedly. Throughout, she has inadvertently typed Willie Loman, rather than Willy Loman. Out comes the correction fluid. Ah, if only the mistakes of life, of choice, of wrong roads taken could be so easily remedied.

She has returned to the university and the house is still again. Rain whispers around the windows. The wind teases the lingering leaves in the great oaks.

From far afield I hear the faint caw of a crow in the November silence. And I hear again the ghosts of Eugene and Ben, the poignant cry that echoes throughout the novel, "O lost, and by the wind grieved, ghost, come back again."

*November 15, 1986*

# 'Do You Serve Colored Here?'

Like excited kids just let out of school, the four mongrel dogs came trotting along Hargett Street. The lead animal glanced briefly at the stoplight before stepping off the curb and into Dawson Street, one of the state's busiest thoroughfares.

A screeching of brakes from three lanes of peak hour traffic saved the dog from certain death. Tail between his legs, he sheepishly retreated to the curb where, obviously embarrassed by his almost fatal leadership error, he apologized to his pals by briefly nuzzling the nose of each.

As traffic resumed, I thought how we motorists had risked our own and other lives by instinctively trying to save the hides of four scrawny, unloved animals.

The animal rights activists would have been proud. And maybe pinned medals on all of us.

Under other circumstances any one of us might have reacted differently. I have thrown brooms at pesky squirrels and aimed curses and rocks at neighborhood cats poised to pounce on unsuspecting baby birds. But I think within most of us there flickers a candle of compassion for animals. Even so, animal righters sometimes demand too much of us.

Oh, yes, animal abuse abounds. Take my friend Hank. When it comes to animals, Hank is bad news.

When he is not stalking the soft-eyed deer in the forest, he is shivering in a duck blind at Mattamuskeet, waiting to blast the graceful wild things out of the sky. And when nothing else is in season, he arms himself with a flashlight and something resembling a pitchfork and spends all night stomping up and down an Eastern North Carolina stream stabbing sleepy, unsuspecting frogs.

"Hey, Hank, what are you killing these days?" I asked when we met in the hall recently.

"Nothing much," he said sadly. "Me and my wife went turkey hunting last weekend. But we couldn't scare up a single bird. Then as we were headed home, danged if we didn't come up on a big old turkey gobbler standing right in the middle of the highway.

"Boy, he was a real beaut! I hit the brakes and reached back and grabbed my gun off the rack. I was gonna shoot him from the truck window but when I started rolling the glass down, I accidentally hit my wife in the head with the gun butt. By the time I got through apologizin' and she got through cussin' that dern gobbler must have been five miles away."

One recent rainy afternoon, my telephone rang. When you pick up the phone and all you hear is uncontrolled sobbing, you wonder a number of things.

Somebody's got the wrong number. Somebody's a little wacky. Or somebody's bringing bad news. Really bad news.

"I know I'm being over-emotional," the woman managed to say between sobs.

"A few moments ago I was out in this downpour we've been having when a plumbing company truck passed. Two white men were sitting in the cab, eating their lunch, and a poor, black kid was sitting in the back, huddled against the cab, looking like a soaked animal, while the rain poured down in torrents."

She said she had gone straight to the telephone and called the plumbing company to lodge a complaint. The secretary had told her the boss was out but she would pass the word.

"I suppose nothing will come of it," the caller sighed. "But I know one thing. My husband is a building contractor and I can assure you that plumbing firm will never get any of his business."

"There was room in the cab for the kid, plenty of room," she continued, her voice again breaking. "I want to know. Is this Raleigh? Is this really Raleigh?"

I tried to be reassuring, reminding her that the two men in the truck no more represented Raleigh than they did North Carolina. Or Chicago or Philadelphia. Or Denver or El Paso.

I told her about the time during the early days of integration here when a black woman walked into the drugstore around the corner from us and timidly asked the young woman behind the soda fountain, "Do you serve colored?" and the confused girl replied, "Colored what?"

That incident didn't signal total victory over racism. But it was a beginning. Cruelty, or total lack of compassion, isn't the sole province of plumbers in pickup trucks in Raleigh, North Carolina. What about those motorists who risked their lives saving that dumb dog on Dawson Street?

The trouble is that too many people still treat a stray dog roaming a downtown street better than they do a fellow human being. That's what my caller was crying about.

*May 5, 1989*

# A Stud Somewhere in Chicago

Not long ago, this newspaper ran a long Sunday article in which a bunch of intellectuals tried to convince us there is no Heaven. It's all just hokum, they said.

Try selling that to the folks at Fairview Baptist Church on Route 3, Dobson!

I've always been hooked on Heaven. As a kid, I was taught that Heaven was a real place where, if we were good, we would all meet in the sweet by and by, walk the streets of gold and listen day and night to the Heavenly choir.

Granted, that sounds like a pretty dull day, but I always felt I could make the best of it. Or change it.

There's nothing wrong with fantasizing about the hereafter. After all, one man's concept of Heaven could be Hell to another. It all depends on what each of us wants out of Paradise.

For example, one day while I was packing for a foothills visit, I heard my wife say on the phone to a friend, "I just wish there were some place I enjoyed visiting as much as A.C. loves going to Surry County. I'm afraid when he gets to Heaven, if indeed he does, he's going to be terribly disappointed if it isn't a lot like Surry County."

She exaggerates of course. But maybe not much. But my hope of Heaven is encouraged by the last line of a poem a minister friend sent me this week:

*If you could get religion like a Baptist,*
*Experience it like a Methodist,*
*Be loyal to it like a Catholic,*
*Sacrifice for it like a Jew,*
*Be proud of it like an Episcopalian,*
*And enjoy it like a Holiness,*
*What a great religion you'd have,*
*Especially if in addition you could go to*
*Heaven automatically, like a Presbyterian.*

As for me, I think I would enjoy doing in Heaven pretty much the same things I enjoy on Earth. Surely they have a newspaper up there. But then again, I might like to try something entirely new and foreign to my nature.

For example, consider the case of three men of the cloth who arrived in Heaven on a terribly busy day. At the Pearly Gates, a breathless St. Peter, wringing his hands, said that due to an unexplained crush of new arrivals, there was just no way their papers could be processed that day.

"I've never seen such a mob," the good saint sighed. "They must have lowered the standards for admission without telling me."

He told the trio they would have to be put on hold for 48 hours. But as a sop for the inconvenience, he would allow them to return to earth and spend the time doing or being anything they wished.

The rabbi said he would like to spend his 48 hours playing golf, preferably in the Masters at Augusta, having all his life wondered why so many men in his congregation consistently skipped services to chase a little white ball around the green expanses.

Father Flannegan admitted sheepishly that he'd like to spend two whole days at O'Malley's Bar, having heard thousands of parishioners confess their inability to pass up the place on the way home after work.

Meanwhile, the Reverend Mr. Pureheart, a Baptist minister, was thinking how throughout his long years in the pulpit, he had been beset by the almost overwhelming desire to engage in extramarital sex with several pretty women in his congregation.

But, unlike the Bakkers and Swaggarts of his profession, he had steadfastly resisted the urge to run off with the choir director or sleep with the church secretary. Now was his chance. He blurted out to St. Peter that he would like to spend his two days on earth as a stud.

Two days later, St. Peter dispatched an angel to retrieve the three clergymen.

"Fetch Father Flannegan from O'Malley's Bar in upper Manhattan," he ordered. "You'll find him passed out cold under the first table to the left as you enter.

"Pick up Rabbi Schonman down in Augusta where, after attending the Masters, he is making a nuisance of himself stopping people on the street, lying about making a hole in one and shooting a two under par.

"Then swing around to Chicago where they're having a terrible snowstorm. You'll find the Rev. Pureheart imbedded in the front left tire of a 1985 Oldsmobile parked at 1313 South Christiana Avenue."

With that kind of communications problem, surely there is a job for me on Heaven's newspaper if that is what I really want to do.

Seriously, folks. I'm not giving up on Heaven, no matter what the intellectuals and the scientists say. Too many strange and marvelous things happen every hour of every day for there not to be a Mr. Big somewhere out there pulling a lot of strings and throwing His weight around.

Besides, I'd hate to leave this world thinking there is nowhere else to go.

*April 27, 1989*

# Behind the State-UNC Rivalry

At 7 a.m. the morning after Michigan beat Carolina in the NCAA quarterfinals, the telephone rang in the newsroom.

"Michigan won," I heard the reporter say.

"Who was that?" I asked.

"Oh, some State fan," he muttered, returning to his work.

"How do you know?" I asked.

"By the way he whooped and hollered."

"Well, it could have been a Duke fan."

"Nah, it's too wet to plow. It was a State guy."

I'm sorry to say that the good-natured office kidding goes much deeper out there in the real world, where the war among State, Carolina and Duke fans is bitter, uncompromising and unceasing.

For many years the feuding was fiercest between Carolina and Duke. Not any more. It's State-Carolina now. And the consensus seems to be that Wolfpack fans are the most ferocious. And, some say, the most paranoid.

Listen to this Carolina fan:

"I have a neighbor I love almost like a brother except when State beats Carolina. Then I hate him the same way I used to hate my brother after he would beat my tail. Most of the time, this guy is a peach. He'd do anything for me. But let Carolina lose and he can't wait to come at me with 'Your Heels didn't do so good, did they?' "

Many years ago, my wife and I were close friends with a younger couple. Tom, a State grad, was everything you could want in a best friend. Except when his beloved Wolfpack lost a ball game.

I dreaded the Carolina-State contests. My wife and I couldn't yell for Carolina without risking Tom's uncontrollable rage. And if State lost, there went the weekend, no matter what our plans. Having to choose between wanting your team to win and trashing the weekend was pretty awful. I don't know if his obsession with sports had anything to do with it or not, but my friend died of a heart attack at 39. I still miss him.

The intense rivalry has left more than one family with a house divided. Including my own.

My elder daughter, an avid State fan all her life although she watered at the Old Well for two years, was home for a brief visit last weekend. As we settled down to watch the UNC-Michigan match, she said matter-of-factly, "Sorry, Dad. Nothing personal. But you know I have to pull against Carolina."

"Not under my roof, you don't," I snapped, startled at the intensity of my anger. She pleaded a headache and went to bed without watching the game.

In my efforts to delve into what makes State fans adore their athletes and hate their athletic rivals with such fire, I consulted a well-known guru.

"I think you'll usually find this sort of over-intensity at many land grant colleges," he said. "There is a feeling, perhaps a little paranoia, at the 'people's universities,' that other schools, especially places like Duke and Carolina, are elitist."

He must be right. Only this week, I remarked to a co-worker that I had pulled hard for Virginia against Oklahoma, even though Coach Terry Holland named his dog Dean.

"Not I," she said bitterly. "I can't stand the whole Charlottesville schmear. The pseudo-superiority and the Jefferson-was-our-boy elitism."

"Remember when State was called 'Cow College' and Carolina was 'Whiskey Hill' or 'Snob Hill?'" the guru continued.

"Yeah, but that was a long time ago. Now State is recognized for so much more than that. In fact, in this new age of science and technology, State's time has come, and in those gung-ho fields the university is outstripping Carolina in national prestige. They're on the cutting edge of the future."

"Yes, but like racism, it will take generations for the scars to heal," the guru cautioned. That's why, when a Carolina team bites the dust, State folks feel the same kind of high that the peasants of Paris felt during the French Revolution when they thronged the streets to jeer Marie Antoinette on her way to the guillotine."

"But why me? Why, after every Carolina loss, do my State friends seek me out to rub salt in my wounds. 'Hey, did you enjoy the game last night?' or 'I'm surprised to see you at work today.' I never did that, not once, when State stunk up the place in Atlanta."

"They want to punish you," the guru chuckled. "In fact your daughter was punishing you by pulling for Michigan. And the reason for that probably lies somewhere deep in her psyche, perhaps going back to childhood."

"Punish me! For what? I *never* spanked her. And the last time I scolded her was when she was 5 and hid in the downstairs shower to keep from going with her mother to the 'Dance of the Sugarplum Fairies' ballet.

"And I have never been intentionally nasty to my State friends. So what's the problem.?"

"Well, you *did* go to Carolina," the guru said grumpily. "And you'll have to live with that for the rest of your life."

That's the last time I go to a guru who got his undergraduate degree in animal science from N.C. State University!

*March 31, 1989*

# Go With Them Through the Dark

I am in the doghouse with some members of my family because I went to the beach for the weekend instead of attending a Sunday celebration of my 97-year-old sister's birthday.

"How could you be so insensitive?" one asked. "With her heart condition, dear Vesta may not be here much longer."

Not bothering to explain that my sister's birthday had slipped up on me, I smiled to myself, remembering that I must have been 14 years old when I first heard that ominous warning. Yet here she is, the matriarch of my family, a lovely lady with great serenity and serendipity, the daughter of my father's first marriage, celebrating her 97th.

A couple of years ago, my wife, picking up the familiar refrain from my family, said, "We must go by and see Vesta. She may not be here much longer."

We did. My sister, then 95, had just returned from a week of camping in the mountains with her daughter and son-in-law.

I never cease to be astounded by the miraculous longevity and exciting lifestyles of many of today's senior citizens.

A couple of years ago on a plane trip to Europe, instead of being assigned a seat beside my wife, I was put across the aisle next to two elderly ladies. They had little to say, to me or each other, but both kept crawling over my legs to go to the bathroom. One of them sometimes forgot the way back to her seat and the other would have to go fetch her.

Much to my dismay, I learned they were on the same tour with us.

The more fragile one, I learned after landing in Germany, was 80 years old. "There's no way she can survive this tour," I confided to my wife.

On the first day out, I watched apprehensively as she tottered down the steep steps to peer into the huge, cavernous wine vat near the University of Heidelberg. Everywhere we went, she and her friend brought up the rear. But they kept coming.

We thought we had lost the little lady for good one morning when our bus driver hit his brakes suddenly to keep from crashing into a reckless driver in Austria.

Miss Josie, perched on the seat by the bus's side door, hurtled headfirst into the stairwell. Then the rest of us, sitting too stunned to move, saw the frail hands reach up for the guard rail as Miss Josie climbed out of the stairwell and back to her seat.

Throughout the tour, Miss Josie never missed a beat. When I was so tired I holed up in my room in Vienna, Miss Josie made the extra six-hour side excursion to the Hungarian border. When I begged off to wash out my underwear in Lucerne, Miss Josie was out with the young crowd on the moonlight cruise on the lake.

At the tour's end, on that last nostalgic night in a Munich nightclub, I danced with Miss Josie to the "Oompah!" music. She was as light and graceful as frothy champagne.

I imagined her as the popular beauty she must have been in those long ago days of her youth.

Ah, would that everyone's golden years could be as dignified and purposeful as those of my sister and Miss Josie. But as we all know, that is not the case.

Dr. Paul Maness, a friend of long standing and great sensitivity, has introduced me to a book of warm, compassionate essays written by a Seattle doctor. What an injustice — that a doctor can perform miracles and write, too, while the rest of us struggle along with one talent at best.

One of the essays in Dr. Robert Colfelt's "Together in the Dark" is about a frail old woman who lives in the chronic-care wing of a hospital.

"The doctor visits her on rounds, careful not to touch her. He is formal, excessively jovial and talks more to the nurse than to her. Even in her twilight awareness, she anticipates his test of her mental condition:

" 'Who is the president?' Her sluggish memory ponders how there ever came to be such an assemblage of doctors, nurses and others who don't know who is the president, and who, once told, promptly forget.

"He leans forward and shouts the question in her ear. She forces a smile, and he repeats it louder and more slowly. She studies the two blurs in front of her and replies, 'Harry Roosevelt.' The doctor and nurse glance knowingly at each other, pat her on the shoulder . . . "

The essay goes on to describe how the nurse roughly puts the old woman to bed, irritated because she will not urinate when taken to the bathroom.

"She drifts into pleasant memories of when Harry Roosevelt was president and how he would never permit people to be treated like this. But Harry Roosevelt is gone and so is everyone else who might help her. She is on her own and there is no escape, only resistance. She empties her full bladder into the bed and falls asleep."

The message here as I see it is that we must deal ever so gently with all those less fortunates who at age 80 do not dance to the Oompah music in Munich or who at 95 haven't just come home from camping in the hills. And have no one to go with them through the dark.

Happy 97th, Vesta.

*June 1, 1989*

# Tough for a '10' in January

Before returning to college after the holidays, my daughter called me aside and suggested that I "re-evaluate" my attitude toward life.

Reading the surprise and perplexity on my face, she said, "You just haven't been yourself lately...really not much fun at all. In fact, you have been downright grumpy and entirely too cynical during the holidays."

Perhaps I should plead guilty to her charge. Obviously I must have let my guard down. I must have at some moment or another forgotten that nobody promised me a rose garden. It wasn't that I didn't have a good holiday. I suppose on a scale of 1 to 10, it was at least an 8.

I can remember some 5s or 6s: The Christmas the fully decorated tree came crashing down on the furniture, the year I sprained my back lugging in the tub of sand for the "live tree" and the year the kids saw me stowing Santa's stuff in the trunk of the car prior to departing for Grandmother's on Christmas Eve.

And this year I was pleased with the wren house and the suet feeder my daughters had put under the tree for me.

I fared better than some of my friends, including the one who sighed and said, "After passing out a few hundred dollar bills right and left before and during the holiday, I don't know what I expected. But I think I expected a little more than the paperback book my two girls had gone in together and bought for me."

Even my mother-in-law did well by me. Instead of investing a bundle in an exotic shirt or tie or something I'd rather pick out for myself, she gave me cash.

"Not my mother-in-law," sighed a fellow here at the office. "Mine gave me a bar of soap — Brut, with a rope around it. You know, the thing you hang in the shower but never use. But she treated all the men in the family alike. Sons, sons-in-law; grandsons: We all got Brut soap — on a rope."

I've always thought of myself as a passable parent. I once received a Father's Day card from this very same daughter that read, "Daddy, you're a 10!" But at the time she was eight or nine and I was somewhat younger. Her perspective on me undoubtedly has changed, along with my perspective on life.

I was still pondering my daughter's departing words the next day as I sorted through the post-holiday avalanche of mail: tax forms, utility bills, a circular urging me to buy life insurance, a reminder to mail in my Alumni Association dues and a letter from a bulb company urging me to place my gladioli order before the special runs out.

Then out tumbled an envelope with "Plink. Splut. Kerplop." printed on it in colorful tones. "When life glooms over, open here," it said.

I opened. It was a subscription offer from The New Yorker, promising to cheer me up for all of 1987, "when the stock market is down...when the bureaucrats have done it again...when rain is predicted for the weekend...when they serve you bread pudding that contains only two raisins."

The brochures included samples of the promised cheer. I confess I chuckled over a reprint of a story Miami Herald crime reporter Edna Buchanan had written about a killing at a local fried-chicken outlet. Bright, snappy leads are pearls of great price in the writing business.

An ex-con named Gary Robinson one Sunday night lurched drunkenly into a fried chicken place, shoved his way to the front of the line and ordered a three-piece box of chicken to go.

Sent to the end of the line to wait his turn, Gary flew into a rage when, finally again at the head of the line, he was told there was no more chicken and would he settle for chicken nuggets instead.

Gary wouldn't. After slugging the waitress in the head, Robinson set off a chain of events that ended with his being shot dead by a security guard.

Edna Buchanan's lead read: "Gary Robinson died hungry."

We don't think a killing qualifies as a sunbeam amid the low clouds of January's discontent. Even if it did, one sunbeam does not a spring bring.

I imagine a lot of parents join me in this post-season letdown, the dead-of-winter doldrums when children like mine have gone gleefully back to the campus, to the friends, to the good times, the loud music and late-night pizza, the post-game parties.

Meanwhile, back home, their parents are picking up the pieces of Christmas, stowing the tree ornaments in the attic, straightening up the rooms left in disarray, paying the piper for all the extravagances they found under the tree.

Soon the calls of woe — collect of course — start coming in from the campuses, hundreds of miles apart. This one has flu and can't keep anything on her stomach. That one couldn't get the psych class she wanted and, alas, had to sign up for a course in skiing at Wolf Laurel.

But, Papa, keep your chin up. Already the red-headed woodpecker is clinging to the suet feeder, and soon Mr. and Mrs. Wren will be flying in to negotiate a lease on the new condo. Spring is always a "10," even to cynical grumps.

*January 17, 1987*

# Salmon Thursday, Quayle Friday

As we rode by the White House one night last week, I wondered if the light on in the Oval Office meant the President was working late.

The weekend before the annual Washington meeting of the American Society of Newspaper Editors, I had attended a North Carolina editorial writers' conference where Hugh Sidey, longtime White House correspondent for Time Magazine, described the working habits of presidents he had covered.

Mr. Sidey, who his introducer said has been "intimate" with eight presidents, says President Bush gets up very early and goes to the Oval Office to work.

Jimmy Carter, he said, used to arise at 5 every morning and go there to meditate. Jerry Ford also rolled out of bed at 5 to exercise his football knee so he wouldn't fall down during the day.

Mr. Reagan was different. This affable president languished in bed or over breakfast until 8:30 or 9, went to the office for an hour or two, had lunch, took a nap and rode horses in the afternoon.

Mr. Sidey described President Kennedy as a "sexual athlete" and the most restless of all the presidents he had known.

"He had 'glandular tension.' If he didn't relieve it by having sex every day, he'd get a headache. I covered Jack Kennedy for years and as far as I know he NEVER had a headache."

President Bush addressed our Wednesday luncheon gathering. Indeed, he does seem gentler if not kinder since last fall's vicious campaign. He spoke to us of ethics — a subject dear to our hearts.

For editors, having ethics is a little like having a hangnail. Both are painful afflictions, so painful that editors want everybody else to have them too. President Bush seems to have come down with a severe, perhaps incurable case of ethics. We hope so.

The program committee outdid itself. Israel's Prime Minister Shamir argued that the rock-throwing by PLO youths isn't just a case of "boys will be boys." You can get hurt. Colombian President Virgilio Barco said the reason Colombia has no drug use problem is because the country ships 60 percent of the country's cocaine into United States. Drug czar Bill Bennett preached for more prisons for drug users and pushers.

Erma Bombeck and Art Buchwald deplored this country's lack of humor and humorists. And on one panel, TV personalities Morton Downey, Jr., Geraldo Rivera and Phil Donahue argued their case as "legitimate journalists."

A film clip of Mr. Downey at work showed him and a member of his studio audience standing nose to nose screaming insults at each other. The confrontation ended with Mr. Downey ordering the dissident out of the studio and inviting him to "suck my armpit." I don't know what Mr. Downey is, but I know what he isn't.

On Thursday the luncheon entree was salmon. Someone at our table referred to it as "salmon rushdie," since we had just come from a session where a California book store operator described what it was like to be firebombed for carrying Mr. Rushdie's book after it was banned by the Ayatollah Khomeini.

After salmon on Thursday, we had Quayle on Friday.

The vice president's appearance was low-key. No dogs to sniff out would be assassins or explosives. No Secret Service agents to examine the contents of the ladies' purses.

Mr. Quayle seems very relaxed these days. He still comes across as a mere boy, a walk-on who hopes, as we fervently do, that the first string quarterback won't get hurt. But he is a boy who can laugh at himself.

I remembered how he told the Gridiron Club he can't get any work done for the Bush grandchildren coming by, knocking on his office door and pleading, "Danny, can you come out and play?"

Our banquet speaker was Jim Brady, the White House press secretary who eight years ago took, in the brain, a bullet intended for President Reagan.

Although still severely handicapped, Mr. Brady read his brief speech almost flawlessly. His devoted, long-suffering wife, who has become the gun-control lobby's strongest weapon, sat beside him, chain smoking, turning the pages as he plowed bravely through the script.

I wondered if the two standing ovations weren't directed as much to Sarah Brady as to her husband.

Later, after the awards were handed out, the speeches given, the gavel passed and the cheering done, Jim and Sarah Brady sat alone in the shadows at the abandoned head table. In a little while, almost unnoticed, she quietly pushed his wheelchair down the ramp and out of the ballroom.

For all their courage, it was a troubling sight, their return to the real, unromantic world of day-to-day coping, of endless days of PT — "pain and torture," as Jim Brady calls it.

Every time they mention a parole for John Hinckley Jr., whom Brady once referred to as "that twit," I will always see the Bradys there, late at night, alone at the head table.

I will see his body hunched in the wheelchair as she lights still another cigarette, while several dozen middle-aged editors and spouses dance "the twist" only half a room but still a world away.

We left Washington in the rain. The morning paper reported the city had met its murder quota for the day. Three people were shot dead, one a barber as he cut a customer's hair, another a 15-year-old shot five times near a housing project. That brought the total to 141 for the year.

We were happy to return to Raleigh, a kinder, gentler place, fresh-faced from the spring rain, with the woodland all aglow and the dogwood white as snow.

*April 21, 1989*

# 'Humpty Dumpty Was Pushed!'

We were riding along the causeway at Atlantic Beach when my wife gasped, pointed to the car just ahead and said, "There it is. That awful bumper sticker!"

Sure enough plastered to the left end of the bumper was the very sticker that has had our honorables the legislature in an uproar all spring.

"Why would anyone want such a bumper sticker?" she asked.

"Maybe he's punishing his mother," I said. "Maybe he hates his mother. Maybe she walked around naked in front of him when he was 13. That's what a shrink might say."

It's interesting how people use bumper stickers to make statements about themselves: their commitments, their frustrations and sometimes their rebellion. Bumper stickers are less expensive alternatives to personalized license plates.

I have subsidized a personalized plate for several years now. My older child's car sports one that reads "GLAD2BEME."

Pretty clever, you say. But she still can't give me one good reason why she wants the world to know she is glad she is who she is. Or why the world outside her family should care. But it comforts me to know that the extra $10 the state charges for it goes toward planting those pretty poppies along our highways.

Perhaps the recent rash of commentary from the backs of cars is symbolic of a society that has become more and more impersonal. A bumper sticker is a way of reaching out to someone, even though the someones are total strangers.

Not long ago at Five Points in Raleigh, I studied the back of a car plastered with stickers. I learned that the driver is an N.C. State fan (This Is Wolfpack Country) who is interested in preserving the environment (Protect the Ozone) and loves animals (Have You Hugged Your Dog Today?)

Just think. I could have sat with the driver for an hour at some civic club meeting, gone to church with him for years or lived down the block from him for half a lifetime and not have known that much about the man.

One of the guys here at the office remembers the first time he saw the offensive "—— Happens" sticker.

"I was on my way to work around 7 a.m.," he said. "I noticed the vehicle first, a rusted-out old pickup truck, the right window broken and replaced with a piece of cardboard.

"The driver was a woman who hadn't put a brush to her hair in days. A cigarette dangled from her lips. And then I saw the bumper sticker. And

I thought, 'You know, it does. It really does happen.' Here was living proof."

State Sen. Robert Shaw of Guilford said our country's fathers did not have dirty bumper stickers in mind when they guaranteed us freedom of expression.

"If somebody had written those four-letter words all over wagons back then, there would have been some hangings. There wouldn't have been any rulings."

Sen. James Ezzell Jr. of Nash, who stands on the other side of the aisle in this debate, points out that the Constitution does not discriminate. "You can paint the same things on the bumper and they will be legal. You can wear it on a baseball cap to church and it will be legal."

Even my old friend, the Rev. Bill Finlator, got into the fray, writing a piece to the newspaper reminding legislators they are sworn to "uphold not the Ten Commandments or the Sermon on the Mount but the Constitution and the Bill of Rights."

A law would put a heavy burden on the police. They'd have to decide whether the sticker reading "If Dolly Parton Worked For the State She'd Be Flat Busted" was obscene or just fair comment on the pay of state workers in Raleigh.

The ruling could go either way, depending on the mind of the cop. So could another one I saw on a car driven by a young woman, "Ask Me. I Might Say Yes."

Yeah, occasionally I feel like chasing down some drivers and scrubbing their bumper stickers with Octagon soap. But I worry more about where it would all end. Clean up bumper stickers and the next thing we know we'll be out arresting people for what they wear on their T-shirts and baseball caps.

Florida adopted a clean bumper sticker law last year. Most of the early charges have been thrown out of court.

One Florida woman was stopped by a cop who warned that her bumper sticker was against the law because it confused children.

It read: "Humpty Dumpty Didn't Fall. He Was Pushed."

See what I mean?

*May 22, 1989*

# Talking Frogs, Freeze-Dried Freds

I think it was the newspaper headline I spotted as I was having my morning coffee that put me in this late February funk I can't seem to shake.

"Gooden will get $100,000 pay cut," read the headline. I wanted to cry. Poor guy. How will the New York Mets pitcher ever get along on only $1.4 million a year? And pay for his drug-rehabilitation program out of that pittance?

The headline reminded me of a little story about the two middle-aged spinsters who were walking along a rural road one spring morning when a frog hopped out of a ditch and landed in front of them.

"Dear ladies," croaked the frog, "pick me up and kiss me and I will turn into a Texas oilman."

One of the women reached down, scooped up the frog, thrust it headfirst into her purse and snapped it tightly shut.

"Why, Mabel," said her surprised companion, "aren't you going to kiss the frog?"

"Heavens, no!" replied Mabel. "Texas oil men aren't what they used to be. There is no limit to what you can do with a talking frog."

There are a lot of talking frogs around these days. Dwight Gooden's pay cut wasn't the only recent news event that convinced me the world is more than a little bit nuts.

Take the case of Ms. Joyce Brown, the now-famous street person who made her home on the sidewalks of New York City before she was carted off to the mental ward as a part of Mayor Ed Koch's street-cleaning program.

Ms. Brown wasn't there long until the American Civil Liberties Union came galloping up and rescued her from the hospital's clean sheets and indoor plumbing.

You see, one of the things that had bothered Mayor Koch and others was Ms. Brown's habit of using the street as a bathroom. Admittedly, New Yorkers may not be very sensitive, but even they don't like stepping in it on their way to work.

Last week, garden columnist Bugs Barringer wrote about a robin that became frustrated when petals from an overhanging dogwood filled the birdbath in an Eastern North Carolina bird-lover's yard. The robin patiently picked out the petals, one or two at the time, with his beak and dropped them over the side until the water was clean enough for his bath.

Barringer reminds us that birds do not foul their nests. But humans can and do, and become national celebrities in the process. Ms. Brown recently addressed the Harvard Law School Forum and is now being offered book and movie contracts. Talk about talking frogs!

Then there are the television evangelists, a veritable frog farm. Brother Jimmy Swaggart has just stepped up and, shedding buckets of tears, confessed to committing a variety of sins of the flesh, including spending the widow's mite on a prostitute in a cheap motel room.

And Brother Jim Bakker, who also got caught with his morals down, is getting excited about the upcoming movie about him and Tammy Faye. Tammy Faye wants Sally Field to play Tammy Faye.

For most preachers, having sex with the church secretary or slinking into a motel with a prostitute would mean they'd have to turn in their Bibles.

Not so for these guys. Why, Brother Swaggart got a standing ovation from 6,000 born-agains for his macho performance at the $10-a-night motel.

A license to prey on public ignorance and gullibility is more precious than pearls, even a talking frog.

As for other frogs, what about a guy featured on CBS news one night this week? His racket is freeze-drying pets. That's right — cats, dogs. You no longer have to bury old Fido when he dies. You can have him freeze-dried and keep him right there in the den, parked on the couch, so you can stroke him from time to time as you relax after work with your book or TV.

The film clip showed one couple going off to bed with their late departed white poodle, the wife stroking her "little girl," as she called the "freeze-dried" dog.

"The possibilities are unlimited," said the guy who does the freeze-drying.

Indeed they are. As I caught the look the woman with the freeze-dried poodle kept laying on her hovering husband, I thought, "Aha! Fred, you're next." Just think — a freeze-dried Fred. Sick, folks, sick.

This week I saw two men cry. One was Brian Boitano, when he won the Olympic gold for his flawless figure-skating.

As young Boitano stepped forward to receive his medal, I waited for the inevitable tears. Although his lips trembled from time to time as the strains of "The Star Spangled Banner" rose and fell, it was not until "and the rockets' red glare" that the tears finally came, singly, like the first raindrops of an April shower, coursing across the windowpane of his emotion. Now *there* was majesty.

Two nights later, I witnessed the weeping of the Rev. Swaggart. Compared to the youth's, his tears were without quality, simulated, salty with shamelessness.

I do not mean to sound cynical. I suppose everyone has his own talking frog. It's just that the warts on some are more pronounced than others. Anyway, February is about over.

*February 26, 1988*

# Blest Be the Tie That Bends

When I think of house guests, I think of Leo and Rusty Wagoner of Chapel Hill.

Last winter, as a part of Chapel Hill's Bridges of Peace program, they hosted a Baptist minister and a rock musician, both from the Soviet Union — a perplexing combination in any language.

The media soon descended. Channel 5 said they'd like to spend 30 minutes with the Wagoners and their guests. The crew stayed for four hours.

"Have you an idea what it's like to wrestle with a slippery chicken under TV lights?" Rusty asked us recently. "Neither the cook nor the chicken maintains much dignity."

"I'm no Julia Child but I finally managed to get the bird in the oven in what I hoped was a half-way professional manner. Then I started cutting up vegetables, and the cameraman zeros in for a close-up of my hands in the sink.

"A while later, I smelled smoke. The chicken had caught fire! The smoke alarm went off. We had to open all the doors and windows, and it was the middle of December. The camera kept grinding away. I knew that those beautiful Christmas decorations I had labored over for hours and hours weren't going to show up on TV because of all the smoke."

As courageous as Scarlett braving a burning Atlanta, Rusty pulled the charred chicken from the oven, and turned to the cameraman in despair. "If you dare show this on the 11 o'clock news I swear I'll never turn on Channel 5 again as long as I live!"

The Wagoners and the Russians sat down to dinner under the camera's penetrating gaze. "You don't have to eat the chicken, just pretend," hissed Rusty to the confused Russians as she smiled brightly at the camera. As soon as the TV crew left, she sent out for pizza.

After the 11 p.m. news, a friend called.

"Rusty," she said, "you have set the woman's movement back 50 years. There you stood working like a galley slave at the sink, doing the best you could with that scrawny looking chicken. And there was Leo, rared back in his easy chair like the King of Siam, waxing philosophically on and on about what a wonderful learning experience the Russians' visit had been for all concerned."

When we have house guests at the beach, the rule is that everybody does his own thing. Some guests would rather talk. Or do needlework. Or take walks.

There is always one athletic type who "slips out" for that early-morning jog. He showers at 5 a.m. as quietly as a brood sow in a hog wallow. He flushes and the commode sounds like thunder across the bay. He slams doors. He whistles softly to himself. Have you ever tried to sleep through someone whistling softly at the top of his whistle at 5 a.m.?

Sometimes your guest list includes the fashion-conscious.

"Did you notice that A.C. wore gray socks instead of white with his Nikes when we walked on the beach?" I heard one of the women remark.

"I read somewhere that that means something — something negative," she said. "I can't remember just what. Oh, yes, now I do. Richard Nixon always wore gray socks when he walked on the beach. But of course he always wore a suit and tie, too."

A word to the wise. Omit politics from your intellectual menu. My wife casually mentioned that she likes Dan Rather.

"I can't stand that man," one of our guests snapped. "He is arrogant and rude. Remember what he did to poor George Bush?"

One of the husbands is in the dog house. And for good reason. He was foolhardy enough to reorganize his wife's recipe box.

"A.C., where would you file 'apple pie?'"

"Under A."

"No, you turkey! It goes under D, for dessert. And behind D, for dessert you file it under sub-category A, for apple pie."

It is lunch, and they are making tomato sandwiches.

"Neither of my boys like tomato sandwiches," one of the women is complaining. "It's their father's influence. He never liked tomatoes. Don't you think it's tragic that two Southern boys won't even taste tomato sandwiches?"

"You just don't know what it's like to have been married to the perfect man all these years," another member of the kitchen crew lamented.

"You can't *complain* about anything, because nobody will sympathize. There is no justice in this world."

So the heroine in one of Ferrol Sams' stories I was reading just then is right. "Justice is blind, you have always heard?" she says as she contemplates suing her doctor. "And they have that statue of a woman holding a set of scales in one hand and a sword in the other? She is fairly flat-chested with one of them hanging out and a blindfold over her eyes? And if you'll notice she's got on sandals, too?

"Any Southern woman could tell you not to trust another female who's wearing a high-waisted evening dress with flat-heeled sandals, and no hose with one shoulder bare and no bra? Justice is not blind; Justice nowadays is what they call a travesty."

Although having house guests at the beach is far more treat than travesty, when forced inside on a rainy day we cannot help but learn how unalike we are. Yet it is partly our differences that draw us together as friends.

And when the weekend is over, guests and hosts alike may go home marveling at the miracle that matches male and female into lasting relationships that would have surely foundered on the rocks had the pairings been cast differently to include one or the other of us.

*September 9, 1988*

# Returning to the Old Well

"Why did you go?" I asked Grady Cooper Jr., who like thousands of other old grads everywhere, went back to his college reunion last weekend.

"To re-establish old friendships," he said.

"Oh come off that."

"Well, to tell you the truth, I went to see how my classmates had aged. And, boy, they have!"

Grady admitted that he himself doesn't look like he just pecked his way out of his shell.

The Ed Rowlands of Newport News, Va., came by from Chapel Hill to say that going back after 30 years was a great experience.

They agreed that much of the weekend was like a grown-ups' "Show and Tell." One classmate reported she is now married to her fourth husband.

"Things just didn't seem to work out," she had sighed.

"In a way, the whole thing sounded like a 'Can you top this?'" Ed said. " In her case, nobody could."

These public recitals seem a bit in bad taste, a lot like those mimeographed Christmas letters you get from people who itemize all their pluses while ignoring the minuses:

"Jimmy has landed a job with a New York stockbroker firm and is making $60,000 a year...Susan has married a lovely boy from Boston — they have a place at Nantucket...We are looking forward to taking the whole family to Europe next summer."

You never get Christmas cards that read: "Tommy was busted for drugs again — his fourth time. Looks like he'll be leaving us for a while." Or, "Elaine has decided not to go to graduate school after all. She became pregnant and has a cute little baby which we are taking care of while she is doing Outward Bound in the Colorado mountains."

That's not quite the way it is at class reunions.

There, you have some guy announcing that he's a full partner with Gernst, Dodecker and Bisset. And he's followed by some unfortunate who says he's selling lawn sprinklers door to door.

"That poor woman was probably embarrassed that she has run through four men in 30 years," I said to my friend.

"Naw, she was bragging, I could tell," said Ed.

My wife went back to her reunion this year at UNC-G. She came home talking about one of the girls sporting a diamond "as big as the top of a saltshaker."

"Well, there are big saltshakers and small saltshakers," I reminded her. "What does her husband do?"

"He owns the Ford place," she said. So I gathered it was an above-average sized saltshaker.

Another of her classmates reported she had recently remarried.

"This one has money, she said. "I've tried marrying a poor man and a rich man, and believe me, the latter is a lot more fun."

There's always talk about the children, of course. How many years it took them to get out of college. What they are doing now. What they aspire to do.

"My son majored in Latin American studies," said one father of a strapping lad who has spent most of his summers perfecting his suntan while lifeguarding at resort swimming pools.

"What does he want to do?" I asked.

"Well, he'd like to be an international lifeguard," the father chuckled. "No, seriously, he's trying to get into the Peace Corps so he can go to Honduras to teach the natives how to raise goats and chickens."

"Does he know anything about raising goats and chickens?"

"Not much really. He's seen a chicken a couple of times."

There is always a bit of levity at these affairs. Art Weiner, Choo-Choo Justice's favorite target during UNC's golden years of football, entertained the Chapel Hill group at a Saturday breakfast.

Art warned of the hazards of aging and mentioned a few of the early symptoms.

"First, you don't remember names. Then you don't remember faces. Then you find yourself always looking for a bathroom. Then you start forgetting to zip up. And then finally, you start forgetting to unzip. And buddy, that's the time to start worrying."

At college reunions, people sit around remembering. Some visit old classrooms or walk the familiar paths of yesteryear.

Here by the Playmakers Theater, he kissed the girl he thought would be his wife. Where is she now?

There in Aycock Auditorium, she played a bit role in "Arsenic and Old Lace." What happened to the acting career that would make the world forget Helen Hayes?

Why do they go back?

Primarily, I think, to chase once more the sweet bird of youth. It all happened so fast, that quicksilver time of high school and college. After that the years flashed by like telephone poles from the window of a speeding train.

And now from time to time during a weekend in May their hearts cry out, "Stop the world, I want to get off. Let me go back and see if it really was the way I think it was."

It never is of course. But as Santa said in "Miracle on 34th Street," after he belched and people looked chagrined: "What did you expect? Chimes?"

*May 26, 1989*

# Heaven and the 'Splitting Headache'

Some years ago, Dr. Albert Edwards, my former pastor, remarked that the lucky people in this world are those who know for sure they're going either to Heaven or Hell.

"It's the ones in between I feel sorry for," he said, his wry, Scottish wit reaching out to those of us who weren't totally convinced that we measured up well enough for Heaven or had fallen so short that Hell awaited.

I come from a family in which there is little doubt. Most are convinced they're headed Heavenward. It is a part of their faith.

"If you don't *believe* you're going, you ain't," I am told by my foothills kin. Most are literalists who question nothing in the Bible, not even the Old Testament. But I am full of questions.

For example, my wife has been helping to teach a series of circle lessons on women of the Bible. You never thought that "feminism" would infiltrate the church, did you?

I have found some of these women intriguing. Consider the fate of Sisera, commander of the powerful armies of the Canaanites, then Israel's oppressors, Israel's hated foe.

Sisera, defeated and fleeing on foot from the battlefield, came to the tent of the woman Jael, whom he thought friendly to the Canaanites but who actually was a sort of Israeli spy. Jael invited him in for rest and relaxation, gave him milk to drink and lulled him to sleep. She then drove a tent peg right through the great warrior's temple.

Miss Manners would have something to say about this kind of hospitality. But those were different times. I wonder if that was how the much-used term "splitting headache" got started.

Another lesson dwells on Jephthah's daughter. Ah, a truly tragic story. Jephthah, you remember, was the fellow who promised God that if He would make him victorious in battle he would offer as a burnt offering the first thing he met upon his return home.

So, what did he sacrifice? The lovely young daughter who came running out of the house to greet her father. One questions why God would have accepted such a sacrifice. One also wonders about the literal truth of the Old Testament.

As recent events illustrate, he who wonders publicly about what the majority already accepts as unquestionable truth is inviting trouble.

For example, columnist Jack Smith recently got into a heap of trouble with some of his Los Angeles Times readers over a column on Heaven.

Jack took a dim view of Heaven, a place without football games, since there is supposed to be no violence there. He imagined it to be like "Art Deco, full of big square white overstuffed furniture, cumulus clouds and unearthly Muzak." He supposed everyone would be issued an all-purpose credit card to use in one great big free shopping mall.

"I'm not sure I would want to spend eternity with the kind of people who would be getting into heaven," Smith wrote. "Most of them just wouldn't be my type. I'd probably get into trouble for peeping at earth or harassing an angel. So count me out."

Mark Twain, in his short story "Captain Stormfield's Visit to Heaven," reminds us that "a man's got to be in his own Heaven to be happy," and that Paradise is divided into districts for that purpose. How true. One man's Heaven could be another's Hell.

Captain Stormfield, like columnist Smith, was disenchanted with some aspects of Heaven — particularly the harp playing. He found the place too crowded. And he spent fruitless hours walking around trying to spot biblical celebrities.

He remembers that back home in Brooklyn, a preacher by the name of Talmage was always saying in his sermons that the first thing he was gonna do when he got to Heaven was fling his arms around Abraham, Isaac and Jacob.

"There's millions of people down there on Earth saying the same thing," Stormfield's buddy in Heaven tells him.

"As many as sixty thousand people arrive here every single day, and they want to run straight to Abraham, Isaac and Jacob, and hug them and weep on them. Now mind you, sixty thousand a day is pretty heavy contact for those old people."

I cannot help but hope that some of us doubters and questioners will be allowed through the Pearly Gates, right along with all those sanctified fundamentalists.

A Texas preacher was once asked if he thought some of the fundamental extremists would really get in.

"I suppose so," he drawled, "'lessn they over-shoot the place.'".

Perhaps it is the newspaperman in me that constantly questions, without necessarily rejecting. And does so without irreverence.

And I trust that the thoughts raised here will be taken in their proper context. I say so with some anxiety after reading in our First Presbyterian Church bulletin last Sunday that the church, where I have been a member for almost 30 years, is seeking contributions for a "Snow Removal Fund."

I have told Elder Paul Hoover that I will go peacefully, provided the church splits the fund with me.

*February 19, 1988*

# Encounter With a 'Moveable Fuss'

As I pulled out of the office parking lot into South Salisbury Street, I rolled the car windows down to breathe the elixir of October, so rare in the gasping city traffic, so free and taken for granted in the foothills.

Suddenly I heard the voice of anger from a car cruising alongside me, I glanced over into the fury of a marital battle in which no prisoners were being taken.

"How could you be so insensitive? So totally stupid!" raged the driver, a woman who looked to be mid-30s. "How could you accuse me of such a thing?" she fumed, pounding her fists angrily on the steering wheel.

The husband sat with head bowed, totally cowed. Two children huddled on the back seat. As in any war, there are always innocent victims.

At the next stoplight, I turned right and bowed out of what Hemingway might have labeled "a moveable fuss." But driving home, I wondered what had caused the emotional Vesuvius to erupt within the young family.

Probably something of no real consequence. That's how most wars, marital or military, are launched.

Don't you imagine that the whole ugly mess that drove Adam and Eve from the Garden also began over some trifle?

In a good mood, Adam might have said one evening, "Hey, Eve, how would you like to walk over to the Serpent's Pit for an apple Danish?"

And she might have snapped, "You ask me that when you know I don't have a thing to wear!" It would have been the first and last time that familiar female complaint was uttered in total truthfulness.

Psychologists used to list as major sources of marital discord the old business of his leaving the cap off the toothpaste tube, her shaving her legs with his razor. Now that we have electric razors and toothpaste in push-button dispensers, any of a vast number of other irritants can set off the verbal fireworks.

Take my friend Elmo who, weary after a hard day at the office, recently decided to stop by The Player's Retreat for a beer before going home.

"To tell you the truth, I had four," he confided to me. "So in order to avoid a DWI on the way home, I had to stay a little longer at the pub."

"Well, when I got home, my wife had declared World War III. Where had I been? Why hadn't I called her?' I told her I was old enough to have a beer after work once a month. And anyway, I hadn't inconvenienced her, had I?"

"'Oh yes you have,' she said. '"I went to the trouble to fix your supper and now it's cold. I have already eaten!'"

"Well, what did you fix?"

"I warmed up last night's chili in the microwave."

I have an irritating habit that has driven my wife up a wall for three decades of marriage. When I undress or just get comfortable in the den, I slip out of my lace-less shoes. But I do it backwards, my wife says, so that the parked shoes' toes are pointing out instead of neatly, normally inward.

She does not understand this phenomenon. Nor do I. It just happens automatically, no matter how earnest my efforts to reform. But I argue that it is to be preferred over womanizing, horse-stealing or wife-beating.

A summer or two ago, my daughter's boyfriend, in town for a social event, spent the night in our downstairs guest room. After the young couple had dressed to go out for the evening, I went down to take fresh towels.

Upon entering the room, I immediately noticed the lad had parked his topsiders in exactly the same formation.

"Come here quick!" I called to my wife who, thinking perhaps I again had left the water running and flooded the downstairs, came running.

"Look!" I shouted, indicating the out-pointing shoes. "Another genius!"

Dr. Mary Kilburn, a Raleigh psychologist, reacting to my earlier column on the "mixed messages" that spouses and lovers send each other, wrote recently to say that decoding those complex messages is the key to achieving satisfying intimate relationships.

"As one person who has difficulty with the nuances of intimate communcation said, 'If my computer would only kiss back, I would never have another date,' " she wrote.

"To my knowledge the danger of the computer overtaking this function is nil," says Dr. Kilburn. "I suspect that human beings, with our complex richness of emotional experience and meaning, will continue to delight and despair over our efforts to be close."

She's right. The kind of "moveable fuss" I witnessed is, while unpleasant, a common ingredient of the moveable feast of life in which two people have chosen to become intimately and deeply involved with each other.

*October 12, 1988*

# 'Togetherness' at the Birdfeeder

Psychiatrists and psychologists are convinced that prolonged bad weather is bad for one's mental health. And marriage.

It's a wonder that during January most of us have not been locked up in the loony house or, worse still, put behind bars for committing mayhem or murder.

Being snowbound with spouse or children for long periods puts terrible stress on mothers especially.

When snow closed Wake schools for seven days, a school official received a call from a distraught mother.

"You don't mean you're gonna close schools again tomorrow!" the woman wailed against a background of whooping children. "Here they come again!" she shrieked. "Hear 'em?"

For cabin-fever therapy I recommend birdwatching. There is something settling and reassuring about the pattern of birds, their coming and going at the feeder, the pecking order, the sense of survival as tiny feet cling to ice-covered twigs.

But then there are squirrels, the curse of any serious birdwatcher.

My wife, tired of hearing me grouse about the furry pests, said, "Someone told me recently that if you put onions on the feeder it will keep the squirrels away. Squirrels just can't abide onions. You might try that."

She promptly sliced an onion into four quarters which I placed carefully on the feeder. Within 10 minutes a squirrel and his frau had climbed into the feeder. Moments later they were happily munching onions, tears streaming from their eyes.

One climbed down, onion in mouth, and scampered across the frozen snow and up to the nest they have made in a hole in my big oak tree. It may be that I used a cheap onion. But more likely, I am the victim of another old wives' tale.

A normally sweet-tempered friend of mine confesses that he turns savage when penned up with his family for more than 24 hours.

For example, he dislikes cats. He even admits to kicking the family cat when nobody is looking. During the January unpleasantness, his wife came down one morning to where he and his two children sat in the den.

"She looked right at me and said accusingly, 'Someone has let the cat in and I'm sorry to say she has tinkled in three separate places on the Persian rug.'"

"Don't look at me!" the husband snarled. "I hate the damn cat. Why would I let it in?"

If the weather hadn't been so bad, I might have better stood the tension of several days' close association with my wife, two daughters and the dog one brought home with her over the holidays.

My rage peaked the night my daughter went off to a party with her friends, leaving me to babysit her dog, a pup that goes by the ridiculous name of Frosty Summer Snow.

Scared out of its wits by the screeching of the attic stairway being let down, the animal had bolted the house when I opened the door. Fearing it would leave the yard and be run over, I dashed out into the freezing night after her.

Prowling through a neighborhood at midnight on a winter's eve yelling "Summer! Summer!" at the top of your voice could get you a free trip to the loony house in a police vehicle. I was not surprised to see a couple of my neighbors peering anxiously out their windows.

During my recent siege of cabin fever I had a terrible premonition. What if retirement, only a few years down the road, should find me confined, mind and body, as I was during the bad weather?

The thought brought to mind a priceless scene from Arthur Miller's play, "I Can't Remember Anything."

In it, an old couple, Leo and Lenora, are having a go at each other and he says, "By the way, if you come in here some night and I'm dead I want you to call Yale New Haven hospital."

And she wants to know what good is a hospital if you're dead, and he tells her he has made arrangements to donate his organs to research.

Leo: For research. So call New Haven. This mortician here used to have a Nixon bumper sticker.

Lenora: What do they expect to find from *your* organs?

Leo: Why? My organs aren't good enough?

Lenora: But I should imagine they would want people with some interesting disease. All you got is arthritis. Aside from that, you'll probably die in perfect health.

Leo: Well, I might get something.

Lenora: Where, for heaven's sake? You never go anywhere but the Post Office or the grocery store.

Leo: I go to the gas station.

Lenora: The gas station! What do you expect to pick up at the gas station?

Leo: I don't know. Gas disease.

Lenora: (laughing) Gas disease!

Leo: This is another one of those conversations.

This sort of thing sends chills down my spine. What if retirement should be like one long, continuous snowstorm?

*January 20, 1988*

# Not a Trip to Sperm Bank

This will be one of the quietest Father's Days ever in our household. The beloved poodle sleeps the eternal sleep on the hillside behind the house. And the two children are several states away at their summer jobs.

These walls, like all walls that have encompassed a family, echo the sounds of children down through the years. In this strange silence, they recall tales and times the heart had almost forgotten.

There was the long, long ago "egg patty" Father's Day breakfast in bed — the cold fried egg with equally cold tough toast, served with a generous dollop of excitement and laced heavily with love. And years later, a hurried teenager's Father's Day note, "Daddy, you'll always be a 10 to me."

When I think of what fathering means, I can't get out of my mind reporter Cornelia Grumman's article on the UNC sperm bank at Chapel Hill.

For too many males, fathering a child has always been the ultimate macho trip, even though it involves one of the most natural, basic and pleasurable biological functions.

Ms. Grumman's story noted that men are paid only $25 for enough sperm to impregnate four women. That ought to tell you something. A mechanic's helper gets paid more for jump-starting a car on a cold morning.

Wouldn't you think that providing the miracle serum for birth would command a more lucrative fee? But one donor put it in proper perspective: "a painless way to pay for dinner and a movie."

One young UNC-CH employee who donates regularly said he started selling sperm when he broke up with his girlfriend. "I was feeling I would never get married, and this was a way of contributing something to posterity, as corny as that may sound."

It does sound pretty corny. But then so does the male's exaggerated image of himself as the great giver of life. The mystique and romance once associated with the biological act of fathering has deteriorated to the level of taking a drink of water these days.

Young males, and many older ones, flit from woman to woman like a bee from blossom to blossom. The difference is, the bee gathers nectar, while the typical young male gathers ego and, too often, impregnates the flower without sticking around to pick up the petals.

The article on the sperm merchants proves that, without emotional attachment and lifetime commitment to the results, the act of fathering a child has about as much to do with manhood or fathering as shaving.

True fathering is cradle-to-the-grave servitude. It's reading "Charlotte's Web" at bedtime when you'd rather be watching the ball game.

It's putting the bicycle together at 1 a.m. on Christmas morning, subsidizing the Tooth Fairy until the kids are 10, their orthodontist until they're 16, and their old Mustang or Honda until they are 25.

It means steeling yourself against kids' wiles and not letting your love for them make you so vulnerable you end up in the poorhouse.

A friend recently received a note from his UNC-CH daughter, describing an experiment in her psychology class. Students were shown movies of girls standing in front of various makes of cars, from Fords to Porsches.

Each student was asked to vote for the prettiest girl. The winners consistently turned out to be the girls standing in front of the expensive cars.

"Would you believe," my friend's daughter wrote, "that they asked to borrow my old 1981 Citation as a background for the girl who, it turned out, got the least number of votes? Dad, can't you see now how desperately I need a new car?"

Fathering is smiling a lot and hurting a little when you get the note from the daughter who insisted she had to go to Nantucket to wait on tables this summer.

"I am standing on my feet all day checking out groceries. Kate and Beth have jobs as chambermaids. Page has to be at her job at the bakery at 5 a.m. It is freezing cold. I am writing you huddled under two blankets because we can't afford to turn on the heat."

Fathering is keeping your fingers crossed until the "oldest living senior" finally walks across the stage on graduation day.

Fathering, early on, is running interference against heartbreak. It's trying to explain away the fear and mystery of death to a child who wants to know why she can't, like Elijah, go to Heaven in a whirlwind. And trying to keep your cool when, not very reassured, she pleads, "When the time comes will you go with me and hold my hand?"

As I walked past the guard's desk at work yesterday, the fellow on duty said, "They just don't pay as much attention to Father's Day as they do Mother's Day, do they?"

"Only the merchants do," I said with a laugh, wondering if our bad press doesn't stem from the fact that for too many men, fathering is nothing more than a $25 trip to the sperm bank.

*January 17, 1988*

# Never Say It With a Chain Saw

I sometimes wonder if St. Valentine wasn't just some poor merchant who was thrown into prison after his retail business went on the rocks and he couldn't pay his bills.

While behind bars, the fellow dreamed up the grand scheme of Valentine's Day and thereby became the patron saint of all candy stores, florists and gift shop operators.

Now this may not be true. But I'll bet a five-pound box of expensive chocolate that St. Valentine, whatever his intent, never envisioned any man giving his lady love $50 worth of roses or perfume and dinner at the Angus Barn every February 14.

According to the myth I grew up with, St. Valentine was imprisoned for secretly marrying young couples, violating the orders of the emperor, who believed that single men made stronger and better soldiers.

One day, Valentine reached through the bars of his cell, plucked the leaf from a violet, shaped it into a heart, stuck a pin through it for Cupid's arrow and sent it to whom I can't remember.

So every February, which as a month doesn't have much going for it anyway, man is pressured into being for one day something he basically isn't — a thoughtful, sensitive, doting human being.

For some reason, God just didn't design us that way. We've had to learn it. With strong coaching from our women.

One of my associates recalls the first Christmas after she married her husband, a nice enough fellow who nevertheless grew up in a farm family that didn't go in much for bill and coo and extravagances. She woke up on Christmas morning with nary a present from him.

"Now listen here," the new bride explained patiently, "It doesn't have to be much. But there has to be *something* for me on Christmas morning. Understand?"

"He did," she chuckled. "Next Christmas he gave me a butcher knife. But things got better after that."

One of Caulton Tudor's buddies got married in September of the year he graduated from Carolina and took his young wife to his first job as coach of a hard-scrabble high school in Eastern North Carolina. He was expected to produce a winning football team without any funds to buy training equipment.

His first Christmas gift to his wife: a tackling sled.

Then there was a fellow I know who for years got away with ignoring Valentine's Day altogether. In his mind, it was just another Wednesday, or whatever.

Finally, after several annual but fruitless hints from his wife, such as mentioning what her friends received from *their* husbands on this special day, she read the riot act to him.

"At least a Valentine!" she stormed.

Next February 14, the guy went out and paid $45 for a dozen red roses. Well, it seemed that too much was worse than too little. She reprimanded him severely for his extravagance. "Don't *ever* do that again!"

"Don't worry!" he retorted. "You have had your last rose from me. There won't even be a dandelion at your funeral as far as I am concerned!"

I remember a Depression-year February when my mother stayed up late making a valentine for Mary Kate Woodhouse, a town girl and the prettiest lass in the second grade. She fashioned a heart from plain paper, appliqued it with bright-red scraps of cloth and bordered it with white lace.

It wasn't "store bought," but it was the prettiest valentine handed out in the second grade at Boonville Elementary that year. And it won for me a fleeting smile of appreciation from Mary Kate, whose desk was always heaped higher than anyone else's with valentines.

"Roses! At $50 a dozen!" exclaimed another macho male friend, still waiting to be wife-broke.

"If it's roses she wants, give her a shovel from Sears and a $4 rose bush from Logan's Trading Post and let her take it from there," he said. "That way, a man can come out way ahead."

"Oh, no he can't" I told him. "How long do you have to live to realize that women are different? It doesn't have to be roses. But it has to be something personal.

"For whatever reason, the undeserving man in whom a woman has invested her emotional security, not to mention any number of other hopes and dreams, has to pause every February and say, in some way, 'You are special. You count for something with me.' "

Another word of caution. The man who said it's the thought and not the gift that counts is dead — shot through the heart by a woman.

A close friend of mine gave his wife a chain saw on her 50th birthday. Now, years later, he swears that although he served throughout the South Pacific during World War II, this was the closest he ever came to being killed.

So, men, go out into the byways and hedgerows of the market place and buy your love a penny dreadful or a gift. And go cheerfully. Consider the alternative.

*February 8, 1988*

# 'No Males on the Hall!'

We are picking up the pieces of summer, not trying to put the puzzle together into a cohesive picture of good times or bad, but examining each piece, enjoying them for what they are worth and trying to ignore those not worth remembering.

There was that bittersweet moment when I again said goodbye to a daughter at a college dorm and returned home to the "empty nest" of which we have so long heard and read.

Katherine and I arrived first with the big load, including the trunk. Her mother was to follow in the other car with the refrigerator. Going to college these days is like going to marriage in my day.

Kids set up housekeeping in their half of an 8 by 10 room that includes kitchen facilities, a bedroom, a year's wardrobe, a rec room, an art museum, and the city dump.

As we were checking in at first floor Spencer, my heart leaped up when I understood the young woman at the desk to say to my daughter, "And no males on the hall."

Could this be Chapel Hill? Or even Mars Hill, where an eon ago, the occasional cry of "Man on the hall!" in the women's dorms sent the girls scurrying to their rooms like chickens fleeing a hawk and caused the more daring to peek cautiously, perhaps hopefully, from their doors.

Alas, I learned later, what the woman had said was not "No males on the hall" but "No nails on the walls!"

That seems to be where today's college priorities are — take good care of the walls and don't give a hoot about the students.

A van with New Bern license plates was being unloaded nearby. When the chore was completed, mother and daughter embraced, each bravely cheerful, and smiling, "Bye Mom, Dad." "Have fun, darling."

The girl walked toward the dorm, a freshet of tears coursing her face. She waited until she turned the corner to wipe them away. The mother, out of sight of the daughter, sobbed into her handkerchief as she climbed into the van with her husband.

I was proud of myself, brave and brusque all the way home. That night when I started to bed and pulled back the covers, I found my daughter's goodbye note under my pillow.

With my wife away for a month's study in Switzerland, this has been a different summer of marching to different drummers, a summer of courting humming birds and managing offspring and dog alone.

Summer is a transient time for children, too, with temporary jobs, summer camp, much mobility and a general restlessness that is contagious.

It's that way for many. A letter from our friends the Jonathan Lindseys in Waco, Texas, includes news about the children.

Daughter Julianna has returned home from her month at a North Carolina camp.

"She left her heart there with a fellow from Alexandria, Virginia," writes the mother. "So the letters travel frequently. He quotes Virgil on the envelopes so at least he's literate!"

There is the amusing incident involving one of my wife's fellow students in Switzerland, a woman from North Dakota. Complying with careful instructions from her travel agency back home, the first thing she did upon arriving in Lugano was to ask the desk clerk to store her passport and traveler's checks in the hotel safe.

Most of the hotel's night staff neither understood nor spoke English.

"Safe!" said the North Dakotan, pushing her passport and checks toward the clerk.

When he merely smiled, she repeated: "Safe!"

Frustrated at the language barrier, she finally pounded on the desk with her fist and shouted, "Safe! Safe!"

The puzzled clerk shrugged resignedly, dropped to his knees, and after rummaging through a drawer beneath the desk, stood up and tossed two condoms on the desk. The woman gasped in astonishment, seized her passport and checks and fled to her room.

Closer home, on an August morning, I find myself in a peach orchard in the mountains near Cana, Virginia, gathering the blushing fruit from row on row of trees burdened with abundance. Before me stretches a clear view of forever.

Nearby, half a dozen young laborers chatter and laugh and clown around as they move through the orchard picking peaches.

One of the mountain youths throws back his head and howls down across the hillside, bouncing his bark into the valley below where a befuddled dog answers back, painstakingly plaintive. The peach pickers laugh and slap their legs. The howling peach picker howls again.

Ah, summer, how fleeting. We need its magic moments to sustain us during winter's woe.

*August 23, 1986*

# With Beans in Their Ears

At a newspaper meeting some time ago, Dr. Robert J. Stamp, a doctor and psychologist from the University of Michigan, dispensed some pretty good advice for a bunch of journalists well out of swaddling clothes.

He said life should be separated into three categories: salad, scotch and sex. "If only a rabbit would learn to like scotch he would live forever," he quipped.

He identified the "salad" of life as the day-to-day living, generally staying in the middle of the road, avoiding the ditches on either side.

The scotch refers to the special things you do for yourself — a trip to the mountains or coast, a new suit or dress, bragging on yourself a little now and then. Even occasionally taking a a different route to work.

Sex? It's what it implies — healthy, enjoyable. But, as Dr. Stamp says, "neither the alpha nor omega of life."

I suppose that wasting a golden autumn day going back to your alma mater and watching a football team that has won only one game all year would fall under the classification of "scotch." Not the best vintage, of course, but still scotch.

Admittedly, I was not eager to spend my Saturday on football which, at one time the alpha and omega of my salad days at Carolina, was now just a take-it-or-leave-it garnish somewhere far back on life's salad bar.

But when it is "parents' weekend" at Chi Omega and your child says come, you go.

I sat in the warm sun in refurbished Kenan, looking down on its green carpet. Beyond the rim of the stadium, the last lingering splash of Crayola on the trees glowed brightly. Far above the earthbound masses, a free-spirited jet pilot turned and tossed with reckless abandon, autographing the cornflower blue sky with scrawling jet streams.

My mind meandered to another day in another time, my first game ever in Kenan Stadium. Across the decades, I heard the swelling roar of thousands chanting, "All the way Choo Choo!" as the Heels of yesteryear thumped arrogant, undefeated Texas 34-0, and at halftime the drawling voice of Andy Griffith reciting "What It Was Was Football."

But on this day, I did not expect much in the way of fireworks. And by then I had immunized myself against the rash of cruelty jokes my Wolfpack friends continued to inflict on me.

The most recent had to do with a mythical telephone call in which ex-Coach Dick Crum suggested to Coach Mack Brown that he come down and commiserate with him and pass on a few tips on how to win at Carolina.

Mr. Crum suggested they meet at Four Corners.

"Well, I've been there a lot and I'm a little tired of the menu," Mr.

Brown replied, whereupon Mr. Crum suggested Slug's. Again, Mr. Brown demurred, saying he had been there a lot too.

Finally Mr. Crum said impatiently, "Well, why don't I just stop by Kentucky Fried and pick up some chicken and you meet me in the end zone. You ain't been there lately."

Well, by golly, by day's end Mr. Brown and his boys had been there quite frequently, five times to be exact, while the new scoreboard flashed such accolades as "Awesome!" and "Sweet!"

Forty-eight seconds before game's end, football fever once more coursed through my veins. I looked forward to reading the Sunday morning accounts of how the Heels had been born-again, even if only with a tie.

But that was before Carolina's final fling in which our young quarterback, on his own 20 and 80 yards from paydirt, passed instead of sitting on the ball. The interception set up the Terps' winning field goal.

Now athletes will tell you that going for a tie is like "kissing your sister." But when you've won only one game all year and the season is fading fast, there is nothing incestuous about kissing your sister.

A disgruntled Democrat described the unfortunate pass as "the sort of play Danny Quayle might have called from the Oval Office if the Russians were coming."

After the game, I ran into Phil Carson at the Chi Omega House where he was visiting his daughter, Margie. He said he sensed the inevitable before the errant pass was thrown. It reminded him of a Carl Sandburg poem which asks, "Why did the children put beans in their ears when the one thing we told the children they must not do was put beans in their ears?"

Today's young are always putting beans in their ears, on and off the football field. It is a prerogative that youth — unpredictable, impulsive, daring — enjoys as never before. I sometimes envy their daring.

But I do not envy youth. Dr. Stamp in his talk on sex, scotch and salad, told us a surprising thing. In one of his studies, he asked hundreds of people past 70 to name the best decades of their lives.

Youth finished last. The "best years" proved to be, by a landslide vote, the decades between 45 and 65. By then, most of us have stopped throwing interceptions and going for the impossible win.

We settle for ties. And we rarely experience the urge to put beans in our ears.

*November 4, 1988*

# 'What Will We Get for Rhoda?'

On the very eve of the big event, two remarks overheard during my pre-Christmas pilgrimage through the shopping malls still ring in my ears.

One came from a weary-looking, package-laden woman who, pushing her way through a crowded department store, said to the man with her, "Well that's it, except for Rhoda. Whatever will we get for Rhoda? Rhoda is so hard to please."

At another store, a couple lingered over the jewelry counter, the woman admiring a ring she had slipped on her finger.

The man with her nodded in agreement as she said to the salesclerk, "I'm looking for something that speaks of elegance but ain't too flashy."

There is a Rhoda in every family. Particular, persnickety Rhoda. She is always last on the shopping list because her tastes are different, her standards higher than anyone else's.

What bugs Rhoda every Christmas? Could it be that at Christmas she always gets Charlie when what she really wants is White Linen? Or vice versa — she wants something practical instead of something exotic?

There are such people, you know. Lacy Hamilton told me of one when he came out last week to measure for a storm door. He had recently installed a handsome new door at a house where the wife fairly danced with excitement as the door went up.

"This is what I wanted *last* Christmas," she said. "But the dear fool gave me a diamond instead."

Or could it be that Rhoda is one of those poor souls who are unhappiest with themselves at Christmas, when we are almost under a court order to be joyful and dispense cheer, even if it kills us? It may be that the only gift she wants is for someone — man, woman or child — to touch her cheek and softly whisper, "Rhoda, I love you."

At our house two rules prevail. The father is never again to "ruin Christmas" by re-telling the tragic tale of how, during the Great Depression, there was one year when Santa never showed at all.

And the children now know better than to say ever again on Christmas morning as they survey the extravagant mound of tissue and wrapping paper and gifts, "Is this all there is?"

To their credit, it didn't take a tornado to get them to begin to realize that all things are perishable and passing, except those gifts that are never found under a Christmas tree, and that all the touchable treasures we have collected over the years can vanish in 30 seconds of howling, twisting terror raging through the night.

In every one of us there is a longing for a Christmas just like the one we used to know, with snow and mistletoe and the rest.

Out of my own past, I remember one Christmas Eve as clearly as yesterday. It had snowed for almost two days. It was the kind of snow that Dylan Thomas remembered as a child in Wales: "Our snow was not only shaken from whitewash buckets down the sky, it came shawling out of the ground and swam and drifted out of the arms and hands and bodies of the trees. . . . "

On this Christmas Eve, it had finally stopped snowing. Still, my mother and I knew that none of my large family would make it home over the frozen roads and the two of us would be spending our first Christmas ever alone there in the foothills.

The night was clear, the stars like diamonds glittering against the black velvet sky. Suddenly, there came to our straining ears the joyful sound of crunching tires on frozen snow. Through the window we saw the headlights of a car, slipping and sliding along the winding road. A favorite brother, then a bachelor, had inched along 38 hazardous miles from Winston-Salem, just to be "home for Christmas."

A good Christmas it was, not too flashy but, in memory, beautiful with a stillness that spoke a little of elegance.

From the beginning, nineteen hundred and eighty-nine years ago, the child has been the centerpiece of Christmas, whether it's a newborn babe in the manger or a 4-year-old at West Raleigh Presbyterian Church.

For it was there that the associate pastor recently gathered the little children around him at the front of the sanctuary and began asking them questions. That is always a dangerous practice with children, sooner or later bound to boomerang.

"Now," the minister said to the wee ones, "tell me, whose birthday is it just two weeks from today?"

"Mine! Mine! Mine!," a little girl shrieked, her bright eyes sparkling, her voice breaking with anticipation.

Wise men seeking the spirit of Christmas still follow a star to a child. The late E.B. White years ago wrote movingly in The New Yorker of the coming of his first grandchild, born just before Christmas:

"Instead of following a star, we simply followed directions given us by the child's parents, took the 10 o'clock train, and found the infant in Boston, where it lay behind glass in a hospital.

"No shepherds were abiding there, but there was a nurse in a mask attending and the glory of the Lord shone round about — a child seen through a glass clearly."

That's the way it is with a child — nothing flashy at first, but something that over the years will, with God's help, perhaps speak of elegance.

Merry Christmas to all of you. And especially to you, Rhoda, whoever and wherever you are.

*December 22, 1988*

# Their Typos Live After Them

Not long ago, Nancy Welch, a bright young UNC journalism student, interviewed me for a term paper. I say bright because, unlike most high school and college kids, she had not waited until the night before the paper was due to grab and interview her "ram in the bush."

In closing, she asked what advice I would give to young people entering the profession. Among other things, I suggested they should "love it or leave it—," not be clock-watchers, read a lot and above all strive to be accurate.

It was not until she left that I realized I had forgotten to warn her to develop a tough skin. Journalism is not for the faint-hearted. Few professionals' work is subject to as much review and criticism.

Not long ago a woman accosted me after church and said she deeply resented the use of the world "elderly" in a headline over a story about a 63-year-old Raleigh woman being raped.

"Why do they need to use such an adjective? Why can't they just say 'woman' and let it go at that?"

"Well, for one thing, the word 'elderly' does convey the victim's inability to resist her attacker " I reasoned.

"Well, I don't like it," she snapped.

I recently fielded a telephone call to the sports department from a woman who angrily asked, "Why didn't you all use Lake Speed's picture in the paper yesterday?"

My mind floundered frantically. "'Lake Speed?' Is it a body of water, a rock group or what?"

"He won his first race ever and you didn't even use his picture," the woman said, rescuing me from my ignorance.

"I know why," she went on. "It was because he is a Christian. If he had had a beer ad painted on the door of his car, you woulda used his picture."

I promised to pass the word.

You never know from what direction to expect the next bullet.

Last month this newspaper pulled the Cathy cartoon for what many of us considered a legitimate reason. The cartoonist was endorsing a political candidate on the comics page. Opinion, and certainly political endorsements, belong on the editorial or opinion pages.

Who would have guessed 600 irate subscribers would call the newspaper? Canceling the Constitution wouldn't have drawn that kind of response.

Not long ago in this column, a line from Carl Sandburg was mistakenly attributed to the musical "Fantasticks," which apparently had borrowed from Sandburg the expression "Why did the children put beans in their ears when the one thing we told the children they must not do was put beans in their ears?"

The knowledgeable fellow who quoted the line in conversation following a football game at Chapel Hill let me know the line was from Sandburg's "The People, Yes," along with "Why did the children pour molasses on the cat when the one thing we told. . . . "

As a cub reporter in Burlington many decades ago, I learned early that every time you go to press, you are playing a kind of Russian roulette.

In a retired colonel's obituary, a reporter accidentally demoted him to retired major.

In writing a correction, the reporter made another error. And in correcting that error, made still another.

Finally the colonel's distraught wife called and said, "Please, just don't run any more corrections. You have already ruined a perfectly good death."

Last spring, at our annual editors' convention in Washington, President Reagan was at his charismatic best, teasing, cajoling, criticizing with tongue in cheek the pesky press that had been nipping at his heels for seven years.

He said he didn't expect to read a retraction of any of the media crimes committed against him and Mrs. Reagan. Anyway, he said, if one ever came, it couldn't possibly measure up to one he considered one of the classic newspaper corrections.

Published many years ago, it had read, "Instead of being arrested, as we stated yesterday, for kicking his wife down a flight of stairs and hurling a lighted kerosene lamp after her, the Reverend James P. Wallman died unmarried four years ago."

There is something in all of us that likes to finger-point when we come across errors in print. I recall a particularly entertaining column by one of our sports writers, one of the best in the business. It was about a bad hike from the center that cost N.C. State a crucial football game.

"Some things you just don't like to watch," he wrote in his inimitable style. "A baby carriage rolling down the hill into the water. A guy going to the chair. A car crossing a collapsing bride. A game won or lost on one mess-up."

Yeah, you guessed it. Someone singled out that one small typographical error, and wrote me a note asking if the collapsing bride ever made it to the altar. Apparently, the writer's clever, colorful style, much like the errant snap from the center, sailed right over the reader's head.

But criticism comes with the turf. Without critics, this would be a boring and purposeless business.

*November 25, 1988*

# Hail the Prince in Tennis Shoes

When the children were small and believed in fairy tales, they would come to me from the sandpile or tree-house, and extending a grimy hand, would plead, "Daddy, tell my fortune."

With my finger, I would painstakingly trace the lines of their palms, predicting handsome strangers they would meet in the first grade, and then, seeing through a glass darkly, sketch on the fresh slate of their imagination a columned mansion called Tara, or a neat farmhouse nestled somewhere along Highway 601 in Surry County.

I would tell them of the great world out there that would be theirs because they were young and would be young for a long, long time.

Occasionally, I would let a little rain of reality fall into their future, reminding them that they would have to work hard, pay the mortgage and the utility bills, not have servants and stay up all night taking care of sick babies.

It was amazing how the light would go out of their eyes for a moment, until I picked up again on the positive. A foolish father, I could not bear to cloud their horizon.

What set off this stream of reminiscing was an article in Sunday's News and Observer having to do with the "lost out" generation. They are today's young people who, born in an age of affluence, now are anxious and fearful for their future.

We don't like to admit it. But we parents are to blame, even though I sympathized when a friend recently complained about his happy-go-lucky 25-year-old son, whom he refers to as 'the oldest living sophomore."

"Ninety percent of his brain is dedicated to women and electronic games," he said. "He has reserved 10 percent for family relationships, holding down a job and molding his future."

The "lost out" generation, as the article said, is struggling to afford the worst house in the best neighborhood. They still want the best cars, the priciest condos and "top management jobs." And they want it now. Yet they spend as they go.

Yes, parents must share the guilt here. They have knocked themselves out providing for their children what they, as children, never had.

"My kids borrow everything I have," another father groused. "My sports coat, my car, my ties. They even borrow my memories, having none of their own."

But some parents aren't as sacrificing. I remember from the long ago a middle-class couple with several back-to-back kids. They were hard pressed to make ends meet.

The mother once remarked that, nevertheless, every Saturday night, they splurged and had a T-bone steak for her and her husband. They could not afford steak for the children, who ate hamburgers.

"Their time will come," the woman said. "Our time is now."

I thought her heartless at the time, since we always put the children first. But in retrospect, she was the wiser parent. And her children have doted on and adored her through the years.

In the newspaper article, one of the "lost outs" told how she chose to attend one of the nation's most expensive colleges.

"My mother went to work three days a week to be able to afford the $10,000 tuition. They did the sacrificing. We didn't." How true.

Another one said he goes around with the constant feeling that "doom is just around the corner."

No wonder. Not long ago, I heard a young woman exclaiming happily to a friend, "We've closed the deal on the house. And the payments are only $1,500 a month!"

As a man who used to lie awake worrying about meeting $103.20 house payments, I realized how out of touch I am with these brave ones who can laugh in the face of fate and the bank.

If time's clock could be reversed, I would have read my children's palms a little differently.

"Aha!" I would say, "I see a Prince Charming riding into your life. At 9 o'clock at night? He is driving a second-hand Honda and wearing rumpled blue jeans, dirty sneakers and a shirt from T.J. Maxx. He must have left his manners at home because he is honking the horn out front!"

I had no way of knowing then that they can no longer count on someone who will support, love and obey until death do them part. Or that they would want to step into a "top management" job the first year out of college. Or the possibility they could end up in the tough, tragic role of "single parents."

If any of you young parents out there find yourself reading the palms of your little ones, be smarter than I was. And more honest.

Yes, tell them fairy tales. But let them know when the clock strikes 12, those handsome steeds may indeed change back into mice, and the golden coach with the BMW emblazoned on the side suddenly may become only a second-hand Mustang.

Tell them that the Prince with glass slipper in hand sometimes takes a wrong turn and ends up at somebody else's house where he finds the perfect size 5. Double A width.

*December 17, 1988*

# Thou Shalt Not Chew Gum

I often wonder whether, if the Lord had it to do over again, He might not come up with a different Ten Commandments. Or possibly add a few, at least to a baker's dozen.

Were He to do that, surely the Eleventh Commandment would be "Thou shalt not chew gum in public; thou certainly shalt not under any circumstances chew the stuff in my holy temple!"

For years now, I have reined in my compulsion to comment on public gum chewing. After attending a funeral this week and observing at least two people pumping away on gum, I can no longer contain my indignation.

During the past Christmas season, as I sat in church, enthralled by a splendid rendition of Handel's majestic "Messiah," I noticed two women in the next pew chewing gum as if it was going out of style. As it is — at least with me.

I am ashamed of the anger I felt at this sacrilegious display of bad manners. How could those two good women not look around, and upon realizing they were the only two people in a crowd of almost a thousand chewing gum, refrain from quickly swallowing the stuff?

I felt the same sense of revulsion when I attended a relative's wedding in the foothills. It was one of the most elegant affairs I have ever witnessed, complete with an army of bridesmaids and groomsmen, a vast array of flowers, soloists, violinists, trumpeters. No expense had been spared.

But just before the bride, arrayed in all her finery, came down the aisle to greet the nervous groom, I noticed that five of the eight honorary groomsmen, handsome lads all, seated second pew from the front, were chomping away on gum.

I see no difference whatsoever between chewing gum in church and munching peanut butter and crackers, working a quid of Red Man, or even dipping snuff in church. The effect is the same: jaws working aimlessly, up and down, as idiotically as a windmill on a windy March day.

I called a couple of retired ministers to ask how it feels to be in the pulpit and look out on the congregation and see folks chewing gum. Do they, I asked, momentarily wonder if they are addressing their carefully composed sermons to a congregation of cud-chewing cows?

Ministers, being ministers, are not anxious to offend.

"I always feel sorry for the sexton," one said, evading the question. "It is the curse of his life. But then I also wonder why grown-up baseball pitchers go around with chaws of 'backy bulging their cheeks."

My friend, retired pastor W.W. Finlator, was, as expected, more specific.

"While it's no cardinal sin, I think chewing gum in church carries a touch of irreverence," he said. "But I prefer gum chewing to crocheting or knitting during my sermons. Or members of my flock going to sleep. I've had all three."

Bill Reaves, now retired but formerly the purchasing agent for the State Highway Commission, shares my paranoia about public mastication. He told me about the headlines he inspired a couple of decades ago when he issued a memo forbiding on-the-job gum-chewing by his employees.

Admittedly, his memo was no masterpiece of diplomacy. But back then the boss was boss and he could be as dictatorial as he pleased.

"I do not approve of Purchasing personnel chewing gum while on office duty," Bill said in his edict of Aug. 11, 1966. "I do not think this practice is conducive to good office etiquette. Your cooperation will be very much appreciated in the discontinuance of this practice immediately."

When the press got wind of the directive, people began taking sides. Mostly Reaves' side. As one newspaper headline said, the gum controversy got "sticky."

When the Associated Press moved the story, it got even stickier. Reaves was bombarded by pro and con letters from around the country, including one from the National Board of Boiler and Pressure Vessel Inspectors in Columbus, Ohio. The state's editorial pages took issue, one noting that good or bad, gum was the only thing that in 1966 still sold for a nickel.

I suppose the choice to chew or not chew gum is one of those individual freedoms we all fought for in the wars down through the ages. It goes along with the right to pick your teeth or nose in public, to take the widow's mite and spend it on an air-conditioned doghouse, or to pave the path to the presidency with pretty girls. Or to call up some columnist at home and say, "Look, Bozo, it's no business of yours if I chew gum in church."

I confess I occasionally chew gum in private, especially when becoming airborne and my ears start popping. Or when, against my family's wishes, I have had spring onion in my tossed salad.

But the best use for gum I've heard yet came from garden columnist Bugs Barringer of Rocky Mount. Responding to a column I had written about problems with moles in my lawn, Bugs recommended I insert sticks of unchewed Wrigley's in the mole runs. The moles, he explained, will come along, chew the gum, become constipated and die. He swears it will work.

Thank you for allowing me to purge my psyche of this peeve. I conclude with a fervent request to those who crave gum during The Lord's Prayer or Handel's Messiah: Please save it for mole killing outings or other similar occasions before and after church. Or bring your knitting.

*May 30, 1987*

# Don't Bring a Hoe in the House

Los Angeles Times Columnist Jack Smith recently received a letter from a young man asking, "If you could offer the young people of today any piece of advice, what would it be?"

Mr. Smith felt stumped, as all of us would, at being asked to capsule all his great storehouse of wisdom for the young into a one-paragraph package.

And, if he is like most fathers, Mr. Smith undoubtedly has huge reserves of unused advice rejected by his own children. Nevertheless, he shouldn't hesitate to advise on the grounds that he feels unqualified.

Fiddlesticks! What have qualifications got to do with it? Only air is freer than advice, unless you're getting it from a lawyer or a shrink.

Mr. Smith recalls Nelson Algren's renowned advice to his readers: "Never eat at a place called Mom's, never play poker with a man named Doc, and never sleep with a woman who has more troubles than you have."

And he remembers Somerset Maugham's short story "Facts of Life" which is one of my own favorite Maugham pieces.

In that story, an English gentleman is telling friends at his club about his young son who has just made the traditional trip to the Continent that all sons of the well-to-do made back then. The father had advised the lad ere he left home to steer clear of gambling, liquor and women.

But as is so often the case, the son has done the opposite, heading straight off to the game rooms at Monte Carlo, where he wins a pile of money and meets a ravishing woman who takes him to her apartment.

After a stimulating romp in her bed, the young man drifts off to sleep only to awaken to find the woman taking his money from his clothes and putting it under a flower pot.

After she returns to bed and falls asleep, he gets up, retrieves his winnings and departs. He later learns that he has also scooped up the woman's savings along with his own money.

Having recounted this saga, the father asks his friends what to make of all that. One replies, "Don't worry, the lad's just lucky."

Algren's advice to avoid eating at a place called "Mom's" applies more to some truck stops these days, since there aren't many "Mom's" cafes or boarding houses still around.

For years, naive travelers thought that the 18-wheelers parked in front of a restaurant represented the seal of Good Housekeeping insofar as tasty food was concerned. I don't know when or why we accepted truckers' tastes as the hallmark of cuisine.

A friend who briefly drove a long-distance hauler right after he got out of school set me straight on that score many years ago.

"Yeah, I used to pull over and park at those places with all the rigs out front," he said. "But I soon discovered that the food was usually lousy. In many cases, what was attracting the truckers like flies to honey wasn't the apple pie and spare ribs from the kitchen but the obliging women in the little rooms upstairs over the cafe."

I have handed out so much unheeded advice to my own children, it is difficult to recall any of it. As children grow and change, the kind and scope of advice from parents also changes.

Some 18 years ago, when my youngest was 3, I found on our street a possum that had been squashed by a car. I walked the youngster out to look at the scene and the victim for an explicit purpose.

"See, honey," I said. "What happened to the little possum will happen to you if you play in the street."

It was one of the few pieces of fatherly advice that made instant impact. She didn't go near the street after that. But for a long time her nightly prayers included, "And God, please don't let any more little baby possums play in the street and get runned over."

As for my parents' advice to their kids, it was very brief and basic: Don't lie, don't steal, don't use the Lord's name in vain and don't bring a hoe into the house.

I am still puzzled by the latter commandment since I cannot fathom to this day why anyone would ever bring a hoe into the house. Perhaps it might have been one of those foothills superstitions—bringing a hoe into the house would bring bad luck.

My friend Nell Styron says I misunderstood the whole message.

"Your dear mother was surely addressing your older brothers and warning them, in her Southern dialect, not to bring a 'hoah' in the house," which, Nell says, is still sound advice for any family with six sons at home.

The British gentleman in Maugham's story was right. Being lucky has a great deal to do with how well we get through life. And I am convinced that if parents reduced the quantity of advice dispensed to their offspring by 75 percent and left more to luck, everyone would be better off.

As for not sleeping with a woman who has more troubles than you do, how can anyone tell before it's too late?

*January 5, 1989*

# Sins of the Flesh — and Runts

In the foothills, folks take their religion seriously. So when I recently went back for a visit it was with no little caution that I brought up the matter of Judge Rufus Reynolds calling a spade a spade, or a shyster a shyster, after he retired as judge in the PTL bankruptcy case involving Jim and Tammy Bakker.

"I don't think he had any business including that part about the sawed-off runt," one of my relatives noted, referring to Judge Reynolds' remark "What puzzles me is why people were interested in that sawed-off little runt."

"Why not?" I asked.

"I just didn't think it was fair to runts...kind of a slur against short people," my relative said. We have some short people in our family.

To be perfectly honest, the folks back home were not as uptight over the Jim and Tammy mess as they are over the loose lifestyles creeping into the foothills from the city.

My two older sisters were not as indignant over Jim and Tammy's shenanigans as they were over a report that a 75-year-old Casanova in the community had, by his own admission, spent the night with a widow out on Route 8. The woman is is a faithful churchgoer and professes to be a conscientious Christian.

Monroe Mattlin's romance with the widow had been on shaky ground for some time because she constantly nagged him to accompany her to Sunday School and preaching. Monroe — one of those "cooled-down Christian" types who frequently let the sins of the flesh get in the way of their better spiritual instincts — resisted stubbornly.

He made the mistake of discussing the problem with his boss who confided it to a friend who confided it to half the people in Surry County and that's how my sisters learned of it.

Things came to a showdown on a Saturday night when Monroe finally talked the widow into letting him spend the night. She had reluctantly given in on condition he park his pickup behind the feed barn so nobody would know he was there.

"As if the Lord didn't know," my sister snorted.

Next morning, Monroe rolled out of bed and was dressing when the conscience-stricken widow raised herself from her pillow and said:

"Monroe Mattlin, I've made up my mind. We are not going to do this again until you get saved and join the church!"

Apparently, Monroe hated ultimatums as much as church. He dodged both bullets by changing girlfriends.

My folks also don't agree with Judge Reynolds' insistence that "Religion is just another consumer item, just the same as selling soap, or washing powder or aspirin."

They say it depends on the brand of religion, the way it is marketed and, mainly, what happens to the money taken in.

Talk about selling soap! I recently received in my mailbox a letter from a Rev. Ewing down in Atlanta, Ga., who wants to give me, free of charge, a "Blessed Golden Metal Cross."

All I have to do is return the postage-free card that also lists a number of things I can ask Mr. Ewing to pray for.

If I were to accept his offer, I would certainly check the box that reads "Pray for my blood pressure," especially with income tax time approaching, the legislature in town and the Carolina Tar Heels' up and down basketball season.

But to check "Pray for me to receive a continuous money blessing" sounds too mercenary, if not downright greedy to me. But apparently it is one of the hottest items on the preacher's prayer menu.

His colorful brochure is chock full of examples of people he has prayed to prosperity.

There is a photo of a smiling woman standing at her kitchen stove, turning pork chops in a frying pan.

"You can almost smell the fish and pork chops frying and those big round biscuits baking," the brochure reads. "Rev. Ewing's assistant visited the Cambrell home. God blessed her with this home and a new Cadillac."

On Page 3, "Sister Emma" testifies, "I was on welfare but I'm not anymore. I've got more money than I know what to do with." Thanks, of course, to Brother Ewing's prayers.

A man in Michigan has been blessed with "a new Cadillac and 2 family flats." A Chicago resident has suddenly been visited with "a new Cutlass, a new Lincoln, a Chevrolet." A North Carolinian thanks Brother Ewing for a new washer-dryer and her new Skylark Buick.

Mr. Ewing makes God sound like an auto dealership, specializing strictly in made-in-the-USA models, with a preponderance of Cadillacs.

"When you go stealing other people's money, you can't say, 'The Bible excuses me. I've been forgiven by the Lord,' " said Judge Reynolds. And I say amen to that.

In fact if I had to vote on whether Mr. Bakker, Mr. Ewing, Judge Reynolds or Monroe Mattlin had the best chance of crashing the Pearly Gates, I'd have to go with Judge Reynolds. But Monroe Mattlin would be a close runner-up. That lecherous old scamp!

*January 20, 1989*

# Under 'C' for Contraceptives

I was pleased to read that the Moore County mother who objected to "The Grapes of Wrath" on the shelves of her child's high school library has backed off. She has decided that even though she doesn't want her child to read the Steinbeck novel, it will be OK for other students to do so.

That is big of her. There are other book-burners among us not nearly so generous in doling out what constitutionally guaranteed freedoms we can still enjoy.

In fact, United Press International in its annual survey found that there were 130 attempts last year to censor library and public school books. That's an increase of 35 percent over the previous year.

When I think of censorship, I also think of an anecdote told by Dr. Raymond Rodgers, an N.C. State University free-speech specialist in the Department of Speech Communication.

Dr. Rodgers tells the supposedly true story of the school librarian in Oklahoma who one day missed volume "C" from the library's only set of encyclopedias. After she issued a memo asking all teachers to be on the lookout for the missing volume, a teacher approached the librarian's desk.

"I have 'C' ", she whispered, glancing around the library. "It has 'contraceptives' in it."

"We'll talk about it later," murmured the busy librarian, turning her attention to a group of children entering the library.

A couple of days later the librarian went to the teacher's room. "I want 'C' back," she whispered. "It has 'Christ' and 'Christianity' in it."

The tale well illustrates the main problem with censorship. Many of us would rather that profanity, obscenity and sexual intrigue not be included in the books our children read. But in rejecting powerful writing, including pertinent and perceptive messages that stimulate intellectual development, we are indeed throwing out the baby with the bath water.

The Moore County mother, for example, objected to "Grapes of Wrath" because it had the word "goddamn" in it. Because of a word that has become almost standardized in the language of many of today's teens, she would deny her child and everyone else's the wealth of understanding, compassion and history contained in Steinbeck's classic saga of a poverty-stricken family fleeing the Oklahoma dust bowl during the Depression in search of the promised land of California.

I called a friend's house this week and found him deeply absorbed in preparing the Sunday School lesson he is to teach tomorrow.

"We're into the prophets," he offered.

"Pretty dull, huh?"

"Either your memory is dull or you haven't been near the Bible lately," he replied. "The Bible isn't dull. Sometimes it reads like a soap opera!" He suggested I browse through Genesis.

I did. Wow! There I met Jacob, a selfish, greedy fellow by anybody's measure, who takes advantage of his hungry brother Esau and trades him out of his birthright for a mess of pottage.

That same Jacob, at the urging of his conniving mother, then deceives his aging, blind father when the old man is ready to dispense the patriarchal blessing that, by tradition, was to go to the eldest son. Jacob, wearing goat skins and passing himself off as the hairy Esau, receives the irrevocable blessing, leaving Esau penniless and property-less and more than chagrined by the deception. Shades of "Dynasty!"

Jacob gets his comeuppance. Seeking a wife in a nearby country, he falls in love with the beautiful, sexy Rachel. So smitten is he that he promises her father Laban to labor seven years for her hand in marriage. Seven years later, on the wedding night, the wily Laban sneaks "tender-eyed" but ugly sister Leah into Jacob's bed in place of Rachel.

Comes the dawn, and the disappointed but determined bridegroom is back at Laban's door complaining about the switch. He agrees to work another seven years for Rachel. Some dish, that Rachel.

A chapter or so further along, we come to the next X-rated episode. Jacob's granddaughter Diana is raped by Shechem, son of King Hamor, the Hivite. The rapist is so enamored of his victim that he goes straight away to his old man and says, "Dad, get me this damsel to wife!"

And Hamor the Hivite, just like today's doting fathers who try to satisfy their sons' every whim, negotiates for Diana's hand. Her brothers, Simeon and Levi, secretly seething with rage over the rape, seize the opportunity for revenge.

They agree to the marriage only on condition that Shechem and all his men be circumcised. The anxious bridegroom readily agrees and puts himself and his men to the knife. While the men are lying around in their tents, weak and sore from their wounds, the two brothers descend on the camp, slaying Shechem, Hamor and all the Hivites, plundering the village and making off with all the cattle, women and children.

How stuff like this gets past today's censors is beyond me. And this is just Genesis. We haven't even gotten to David and Bathsheba yet.

*October 25, 1986*

# Was It a Hand on His Thigh?

Days before the all-female jury decided in favor of the man in the sexual harassment case involving employees of First Citizens Bank and Trust Co., thousands of folks on the street, in the pubs, the office snackbars and at the bridge club had already voted.

Unfortunately, most of the people I heard casting ballots voted according to their gender. That makes the real jury's decision even more remarkable.

Sexual harassment is no laughing matter, however difficult it is to define. One woman may welcome a man's overt attention as a compliment. Another may regard it as a potential $2 million insult.

At a newspaper meeting in Chapel Hill, I overheard three women talking about sexual harassment. One actually complained that never in her entire life had she been propositioned by a man.

"Well, *I* was once," piped up Kathy Wilson. "It was in a high-class bar in Cheyenne, Wyoming. I was absolutely thrilled, although my husband insisted it wasn't a proposition. Ken said the fellow was drunk and was asking directions to the men's room."

Louise, the third member of the group and a former nurse, said she was propositioned once right after graduating from nursing school.

"He was from New York, a friend of a patient I was nursing at the time. He called me at home and asked me to come to his hotel room. Wouldn't you consider that being propositioned? I refused, of course. But he sent me a box of chocolates anyway.

"I recall that it was a one-layer box of chocolates. I suppose I expected more. But it confirmed my good judgment in not meeting the guy. I imagine he would have been a one-layer man in everything and for all his lifetime."

At lunch last week, none of the men at my table could recall ever being sexually harassed. "Wives don't count," one said, quickly establishing ground rules.

I wasn't surprised. Traditionally, men are neither the chaste nor the chased.

Modestly, I admitted that I might have been a borderline victim of female harassment many years ago, when I first came to Raleigh as a young reporter.

Yes, once I had a secret love. She would call me every few weeks, late at night. Her voice was as gentle as dawn, her conversation as pure as the driven snow.

She'd say she had liked something I wrote. Or inquire about my general health. Also — and this bothered me a bit—she would tell me where she had seen me that day — walking across Capitol Square, leaving the library or lunching at the Sir Walter Hotel coffee shop.

One spring day she sent me flowers — a bunch of pressed violets in a typed envelope. She never identified herself.

The "affair" lasted only a few months and ceased abruptly when my engagement was announced in The News and Observer's "Women's Section." The week before I was to be married she called to say goodbye.

"Have a happy life," she said — sadly, I thought. "I won't be calling you any more." And she never did.

Men are likely to lie about their sexual conquests. I know a fellow who insists he is frequently harassed by women he encounters at conventions. More than once he gets a faraway look in his eyes and recalls the time when, lunching with a certain woman he hardly knew, he felt her hand on "the inside of my thigh."

"It could have been an accident, you know," I countered. "She might have been just reaching for her napkin. That's hardly harassment"

He pooh-poohed my idea, treasuring the moment. Former athletes are like that. Once the cheering stops, they tend to fantasize over the number of touchdowns they scored and women they seduced.

Imagine the futility of suing for sexual harassment in places like Paris and Rome where womanizing is a work of art and sexual propositions are as commonplace as a flashy smile?

Not long ago I read a Jack Smith column in which 34-year-old Elizabeth Dobbs described the heavy sexual atmosphere she encountered during a vacation in Paris. Mrs. Dobbs, no shrinking violet, is married, mother of two sons born at home and the first female firefighter in her community.

"The taxi driver asked me if he could father a child for me on the way to the hotel," she said. It was not clear whether the fathering was to be done in the taxi or at the hotel.

"Just smiling at a student caused him to run across the street to talk with us. (The language barrier was too great; he left.) Everywhere we went, we felt the open appreciation of men."

"I saw women being valued for their specialness as women. Their sense of style, and the way they take care of themselves," Mrs. Dobbs said.

Many American women may agree with Mrs. Dobbs. But a romantic flirtation in the moonlight by the fountains of Rome or a brazen invitation to copulate in a cab in Paris is one thing. It's something else to be chased around the desk or pinched in an elevator by some lecherous guy back home in Wide Prairie, Chicago or New York.

A man will do well to keep that in mind when he thinks he feels the touch of a hand on his thigh during dinner with a charming stranger.

*March 10, 1989*

# Maybe as Much as Magic Johnson

Eating breakfast out one morning, a friend was asked why she gave up teaching at a woman's college to spend her life with computers.

"I finally left the classroom when I realized the girls valued their suntans more than they did an education," she said. "I just couldn't fight that."

A recent series in this newspaper on student apathy touched on why more and more teachers feel like my friend and go off to do something else. If only the poor ones left, it would be a blessing. But too often it's the great ones who go.

Every one of us can recall one or two fantastic teachers. During our breakfast session, Lou Rosser mentioned the well-remembered May Bush who taught Victorian literature at UNC-G.

"She was a fabulous teacher," sighed Lou. "And one of the few with a keen sense of humor. She kind of brayed when she laughed. But we got used to that."

Dr. Bush always introduced herself on the first day of classes with the anecdote about the time she returned home from a vacation trip and caught a cab at the train station in the little town.

"Take me to the Bushes," she instructed the startled cabbie. May Bush always brayed a bit at her little joke and then got down to the brass tacks of making learning an exciting and memorable experience.

In college, one of the greatest teachers I had was Dr. Ella J. Pierce. She had a unique and at first disconcerting speech habit. She added an 'a' to nearly every word she spoke.

"Mr. Snow-a can you tell me-a the general theme-a of Beowulf-a?"

She was so enthusiastic, so in love with English literature and so bent on sharing every shred of what she knew with us that within a week we had became accustomed to "Dr. Pierce-a's" unusual speech pattern.

Dr. Pierce was one of those totally committed teachers, a pearl of great price. When it came to classroom performance and homework, she rode us hard and put us up wet. She lectured so furiously during the class hour that more than once she had to shout the next assignment out the classroom window as we fled across campus to our next class.

Eudora Welty describes such a teacher in "One Writer's Beginning."

One Friday afternoon young Eudora and a little friend were in the school toilet making Saturday plans from adjoining cubicles:

"Can you come spend the day with me?" she had called.

"I might could," her friend had called back.

"Who—said—MIGHT—COULD?" came a voice out of nowhere.

"It sounded like Fe Fi Fo Fum!" Miss Welty recalled.

"That was the voice of Mrs. McWillie, who taught the other fourth grade across the hall from ours. She was not even our teacher, but a stern lady who dressed entirely in widow's weeds with pleated black shirtwaist with a high net collar and velvet ribbon and a black skirt to her ankles, with black circles under her eyes and a mournful, Presbyterian expression.... We children took her to be 100 years old.

"You might as well tell me," continued Mrs. McWillie. "I'm going to plant myself right here and wait till you come out. Then I'll see who it was I heard saying 'MIGHT-COULD.'"

I have said that a good teacher is a pearl of great price. But what *is* a great price for teachers?

Los Angeles Times Columnist Jack Smith once got in trouble with a reader when he wrote that a certain teacher he knew was worth as much money as Magic Johnson. Well, the last time I looked, Magic was getting $2 million a year to bounce a basketball for the world champion Los Angeles Lakers.

One of Mr. Smith's readers fired back that no way was a teacher worth as much as Magic.

Using a very subjective formula based on the teacher's per pupil contribution to earning power, he concluded that a teacher is worth $26,000 a year. And he added that because they are paid from tax dollars, and Magic is not, the teacher is "merely a step removed from a mugger."

To teachers, "them's fightin' words, podner." But they and the rest of us must consider the source of such heresy—a California jock addict.

I don't think there is one among us whose life has not been directly influenced by a teacher—for better or worse. Primarily because of my teachers, I am doing what I do today for a living instead of being what I suspect would have been a very inept lawyer.

That one of my children hopes to follow in my footsteps is due not to me but to one particular teacher at Chapel Hill, a fellow whose teaching magic can match the magic of Magic Johnson any day. I seriously doubt he's taking home $2 million a year.

So be careful, Mamas. If you don't want your sons or daughters to grow up to be cowboys, or journalists or whatever, you'd better steer them away from a good teacher.

As for pay, if you gave a good teacher the kind of TV exposure that Magic Johnson gets, and the sex appeal of Estee Lauder's Paulina, she could knock down $2 million too.

Or anyway she might could.

*June 9, 1989*

# You Can Go Home Again

When Town Manager Bob Comer asked me to come to Dobson last weekend to autograph books, nothing was said about "A. C. Snow Day." The proclamation by Mayor Jim Davis and the reception at the library were a total surprise.

Certainly God, if not many of the townspeople, took a dim view of such goings on. It rained as if the Ark were about to be re-launched. As we drove to town on Friday morning, the cows in a roadside pasture were ambling toward the barn, two by two.

Being honored by homefolks especially these proud, foothills people, who come through the rain to say hello and purchase the stuff you have written is a gratifying and humbling experience. Meeting with friends, former teachers, and men and women with whom I had gone to church or school seemed a satisfactory substitute for the high school class reunion we have never held.

Classmate Ida Lambert Johnson brought along some snapshots of the way we were, and briefed me on the current status of many of my peers. At Hardee's, I encountered Rom Folger having breakfast.

I remembered that long-ago time when as the new boy in town I had to deal with Rom. The toughest kid in the fifth grade, he was also the marbles champ. I finally achieved a truce with Rom the day I emptied my pockets of what few marbles I owned and staked him the ammo he used at recess to clean out every other marble-shooting kid on the playground. In fairness to Rom, he split the take with me.

My nephew Stephen, who works at the local Extension Service, dropped by. He allowed as how "Snow Day" wasn't much of an occasion if you didn't get a day off from work. And another cynical relative wondered if "A. C. Snow Day" is going to replace Ground Hog Day in Dobson.

The Norman sisters came. At least two of them, Louise and Betty, did. Elizabeth, hampered by injuries suffered when she was struck by a motorcycle the day she retired from teaching many years ago, doesn't get about much, certainly not during floods.

Ah, the Norman sisters. Every town should have such a treasure. Universally loved and spoiled, the three elderly women live just off the main street, surrounded by rich memories, Old South traditions and the handsome heirlooms of a prominent family of lawyers. They are the town's three graces, gentility personified, the last of the aristocracy of a time and a place that was.

Dobsonians still chuckle about the time the Norman sisters journeyed to Concord to visit friends. At the motel where they usually stayed, the manager had welcomed them with a message on the outside marquee: "The Norman sisters are here!"

Inside they found the manager busy at the switchboard, fielding calls from the curious, mostly males, who wanted to know about "the Norman sisters."

"Are they, you know, that kind of women?" one man asked, to which the indignant manager snapped, "Absolutely not!"

"Do they sing?" another caller asked. One wanted to know if the sisters perhaps danced. And another wondered if they told fortunes.

"Well, if they don't sing, or dance or entertain, what in the hell do they do?" one man asked.

"One can't half-hear," the manager explained. "One can't half-walk. And the other one talks all the time."

After the autographing, we spent a delightful hour at the home of the Norman sisters. It was the highlight of my visit, and I look forward to the time when Dobson will have a "Norman Sisters Day."

At the brief ceremony at the library, I remarked that sometimes people who have read about my hometown cut off U. S. 52 and drive over to Dobson to look around or have lunch at The Lantern. One such tourist once complained, "I don't know what's so special about the place. It's no different from most other two-stoplight towns. A courthouse, a liquor store, a few churches, a couple of banks."

But, as I reminded my friends last week, the man saw only the buildings, the streets and the stoplights. He didn't meet the peoples. Nor savor the memories. These are what make anyone's hometown worth going back to.

Early Sunday morning as I drove along Highway 601 toward Mount Airy to catch 52 back to Raleigh, the Blue Ridge range loomed bold and blue against a clear sky. Along the fallow fields on either side of the highway, patches of fog rose like smoke signals announcing the arrival of spring. To my right Mount Pilot reared its hoary head. The magic missing during the previous day's deluge came rushing back.

I remembered when my children used to come here with me. Homeward bound, they would sit in the back seat, weeping bitterly as they gazed longingly out the back window toward the receding hills, berating their father for ever having left such a pleasant place for Raleigh.

They do not go there now. Other things and other places claim higher priorities. But I suspect that some day they will, when they, too, feel a need to go back in time to a place in the heart that can refurbish the soul.

*June 16, 1989*

# Is God Really a Tar Heel?

I did not watch most of the ACC championship game. Close ones like that tend to stretch my nerves as tight as a watchspring. So, during most of the game, I strolled around my brother's farm in the foothills, studying the forsythia's bursting buds, savoring the sweet smell of the silage and trying to identify birds common to the mountains but not to Raleigh.

After all, I had escaped to the hills just to ponder the purpose of life and get away from the world's tensions — including the ACC tournament.

Occasionally, I would stroll back into the house to see how things stood. "He'll probably die of a heart attack during a basketball game," someone was saying.

"He should be so lucky," drawled cousin Joe.

Then I overheard my sister, who is a "messenger" in Fairview Baptist Church, say, "I do wish he could get as excited over religion as he does basketball. I wish he cared as much about something that is important."

I tried to explain to her that at the moment this game was very important to many people. Why, I wasn't sure. But it was. After all, every man is entitled to waste a few moments on the unimportant things of life.

I remembered what Grandpa said to his 14-year-old grandson Will Tweedy in Olive Ann Burns' wonderful book "Cold Sassy Tree."

"There's a heap more to God's will than death, disappointment and like thet," Grandpa explained to Will the night after the boy had been trapped on a high trestle and run over by a passenger train and lived to tell about it.

" . . . Folks who think God's will jest has to do with sufferin' and dyin', they done missed the whole point." Grandpa said.

I watched the game for a few moments, but as Duke crept within four points, I started out the door again.

"I thought you told me you had outgrown such foolishness," teased Cousin Ann.

"Well, I *am* better," I said. "At least I don't *pray* for Carolina to win anymore."

"I should hope not," she said. But I noticed she had her fingers crossed as Jeff Lebo swished a three-pointer.

Yes, I decided many years ago that God does not play basketball, although many Catholic lads still cross themselves before shooting their free shots.

And from time to time, you will see a coach kneeling in prayer on the sidelines during professional football games. Really, why should God give a fig who wins any sporting event?

Can you possibly imagine a scene in which St. Peter enters the

Heavenly Board Room during the second week of every March and says, "God, it's time to decide who's gonna win the ACC tournament this year."

"Well, what do you recommend, Pete?"

And St. Peter says, "Well, I've been going over all the standings and the stats and the records for the past 10 years. I guess it's old Dean's time this year. He ain't won one since 1982. And besides, he is — or at least was — a deacon in Binkley Baptist Church down in Chapel Hill."

And God says "Selah" which is Bible for so be it.

No, I don't buy that scene. And I don't think my sister would, although she is pretty much an inerrantist and thinks God has his fingers in just about everything that goes on down here.

That brings me back to Grandpa's lecture in "Cold Sassy Tree," which should be on everybody's library shelf.

That night, just about everybody in Cold Sassy had come by the house to look at Will Tweedy, who had survived the train. Many had brought food. It was much like a wake, except nobody had died.

On the conrtrary, Grandpa had just returned from his honeymoon. Much to the great consternation of his family and the whole community, he had eloped with Miss Love, the milliner who designed hats in Grandpa's store. And only 10 days after he had buried Grandma!

"Grandpa, do you think I'm alive tonight because it was God's will?" asks Will as the two sit alone in the kitchen, eating chocolate pie.

"Naw, you livin' 'cause you had the good sense to fall down 'twixt them tracks."

"Maybe God gave me the idea."

"You can believe thet, son, if'n you think it was God's idea for you to be up on thet trestle in the first place. What God gave you was a brain. Hit's His will for you to use it — p'tickler when a train's comin'."

Later on, Grandpa tries to further explain the complex puzzle of life and death and God that all of us spend our lives trying to untangle to the point that we can live with it.

"If you'da got kilt, it'd mean you jest didn't move fast enough, like a rabbit gets caught by a hound dog. You think God favors the dog over the rabbit, son?"

As I see it, that's the way it is with basketball. God had no more reason to favor the Heels over the Blue Devils than He does the hound over the rabbit. "Them Heels" finally got off the trestle because they saw a train a'comin.

*March 16, 1989*

# Read My Lips! Buy Hearing Aids

An elderly friend who recently lost her hearing aid was embarrassed that she couldn't tell her doctor when or where she had lost the tiny device.

"Oh, don't be embarrassed," he soothed. "People lose hearing aids anywhere and everywhere. I even had one patient who swallowed hers."

"How on earth could she have done that?" my friend asked.

It seemed the unfortunate woman always took several pills at bedtime. On this occasion, her husband had placed the pills, along with a glass of water, on the bedside table as usual. But his wife had absent-mindedly laid her tiny, hearing aid capsule on the same table.

Before turning out the lights, she scooped up the handful of pills — along with the hearing aid — and gulped them all down with the water.

I am telling this story for the benefit of our younger generation.

Why them? Because 95 percent are going to be deaf before they're dead. And they're going to be buying a lot of hearing aids, which, at prices between $600 and $1,000, they can't afford to lose — or eat.

Everywhere you go these days you run smack into a wall of noise, much of it masquerading as music. Especially in restaurants.

Wouldn't you think that restaurant owners would know by now that if people wanted to dine in a din they would park their lawn mower by the dining room table or pack a picnic lunch for the Spivey's Corners Hollering Contest?

We were delighted when a few months ago a new little restaurant opened around the corner from the newspaper office. I like to go there sometimes at mid-morning to sip a cup of coffee and regroup my thoughts.

The food is good. Normally, the place is an oasis of serenity. The morning sun pours through the front windows, making patterns on the clean white tablecloths and chases the January doldrums. The low hum of conversation from the coffee and croissant crowd is relaxing.

Imagine my surprise to walk in one morning and find the walls vibrating with ear-piercing rock music pouring from a "box" parked atop the cashier's counter.

Time was when I would have endured in silence. But more and more of us are speaking out these days, subconsciously harking back to that line in the old movie "Network," "We're mad as hell and we're not gonna take it any more."

"Look, would you mind turning the volume down a little," I asked the young person on duty. "We come here to drink coffee, think and talk, not to listen to the loud metal."

"Well, MOST people like the music!" I was told in no uncertain terms.

"But we are not MOST people," I smiled. It took a while but we have made peace with youth. The music, if there is any at all, is *sotto voce*.

A Raleigh woman I know is crusading for legislation that would make theater owners responsible for keeping kids out of R-rated movies.

Nothing irritates her more than attending a movie that even she finds barely bearable and seeing a child there. Her husband dreads such times.

"Not long ago we were at a theater when, suddenly, without warning, a couple of earthy types were sweating through an explicit love scene on the screen," her husband recalled recently.

"Unfortunately, about that time my wife spotted a little girl sitting two rows down from us." he said.

"What is that child doing here?" she hissed.

"Shh! 'that child' belongs to that 250-pound man she's sitting with, the guy who is going to beat hell out of me if you don't shut up!"

"Tell him that the child has no business being here!"

"No need to. He's already heard you," the husband said as he hurried the reform movement out of the theater.

During the last game of the season at Kenan Stadium, my friend Joe, a reformed cigarette addict, was incensed when a woman in the seat beside him kept extending her cigarette hand into his territory.

"Would you mind getting your cigarette out of my face," Joe asked, none too pleasantly, I fear.

"Really!" the woman snapped haughtily and turned to say something to her husband. Three minutes later, another cigarette was burning under Joe's nose.

"Lady," he said, "I warned you once. If you do that again I'm going to pour this Coca-Cola all over your expensive fur coat."

The woman jumped up, seized her fur and flounced angrily down the stadium steps to another seat, leaving her red-faced husband behind.

"I just want to say I'm glad you told my wife off," the guy said as he was about to follow. "She asked for it. She does the same thing to me. I warned her that one of these days she was going to run up against some mean S.O.B. like you who would tell her where to get off."

I don't know if we will ever win the war against insensitivity, especially noise. Probably not. American Health Magazine recently reported that hearing loss has moved ahead of "back ailments" as the fourth leading chronic physical disability in the United States.

Read my lips. If you've got extra bucks to burn, invest in hearing aids.

*January 25, 1989*

# Beware the Ides of Spring Break

I never understood why parents thronged Wake School Board meetings last fall to bewail the shortening of this year's spring break.

"My good man," I reasoned with one parent who called the office, "shortening spring break can save you a bundle, as well as help your kid get an education."

"I don't care about that!" he stormed. "Have you forgotten what it's like to have the kids out of the house for a whole week? It's worth every penny of the cost. It's my favorite week of the year. And now the school board wants to ruin it for me."

Spring break usually begins at most teenagers' homes with the announcement, "We're going to Atlantic Beach this year, if it's all right. And Mother, would you make another pound cake and one of your wonderful chicken casseroles to take down."

(We always drew the pound cake-chicken casserole chore when assignments were passed out — never the Fritos and Girl Scout cookies some parents got away with.)

In the freshman, sophomore and junior years, you ask about chaperones.

"Oh, yes, we have a chaperone."

"Who is she?"

"Oh, she's a friend of Jan's aunt who lives at Morehead City. Her husband operates a shrimp boat off Ocracoke. Mom, you know how you love shrimp."

Or "Chaperone? Oh, yes. You know Miss Dixley who teaches science at Broughton? Well, her sister is willing to chaperone us if we will let her bring a friend. You know how you've always liked Miss Dixley, Mom."

You don't dare ask the sex of Miss Dixley's friend.

I usually got stuck with the job of travel agent, finding a beachfront castle that rented at peasant prices.

One year I procrastinated.

"There are only two places left," I apologized to my daughter, after I had called a rental agency. "One is a nice house up the beach toward Salter Path — four bedrooms, three baths and right on the ocean. The only other thing available is a dinky little cinderblock place two blocks behind the police station. But it has only two bedrooms and one bath."

"We'll take the cute little house behind the police station," my daughter said instantly.

"You must be kidding! Nine girls in two bedrooms? And only one bath? The big place with four bedrooms and three baths is only $50 more."

"We'll take the cute little place behind the police station, Daddy," she said firmly. "Would you mind reserving it first thing tomorrow?"

"But why?" I pleaded.

I learned why later. Down around Bert's and the causeway, that's where the boys were. That was where the action was.

In a high school senior's mind, being marooned up the beach with eight other girls, chicken casserole and a bag of Fritos is like being sent to a nunnery. It's the kind of thing that can destroy a girl's destiny.

So, in the end, they went to the cute little house two blocks from the police station. Half of them slept on the floor. All of them froze to death during the coldest spring break on record. But they learned bladder control that should last them a lifetime.

The next spring, on a weekend trip to the beach, I drove my wife to the cute little house behind the police station to find the favorite casserole dish my daughter had left behind.

I walked up the steps of the cottage where a bevy of wide-eyed, anxious-looking teenagers perched about the porch.

A harried-looking woman rushed out the front door and blurted, "Oh, you're from the police department. Thank God!"

"No, I'm from Raleigh, and I've come for the casserole dish."

The wife of a Greenville attorney, the woman was chaperoning a group of junior high girls whose boyfriends were staying nearby. But for the past 24 hours, a band of local roughnecks had encamped outside the cottage, beating up on the Greenville lads every time they tried to make contact with the girls.

As my wife searched the kitchen cabinets for her casserole dish, which she found intact with remains of chicken cemented to its sides, she had some good, straightforward advice for the poor chaperone: "Pack up and go back to Greenville. At once!"

Spring break is no sweat for parents of boys, who generally prey upon the hospitality of the girls.

Like the lilies of the field, the boys neither toil nor spin. They forage for food. They sleep in dumpsters. They go to the girls' parties and trash the cottages the girls' fathers have rented.

A friend of mine recalls with horror her daughter's junior-year spring break.

"Would you believe the real estate agency billed us $154 each for damages? There must have been 300 girls in that house. I figured from the size of the bill that the whole place had been demolished and only the pilings left standing. The best I can remember, they charged $30 per yard to replace the carpet.

"Beware the Ides of March," warned Caesar's soothsayers. But I say unto you 20th century parents of high school and college girls, beware the rites of spring break!

*March 5, 1988*

# How Long Is a Little While?

A survey by the Hilton Hotels chain has found that 60 percent of Americans come to work Monday morning more exhausted than when they left Friday afternoon.

I have a solution to this disturbing phenomenon: Skip Monday. Don't go to work. I tried that last week. The results were more than satisfactory.

At the beach, Monday is a very special day during which nothing happens. The sun comes up. The waves roll and slosh against the shore. The sun shines. Or it rains. Pure ecstasy!

On Monday, many husbands have gone back to Raleigh and Durham and Chapel Hill and the places in between. And Mom is left with the children, the sunburn and the sibling fights. At least Monday is not wash day at the beach.

At our place, two boys, about 9 or 10, splash aimlessly in the pool. They have done the beach, built their sand castles and watched the tide sweep them out to sea.

They are tired of teasing sand crabs and bobbing in the surf. Now they are bored, bored, and bored.

"Hey, Mom, when can we go to the water slide?" one calls up to his mother on a balcony four floors up. We cannot hear her answer.

"What did you say?" he shouts. "Can we go after breakfast?

"Did you say 'In a little while?' Do you mean in a little while after breakfast or just in a little while? Hey, Mom. How long is a little while?"

Out on the boardwalk leading to the beach, a father and two little girls trudge past the bench where we sit, enjoying the breeze and the ocean.

The dad is talking to the older child, about 7. The 5-year-old tags along behind, sulking, dragging her inflated fish and carrying her sand bucket.

She stops in front of us, stamps her little feet and screams angrily, "Daddy!"

"Ah," I murmur to my wife. "We are witnessing a revolution."

The father turns. "What do you want, Amy?"

"I LOVE you, Daddy," she says, and runs to catch up, dragging her fish.

In the surf, another father is trying to entertain his little girl.

"Woof! Woof!" he barks, thrashing among the waves like the Loch Ness monster. The child shrieks with fear and excitement.

Long ago, I did the same thing with my own children. Ours was the time of the movie "Jaws," and I would swim under the water and seize the victims' legs and yell "JAWS!" There would be great shrieks, much splashing and happy laughter.

I am glad the young father does not know that as time goes by, his little girl will not shriek with laughter as often or as easily as she does now. It will take much more than a "Woof! Woof!" in the waves to elicit such cries of delight.

At about the same time, my friend Glenn Keever advertised his son's sports car for sale. He is a lot like me. Every time a client came to call, he would start downgrading the car by telling every thing that had gone wrong with it, even though he had replaced several defective parts, a bad paint job and put in a new carburetor.

"The insurance on this car is terrible," Glenn told the father of the 17-year-old boy who sat in the driver's seat, fondling the gear shift and salivating over the colorful upholstery and the gadget-studded dash.

"Dad, please!" the boy said, in much the same way my friend's own son William had said "Dad, please!" when against better judgment he had bought him the car two years earlier.

"It's not very good on gas, either," Glenn added while the father kicked the tires.

"Dad, it's all I ever wanted!" the boy wailed from inside the car.

We both sold our cars for considerably less than advertised because we hoped our price cuts would cover potential problems to the new owners.

Someone told me long ago never to look back when you sell a car.

"When people buy a used car, they should know they're buying future trouble," he said. "That's why they don't pay new car prices."

He was right. But a few weeks later I called the man who bought the Honda.

" Would you believe it, the motor blew up the week after I bought it," he said sadly. His grandson had never driven it.

Instead of saying, "Oh, gee, that's too bad," and forgetting about it, I got on the phone trying to find a mechanic who would put in a salvaged motor he had a line on. And before the day was out, I had promised to send a check to help with the unexpected expense.

I wonder. Are used car salesmen's dreams ever visited by The Ghost of Car Sales Past?

Does some spirit appear, drag the salesman from his bed and lead him through the pouring rain at midnight out to the Raleigh Beltline where the little old widow to whom he sold the overpriced, "good as new" 1978 clunker only last week is stranded, frightened and alone because the car's transmission has fallen out?

Probably not. Used car merchants can't guarantee that every car they sell will last forever, any more than I could mine. That's why they must keep some things to themselves. Why shouldn't they sleep the sleep of the untroubled?

Maybe that's why you don't find Diogenes hanging out at many used car lots.

*January 13, 1989*

# Wedding Band in the Men's Room

I came to work one morning and found the following message on my computer screen:

"Anyone lose a men's wedding band? I found one in 2nd floor men's room, sitting on a wash basin next to a recently used bar of Ivory. It is of rather cheap quality and appears to have been well-worn (as opposed to worn well). I am accepting offers."

I wondered about the ring. Was this just an absent-minded husband who had wandered off without the symbol of his lifetime commitment? Or was it someone literally washing his hands of a burned-out marriage?

The latter seemed entirely possible since a recent survey has found that 75 percent of all American first marriages will end in divorce. Three fourths! And that doesn't include all the young people who are living together but haven't bothered to get certified.

Used wedding bands are common stock in today's pawnshop. Before starting this column, I stopped by after lunch at the local pawnbrokers' where two full trays of second-hand bands were in display.

The lady behind the counter told me I could borrow up to $25 on the band of 14 karat gold I have worn night and day for almost 31 years. It is not for sale.

Like the flag, the wedding band is only a symbol of what two people want and expect from each other. Some bands are worth nothing. Others are beyond price.

Some men lose their rings via the divorce route. Some lose them down the shower drain. Others while fishing or golfing or water-skiing. My friend Mac MacGrew is the only man I know who lost his in a dog fight.

Last week, almost on the very eve of his 33rd wedding anniversary, Mac was ambling around in his yard when a huge dog bounded across the lawn toward him. Thinking his master was in danger, Mac's little cocker, normally shy and retiring, came charging out like a lion and tackled the enemy front on.'

The little dog was about to be eaten alive when Mac waded into the fray. While separating the snarling animals, he lost his wedding band. Some marriages endure all kinds of conditions.

The absence of old-fashioned romance may account for some of the fragility of the marriage vows.

In an Ann Landers column, a woman is complaining about her finance smoking in bed. "Several cigarettes a night," she says. "On occasion I have seen him fall asleep with a burning cigarette in his hand," she says.

A couple of decades ago, a reader would ask with alarm, "What gives here? What is the fiance doing in bed with the fiancee before the wedding?"

There was a time when in North Carolina, such carryings on would earn you 30 days in jail or a trip out of town on a rail.

But financees sleeping with fiances is socially accepted these days. A couple of years ago I ran into a young fellow who was about to be married to the pretty girl he'd been living with for some time. I inquired about his honeymoon plans.

"Honeymoon?" he said, grinning at me in a condescending way. "What does one do on the honeymoon that one hasn't done before?"

In a recent TV commercial, a lovely bride is being embraced by her handsome groom at the end of the wedding ceremony. Friends gather around. Rice is being thrown.

You know what the commercial is about? Jock itch! The ad is promoting a product used to quell the irritation of jock itch! Can you imagine? Athlete's foot, perhaps. But not jock itch! Not on the honeymoon!

When I was a young fellow and read Ernest Hemingway's "For Whom the Bell Tolls" for the first time, I kept going back to the scene in which Robert Jordan and Maria, caught up in the Spanish civil war, have a sexual encounter when she sneaks into his sleeping bag.

Unlike today's writers, who can strew all kinds of steamy descriptions throughout their work, Hemingway was restricted by time and custom. And was the better writer for it.

" . . . I felt I wanted to die when I am loving thee," says Jordan."

"Oh," she said. "I die each time. Do you not die?"

"No. Almost. But did thee feel the earth move?"

And later on, she wants to know if it had been thus with other women he has slept with. Had the earth moved then?

"Nay. Truly never," he says. And we have no way of knowing if he lies or not.

With the horrendous strike-out rate among marriages, it may be that for many couples, the earth doesn't move any more. Or it never did. Or that too many married couples expect a 10 on the Richter scale instead of settling for a slight tremor.

*June 29, 1989*

# Mama's in the Bathtub With Daddy

One of the most amusing and also irritating commercials I've heard lately is the one in which the guy calls his telephone company and a flaky-sounding operator answers in a high pitched, nasal voice, "Megaphone Company. We're bigger than the world!"

The fellow wants to talk about his account and the girl asks for the first letter of his last name.

"Thank you," she whines. "I will switch you to the person in charge of the A's." And then he is put on hold, listening to canned music, until finally an operator comes on and says, "Sorry, all the operators in charge of the A's are busy." And he then gets another dial tone.

This kind of foolishness isn't unusual. It's a part of our daily lives. The wonderful invention that Alexander Graham Bell brought forth with his "Mr. Watson, come here, I want you" is about to self-destruct through bureaucratic red tape and gimmickry.

At our house, we have only three phones. We don't even have one in a bathroom. We don't even have "Call Waiting."

I get a collect call from my daughter at college. We are in the midst of resolving crises of mammoth proportions — What happened to last week's allowance? How did she do on the mid-semester exam in J-54?

Suddenly, she says, "Just a minute, Daddy" and disappears into the never-never land known as "Call Waiting." No coed I know is going to miss a call from a guy in order to converse with her father about anything.

Equally infuriating is calling a public service for information and being told by a recording to punch in numbers for the information you need.

Recently, Cablevision of Raleigh signed me up for a new level of service that I neither needed, asked for nor wanted, but nevertheless must pay for.

The letter bringing me this good news said I might or might not need to add an adapter to my TV to get the new channels. I dialed and dialed before I got an unbusy number that turned out to be Cablevision's recorded hotline.

"If you know the three digit number of the message you wish to hear, punch it in at this time," the recording advised. "For listing of the information available, punch in 1, 3 or 9."

Not knowing what I wanted to hear, I chose the number 9 at random and punched. And waited. Until I got a dial tone again. I tried again. The line was busy.

What I really wanted to know was did I have to pick up a converter in order to get the new service I didn't ask for but would be paying for. When, by dialing another number I found in the telephone directory, I finally got a human being, she advised me that yes, I would need an adapter. I could come by the office and pick one up.

"Who will put it on the TV?"

"You," she said. "It comes with instructions."

"Ma'am," I protested, "my wife says that on a good day I can put in two light bulbs. There is no way I am going to install a converter on anything."

Then there is the business of "We are not at home at the moment — at the sound of the tone, please leave your name and number."

That takes some getting used to. Carol Dykers, a friend who raises beef cattle over in Chatham County, has a message taker on her phone.

I fully expect to call her some day and hear something like this:

"Sorry we can't come to the phone. We are down at the South Pasture. The neighbor's bull has broken into our heifer herd and is going to town! We've got to get him out before he impregnates the whole lot."

You may not know about things like that. But Carol, who said this actually happened one night recently, tells me that young heifers shouldn't be bred until they are a certain age. She is presently chewing her nails, hoping the wayward bull has not messed up her heifers.

"Well, all you can do is pray," I said. "Because President George Bush sure ain't gonna let your heifers have a bunch of abortions."

Having to listen to canned music while you are kept waiting doesn't do much to soothe the savage breast within us either. Usually, it is a song you neither know nor like.

I even heard recently of a man who, calling a mortuary about arrangements for a friend's funeral, was put on hold to the strains of "Hawaiian Love Song."

Telephones are dangerous weapons in the hands of the young, from toddlers on up to teenagers. Teens have been known to run up astronomical telephone bills by talking to friends long distance or dialing those recordings of sexy-sounding women talking dirty stuff.

Years ago, a friend of mine threatened to have his phone taken out after someone called his house and his toddler son answered the phone.

When the caller asked to speak to the boy's father, the youngster said, "Daddy's in the bathtub."

"Well can I speak to your mother?"

"No, Mommy's in the bathtub with daddy."

Ah, yes, there are times when I think that if Mr. Watson had replied, "Mr. Bell, I can't hear a word you're saying," we might all be better off today.

*November 10, 1988*

# Passing Grade on Parenting

I thought about the report card that the nation's children have issued to parents as I set out on my evening walk.

Almost nightly, I set out through the neighborhood on a boring expedition past the same driveways, the same lawns, the same monotonous but painful hills and the same assortment of dogs who feel duty-bound to bark as I walk by.

Joyful jogging, or walking, requires, at least for me, a stimulating conversationalist as company, or, if not, the sound of an ocean to walk to, or purple hills in the distance for serenity.

On rainy days, my longtime friend Herb O'Keef walks in his house, round and round, down the hall, turn left through the living room, out through the dining room, left again into the kitchen and back around, again and again. A Beethoven nut, he walks to the symphonies. Beethoven's Ninth is the equivalent of 1.2 miles.

But back to the report card.

Our children, in a recent poll of 1,000 of them across the country, gave us a better than passing grade on parenting. They graded us higher than we graded ourselves in a Roper poll a few years ago.

I was not contacted during the Roper poll. It's just as well. Instead of wringing my hands and wailing "What did I do wrong?" when the kids mess up, my first impulse is to wonder with irritation, "How could they have done such a stupid thing?"

This is the typical fatherly reaction, as opposed to mothers, who are quick to don the sackcloth of guilt for their children's disasters.

When I mentioned the survey to the fathers I lunch with at the Capital Room, one immediately responded, "We should have gotten an A. We've given them everything they've asked for."

But let us not rest on our laurels. In the poll, our youngsters say we can do better. For example, we don't give them enough independence. I thought of independence one night recently when the telephone by my bed rang at midnight.

Imagine the terrible tragedies that parade across a parent's imagination when he picks up the phone and hears only strangled sobs. But the words that were trying desperately to push past tears finally came rushing out: "Oh, Daddy, at the mall today, I saw a little black poodle just like Gracie. . . . "

It is an "independent" child's long-delayed, pent-up grief over the months-ago death of the family's poodle, grief finally overflowing over the long miles to parents who are there to understand and say the right thing.

And what about the father who called me at work last week to check the spelling of a tennis player by the name of Hana Mandlikova? Much to the chagrin of the young turks in the newsroom, I'd never heard of Hana Mandlikova. I am not into tennis.

"Why on earth do you need to know that?" I asked.

"Oh," he said somewhat abashedly, "I'm typing a research paper for my daughter in graduate school. And I am checking her spelling. I'm supposed to have it finished and in the mail today."

Yes, kids want more independence. But not too much.

America's youngsters also said life at home would be better if they could be treated more like adults.

"I remember one time I tried to treat my son like an adult," a veteran father told me. "I asked him to take out the garbage. He went into orbit. Said he was swamped with homework. And when I insisted, he threatened to call the Civil Liberties Union about his right not to take out garbage being violated."

The polled youths complained that parents don't spend enough time with them.

"To do that," said one of my friends, "I'd have to chase him down, tackle him and tie him to the bedpost. Or I could just sit up every night until he came in at 2'clock."

Parents are constantly being graded by their offspring. On an out-of-town trip it's always a pleasant surprise to open your suitcase and find a love note tucked in your pajamas. And when they go away, back to college or on spring break, you sometimes pull down the covers at night and find under your pillow a message telling you that on a scale of 1 to 10, you're a 10. In moments like these, you tend to think it's all worthwhile, this parenting that never ends.

These billets doux are like priceless pearls to mothers who sigh over them and file them away in a drawer to be re-read on some darker day when they feel rejected and are convinced that they have once again flunked parenting.

The fact that some of those notes — as well as the occasional brief letters of endearment from college — come when allowances have been trifled away or a big weekend is coming up is purely coincidental.

Poll or no poll, parents still know how to appreciate an A. It can make that walk around the block a little more tolerable. But when will the poll come out on grades parents give their children for their performance in the classroom of life?

*March 21, 1987*

# Burning Flags and Apple Pie

A few of the neighbors were standing around in the street last weekend and someone asked, "What are you going to do on the Fourth?"

"Why, I'm going to burn an apple pie," one of the women said.

"On purpose?"

"Of course. Apple pie is the third element of Americans' 'flag, motherhood and apple pie.' I figure if I burn an apple pie I will get my name in the papers and be on the Today Show. I may eventually be interviewed by Barbara Walters."

For someone who usually burns only beans, this was an audacious statement. But then flag burning is an audacious issue.

I found that to be true that same morning when I called my mother-in-law long distance. My timing was poor. She had just been stopped by a police officer. The full works — screaming sirens and flashing blue lights. Fortunately, she wasn't frisked. Or beaten.

"Since I knew I hadn't done anything wrong, I wondered who the victim was going to be this time," she said. "And then I noticed he was motioning me to pull over. I pulled into a service station, got out and walked back to the police car and said, 'Officer, please tell me what I have done wrong.'

"He was so young. I could tell this was his first attack. He had an older officer with him who never opened his mouth.

"You know what my crime was? I had absent-mindedly pasted my January renewal sticker on the left-hand side of the license plate instead of the right. Just think. It took them six months to catch me!

"And I said to him, 'Officer, with all the things that I know and you know going on in this town, do you mean to say you would stop a lady, scare her half to death and issue a citation for something like this?' "

"Well, it would never have happened if you'd been driving with the American flag draped around you or flying from your radio antenna," I said.

"Stop that foolishness," she snapped. "I don't believe in flag burning any more than you do."

She's right. Neither of us believes in flag burning. But neither do I believe that the sky is truly falling because some jerk in Dallas, Texas, once upon a time burned a flag as a gesture of protest against the government.

When I think of how our flag has been humiliated in other ways, burning it almost seems like the lesser evil.

I have seen it dragged through mud, sewn into the backs of filthy jackets or stamped on faded t-shirts. I have seen it drooping sadly from residential flagpoles in the pouring rain. On TV I once saw a couple at a stock car race sleeping under the American flag in a field near the speedway.

Today, I share with you the true, deep feeling of Dr. Cooper Smith, a Gaffney, S.C., flag lover who wrote to The Charlotte Observer following the outcry over the Supreme Court ruling:

"I knew the pledge to the flag before I knew the Lord's Prayer or the Shorter Catechism of the Presbyterian Church.

"I've pledged my allegiance to it a thousand times in segregated two-room schools — sometimes after being spat upon by white students riding by in buses as I walked to school.

"I've 'snapped to' with pride when the flag passed in review at a half dozen military bases from Camp Kilmer to Fort Sam Houston.

"More than once I've taken it down at sunset from its proud pole on a cold, windy hill near Inchon, Korea, folding it into a triangle under strict orders never to let it touch the ground.

"I've helped amputees stand trembling from wheelchairs to salute it.

"I saw it drape my father's and two brothers' coffins, veterans of World Wars I and II and Korea. And when I die — even if no one sends a single rose or a dime for cancer, which I'm likely to die of — I fully expect Old Glory to grace my bier.

"There then is no alienation between the flag and me. We've had a long and rich relationship. I would not burn it and wish others wouldn't. Yet I think the recent Supreme Court decision on flag burning is right."

I do, too. Because if we amend the Constitution to prevent some misguided malcontent from burning a flag, the next thing we know we will amend the Constitution to keep someone from shooting an eagle.

And close behind will be an amendment that says I can't write what I have written today. Or, even more fearful, that my mother-in-law can't talk back to a cop whose flashing lights and screaming siren have left her trembling hours later just because she accidentally pasted her January renewal sticker on the wrong end of her license plate.

Yeah, I still get misty-eyed when Old Glory flaps in the breeze during certain moments of my life, such as when they play the "Star Spangled Banner" after we have beaten out the Soviets for an Olympic gold or when I think of Francis Scott Key looking through the fire and smoke of battle and seeing our flag still fluttering there over Fort McHenry those many years ago.

But what my flag means to me has to do with me, not with how someone else regards or treats it. And no Constitutional amendment can change that.

*July 7, 1989*

# A Bird and Pee Wee Reese

I found it incredible that two birds had no more sense than to mate and build a nest in February amid a five-inch spring snow. But as we all know, passion passeth all understanding.

My niece Jo Lynn had called to say that she had found two birdlings, one dead, on her lawn and had been trying to spoon milk into the beak of the survivor.

"The worst thing possible," I, the bird watcher, advised. "It must have worms."

I could not, though, imagine anyone in the role of surrogate parent, munching earthworms and regurgitating them for the infant bird. Compassion, unlike passion, does have its limits.

"The experts say put the bird back where you found it," I continued. "If a cat doesn't get there first, the parents may come along and take care of it far better than we humans can." We agreed that since it was already dark, she should keep the bird overnight and put it out next morning.

It's true that tragedy has no game plan. But it could not have lucked upon a better yard on which to deposit its tiny victims. My niece is one of those who all her life has been cursed with compassion.

I remembered the bird incident a day or so later as I read of a senseless tragedy at a rural Missouri school. A 12-year-old boy, taunted for years by his classmates for being fat, pulled a gun, shot one of his tormentors to death and then turned the gun on himself.

"Everybody always teased him, he was overweight," said one of the seventh graders. "Nobody had anything against him. He was just someone to pick on," added another.

There are two needless victims here. In the summing up, I am not sure but what I feel more compassion for the fat little boy who, day in day out, had to dread and endure the relentless torment of his classmates before finally being pushed over the brink.

Tell me. How do you teach compassion? Or can you? Is it inborn? Taught by example? I'm not sure.

But to this day, I remember a dreary day in my own first-grade experience when, as a shy youngster from the rural foothills, I raised my hand to go to the bathroom and the spinster teacher, unwise in the ways of nature and little boys, said no.

"You must wait until recess," she said, firmly. "You must break your habit."

Within a few moments, the error of her ways was evident in a torrent under my desk. And at recess, the entire class suffered the consequence of her poor judgment as I moved over to the steam radiator to dry out. It was a bitterly cold winter's day, but windows were quickly opened.

I doubt I would have survived that humiliating experience without lasting scars were it not for Mary Lou Woodridge. The prettiest and most popular girl in the class, Mary Lou walked over and murmured sympathetically, "Miss Hinshaw should have let you go."

Her courageous display of compassion quieted my classmates' giggling and quelled the otherwise inevitable storm of teasing before it ever got started.

Dr. Albert Edwards once told a true anecdote about Jackie Robinson's 1947 debut as the first black baseball player in the major leagues. As Robinson stepped up to bat for the first time, the Cincinnati stadium swelled with boos. Robinson stood with bowed head until his Brooklyn Dodgers teammate, the popular Pee Wee Reese, stepped to the plate and laid his arm across Robinson's shoulders. The boos were stilled, never to be heard again. And Robinson was voted Rookie of the Year.

Several years ago, my younger daughter, competing in an Optimist Club speaking contest, had reached the semifinal round. We warned her that the competition was tough and that she should be prepared to lose.

Upon being declared the winner, the youngster impulsively blurted, "Before I left home, Mama said I probably wouldn't win. But I guess I showed her."

On the way home, she was very silent for a winner. Her face was clouded with sadness. Realizing her embarrassment over her inopportune remark, I tried to reassure her.

"Oh, it's not that," Katherine said tearfully. "I just keep thinking about the girl who was runner-up. Her parents were there and her grandparents and her brothers and sisters and her teacher. I'm really thrilled about winning. But I keep thinking that maybe she needed to win more than I did."

I drove home silently grateful for this spark of understanding and compassion in my child, at the same time sadly aware of what her sensitivity to hurt and pain in others would cost her all her life.

The baby bird died within a few hours. "I suppose it is just as well," my niece said. "I don't know how I could have brought myself to set it out to fend for itself anyway."

On Wednesday in Missouri, two grieving families went to the cemetery and said goodbye to two 12-year-old boys, who died because somehow we have not yet learned how to teach our children that basic tenet of civilization, "Do unto others as you would have them do unto you."

*March 7, 1987*

# Coach Woody Hayes' Funeral

I have never envied the minister faced with the task of preaching Coach Woody Hayes' funeral. Or mine either, for that matter.

While many of us were following the NCAA basketball road to New Orleans, the Ohio State University football coach died mercifully in his sleep. His going was much more peaceful than his living.

I had often wondered how the sports media that helped create the legend of Woody Hayes would handle this exit from life. I was not surprised. Even during prime time basketball they sent the "great" coach away to that football stadium in the sky in fine style, dwelling upon his devotion to discipline, his exacting demands upon the young men who played for him and his impact on the game of football.

Not much was said about the dark side of Mr. Hayes' character, although one network treated us to film clips revealing his uncontrollable anger and violent nature. His contorted face, his foot-stomping, leaping into the air, lashing out with arms and fists, shouted oaths and threats suggested the mannerisms of a madman more than the "father figure" role former players accorded him.

I still wonder how many young sons this "father" psychologically scarred with his brutal disciplining before hundreds of thousands on those autumn Saturdays.

Perhaps Mark Antony's approach to funerals was right when he said, "I come to bury Caesar, not to praise him." But that is rarely the case today — and never the case at the Baptist funerals of my foothills childhood. Funerals were to praise the dearly departed. The burying was only a secondary essential.

Everybody back home had a "Southern funeral" like the one described in Lois Holt's fine poem, "Southern Style."

*I want a wreath put on the door and*
*neighbors to bring food in.*
*old friends to stand over me crying*
*and carrying on*
*like I was once of their own,*
*saying, "Lord, don't she look good.*
*I want "Precious Memories"*
*and "When the Roll is Called up Yonder."*
*When I die — if indeed I do.*
*don't throw my ashes off the nearest bridge*
*or fling them into a summer breeze or*
*winter wind to settle on some unplowed plot,*
*God only knows where.*
*I want a proper funeral — Southern style.*

In funerals, Southern style, nobody was ever dispatched in disgrace, no matter how barren the life he lived. Mr. Milo Crinshaw was considered the meanest man in our county. He was a poor provider, drank too much, had a profane mouth, intimidated his children and beat his wife regularly. About the only complimentary thing I had ever heard about Mr. Milo was, "He's good to his dogs."

At the funeral, the Baptist minister struggled so diligently to present the late Mr. Milo in the best light possible without lying outright, that I was fully prepared to hear him blurt out, "And he was good to his dogs."

So gifted was the minister in his art that by the time he was half through the funeral, I was sure his poor wife was ready to whisper to one of the younguns, "Tommy, go up there and see if that's your Pa in the casket."

When it comes to propriety, the Episcopalians have it all over the Baptists. They don't editorialize.

At the funeral several years ago of one of the influential women in my life, however, I longed for a Baptist farewell for her. For once, the Episcopalian service was too democratic, too impersonal. It said nothing about this wise, witty and unpretentious doctor's wife who scorned the country club and the bridge table for service to mankind.

I wanted the minister to tell how she had single handedly browbeaten an insensitive town council into oiling the streets and installing water and sewer lines in the town's dusty ghetto. Or how she secretly provided money and encouragement for black children to go to college.

Or how in the spring twilight, she would take her chair to the edge of my woods and sit there patiently, her good ear turned to catch the silver notes of the wood thrush calling from the shadows.

If Shakespeare was right and the evil that men do does live after them while the good is interred with their bones, then it's quite possible I have offended the memory of Woody Hayes, whose good, to me, was obscured by his violent nature. But Shakespeare can be wrong, you know. Why can't the good live after us and the evil be interred with our bones? That's the noble purpose of Southern funerals.

*March 28, 1987*

# Counting Robins and Sex at Sea

At breakfast, through the windows, we see the sun rise "a ribbon at a time." The red-bellied woodpecker drums his mating call on the gutter.

Red-breasted robins dart jerkily across the lawn, their feet sensitive to the stirring of awakening worms just beneath the earth's thawing crust. My brother-in-law in the foothills reports five bluebirds in the back yard.

Despite February's vicious blows, something tells me spring is waiting in the wings and that it is time to clean out not only the ugly debris of winter's despondency from my mind, but also the clutter from my right hand desk drawer.

I have saved from The New Yorker this quip, in a review of a new movie: "He's the kind of actor John Wayne would have been if he'd been an actor." Somehow, this translates for me into "President Reagan is the kind of president he is because he was the kind of actor he was."

The drawer contains a scrap of envelope on which I had scribbled a bumper sticker spotted on my way to work one morning. Gracing the back of a pickup truck driven by a burly, sandy-haired fellow, it read: "I am a virgin. This is a very odd bumper sticker."

Indeed. But no more odd than the Bible Belt sticker the Rev. Rick Brand saw not long ago: "Tithe if you love Jesus. Anybody can honk."

Here is a yellowing copy of a speech by Ben Bagdikian, the Ralph Nader of journalism, who reminds us of our privileges and responsibilities as journalists. Sometimes in the past, I have underscored a paragraph that seems to fit these times when many see the media as a pack of wolves howling outside the embattled White House.

"I think we have retrogressed in the sense that too many public officials believe that informing the public of the most important acts of their government is meddling. But this country was founded on the principles that the multitude have a right and license to meddle with their government. If we restrict the right and license, to that degree we diminish democracy."

I clipped this item from The Charlotte Observer last summer when I was in the market for a new lawn mower. At that time, I was leaning toward a Honda, having been attracted by one of the few TV commercials I have paid attention to.

In the commercial, the voice says, "In Alamance County, North Carolina, Honda lawn mowers are assembled from the wheels up."

And then the camera moves in close on Clara Johnson, the plant inspector, who is about to test the mower for a quick, easy start. After all, what kind of a man would buy his wife a lawn mower that she'd have trouble cranking?

"If Clara pulls it and it starts, it's a Honda," says the announcer. Clara pulls and it starts. (I'm waiting for the day when things don't work as promised on commercials.)

Like most newsmen in hot pursuit of truth,, the Observer writer checked out the commercial. Yes, Virginia, there is a Honda plant in Alamance. But Clara Johnson is no plant inspector. She's a California actress. I bought a Toro.

As you know, dear readers, we do not publish unsigned letters to the editor. That policy, necessary though it is, deprives you of some of the most original and colorful writing of the day.

Near the bottom of my drawer I have come upon this 14-month-old opinion from one of our subscribers commenting on an editorial called "Sex in space."

"Sir, you were awfully naive in your recent editorial about sex in space. First off, hundreds of thousands of people in the military do not go without sex for any length of time. Normal, healthy people just do not.

"There were homosexual relationships going on all around me at sea. The same is true in other services, on college campuses and other areas of life. Psychologists know this if you don't. And sex has to be allowed for normal, healthy people.

"People who have psychiatric problems, major or moderate, might be able to abstain for longer periods than three months due to their illness, but average, everyday people cannot and do not.

"Why is it that for a supposedly liberal paper, you pen so many Moral Majority type editorials? With them, it's hypocrisy. But you hurt people with your ostrich-like position. You are unrealistic as to what people can live up to."

There is more, since the drawer seems bottomless. But what better place to stop, go home and count the robins?

*February 28, 1987*

# A Wedding at Ballard's Bridge

It was a long way to go for a wedding in winter. But these were special people. The groom's dad had come down from the mountains on a hot August day 28 years ago to comfort and sustain me through my own last hours of bachelorhood and get me to the church on time.

His mother and I had been friends even longer, since I was a city hall reporter in Burlington and Eva was public health educator there.

In fact, on our way home from our honeymoon we had stopped by the boy's home for a couple of days and, as she occasionally recalls, my wife had hung the little fellow's diapers on the line.

And when Eddie was a student at State and returning home from the holidays, he never failed to bring me a bushel of juicy, Winesap apples and a couple of loaves of his mother's mouth-watering yeast bread all the way from Andrews, a hundred miles west of Asheville.

I had estimated it would take over four hours to drive from Chapel Hill, where we were attending a newspaper meeting, to the wedding at Ballards Bridge Baptist Church between Elizabeth City and Edenton.

"Oh, let's not leave so early," insisted my wife, who will be the last one on the bus when it leaves for Eternity. She gambles with time. To a newspaperman who has lived most of his life by deadlines, being late to anything is the eighth deadly sin.

"We need to allow 30 minutes for getting lost," I argued. "And besides, if I am going to drive that far to a wedding,, I don't want to go down the aisle just behind the bride."

We drove steadily, arriving 20 minutes before kick-off time.

Sitting there in the lovely 204-year-old church, with sunlight streaming through the stained windows, I listened to the wind crooning a duet with the organ's soft serenade to love. Such serenity.

My thoughts wandered first, sadly, to my good friend, the boy's father, who had been cut down by a heart attack three years ago. And then, anxiously, to my wife. Surely she wouldn't mention that she had changed the groom's diapers to anyone at the reception.

Following the wedding, I watched though the church windows as the young people went about desecrating the couple's car. At least they were half-way compassionate — no live crickets turned loose in the car. No obscenities on the windshield.

"Where are they going on their honeymoon?"

"I don't know. All Eddie would say is, 'Loose lips sink ships.'"

"Oh, a cruise, huh?"

"No, man. That just means he ain't tellin'."

Eddie and Rebecca posed briefly beside their stricken car, the door open, ready to get in and ride away. Suddenly, like a scene out of a wild west movie, a car roared into the churchyard and came to a quick stop. Bride and groom jumped in and were swiftly spirited away, leaving behind an astonished and highly irritated group of friends. Foiled again! Mountainboys aren't dumb.

After the reception, we drove across the benign countryside toward the little town of Edenton where we had made reservations at a bed and breakfast place.

The wind was still high, kicking up little whirlwinds of dust on the tabletop of rich farmland dotted with spacious old two-story homes, many of them pleading for paint and attention. Driving across the flat expanse of land meeting sky, I, born to the rolling terrain of the foothills, felt an uneasy, haunting loneliness within me.

We chuckled over a sign standing in the middle of a field: "We should be taxed on what we earn, not what we own."

After checking into the handsomely restored and beautifully decorated 86-year-old inn, we enjoyed tea and crumpets by a warm fire in the parlor while our personable hostess shared interesting details of her own and the house's life. And we learned we were the only guests for the weekend.

Before we went out to dinner, she came to us and said, "My husband and I will be leaving shortly for our home up on the river. But we'll be back in the morning to fix your breakfast."

"You mean we're going to be here in this big house all alone? And are we supposed to lock up?"

"Oh, I meant to tell you. Don't lock the doors. You'll be all right. This is the Lord's house."

That night, before I climbed into the big canopied bed in the huge bay-windowed bedroom, I locked the bedroom door.

"This may be the Lord's house," I said to my wife, "but not everybody out there knows that. Besides, I don't think the Lord minds me helping Him look after His place a little bit by locking our bedroom door."

We drove back to Raleigh the next day, refreshed by the winter weekend away from the madding crowd. In it we had found the much-needed promise of spring: the renewed faith in life that wedding brings, courageous crocuses in bloom in an old churchyard.

And a quiet but firm lesson in faith that gently reproaches me every night as I lock and bar the doors of my home.

*February 14, 1987*

# Prayer Before the Kick-Off

MARS HILL — It had been a long time since I attended a football game opened with prayer. I have always had the sneaking suspicion that God doesn't suit up for football, with all else He has to attend to in this crazy, mixed-up universe.

But prayer preceding the opening kick-off seemed not out of place in this setting. As the student's carefully chosen words fell across the hushed crowd, I stole a glance at the mountains, looming darkly in the night, riding the ocean of sky like hump-backed whales. A far cry from Raleigh, I thought.

When the man, his small son in tow, arrived and asked me to move over a bit, the cheerleaders were leading the fans in a yell called "Messy Bunch! Messy Bunch!" that I never quite understood. And the Lions, ranked No. 2 in the country, were three points behind.

The guy beside me asked how it happened. "A field goal after a 15-yard penalty for unsportsmanlike conduct against the Lions," I said.

"That's a damn waste!" he exploded. "A guy oughta be benched for that!" He was a Mars Hill grad of the '60s, a basketball star. He had married during his senior year.

"Talk about poor. Her dad gave us a country ham once. We were so poor we couldn't even buy bread to go with it."

It was Parents' Day on the 1,000-student campus nestled in the curve of mountains 19 miles north of Asheville. Here, where I went to school in another age, my daughter is now a student.

On this "Christian" campus, there seems to be an absence of the fundamental extremism sweeping the country, only a calm, happy, matter-of-fact acceptance and mutual respect among students and faculty. The campus, the customs, the rules have all changed since my sojourn here after the war. But the almost incredible caring hasn't.

The Bible-spouting ministerial students of my day apparently are no more. Male and female now sit together in church, hold hands on campus. Everybody knows everybody else and speaks. The president's wife moves about the campus, as charming and effervescent as any vivacious coed.

Like many private colleges, this one can use some fresh paint here and there and new springs and mattresses in the dorm rooms. But it is in the black, and that says something about the quality of recruiting.

In the afternoon, in the sunny parlor of Huffman Dormitory, I sit on the couch watching the last half of the Clemson-Georgia game on TV. My daughter brings me the remains of a tattered, time-worn scrapbook she has found on a shelf in the kitchen. It is the diary of the life of the dorm that opened in 1947 when I was here.

I try to match the signatures of the dorm's first occupants with the once-familiar faces in a yellowing photograph on the opposite page. How have time and fate treated these eager young women who 39 years ago came, apprehensive and homesick, to the hills and made this place a cornerstone of their lives?

A father and his son are lugging a love seat past me toward his daughter's room just as the TV game is about to be decided by a field goal.

"Set it down, son" orders the father. The two drop the couch and stand transfixed as the boy boots the football. The field goal is good. The Clemson men dance a little jig in front of the TV, pick up the couch and head happily up the stairs.

I return to the scrapbook and a fading newspaper account of Old Joe, a college trustee's slave who was jailed for three days in 1856 as a kind of escrow until the trustees got together $1,875 still owed on the first building.

When I was a journalism student at Carolina, the Winston-Salem Journal paid me $10 for a feature I wrote about Old Joe, whose grave and stone are high on a hill behind the president's house.

From my hotel window in Asheville next morning, I can see My Old Kentucky Home, the aging, peeling boarding house that was home to Tom Wolfe, North Carolina's most famous author.

While my wife packs, I walk up the street and spend a few quiet moments in Eliza Gant's dining room. There amid the Gant ghosts, I imagine the noisy chatter of the boarders, wolfing down their dollar-a-day meals.

Every boy or girl who has gone home again to an old, rambling Victorian house can easily identify with Tom Wolfe's words: "I was a child here; here the stairs, and here was darkness; this was I, and here is Time."

We drove to the Grove Park Inn for breakfast, meeting Dot and Ed Preston, our daughter Melinda and their son Joe who is also a student here.

Ed chuckled as he pointed out a headline on the Asheville Citizen-Times' sports page: Christ School Edges Christ Episcopal.

"I'll bet the good Lord had a hard time deciding that one," he said.

The headline only reinforced my thesis that God doesn't suit up for football. But as I looked out the dining room window into the fog rising over the eternal hills, I was convinced that He is partial to this part of the country. There is too much majesty and serenity here not to believe that.

*September 27, 1986*

# 'The Neighborhood Boy'

Early this fall, a West Raleigh couple hired a commercial lawn firm to aerate and reseed their lawn.

Three weeks later, as the couple stood on the porch admiring the lovely new grass, the husband remarked, "Now we'll have to find us a neighborhood boy to come mow it and rake the leaves."

"Have you lost your mind?" the wife wondered. "You're really out of touch with reality. Surely you know that there is no neighborhood boy any more. They have quit making them."

How sadly true. The neighborhood yard boy is no more. I long for a neighborhood boy like the one I had in the yesteryears, an engaging lad by the name of Ed Gainor, reliable, hardworking, appreciative. He looked as if he had walked right off a Norman Rockwell Saturday Evening Post cover. But alas, he grew up and is now principal of a Raleigh school.

Dave Jones and I were lamenting the loss of the neighborhood boy only this week, as we faced the annual autumn ritual of leaf raking. Both our lawns are dominated by huge, lusty old oaks that already are shedding cascades of leaves and raining down those fat, pesky acorns.

Neither of us has any hope of hiring neighborhood boys to bail us out. One year, when his wife wasn't looking, Dave let his leaves lie until spring when he engaged a trio of young men to help move the thick mass of wet, half-rotten foliage.

"I went into the house to get some drinks and when I came back the young men had roared away in their pick-up truck, not even bothering to collect for the hour they had worked," Dave remembered.

Neighborhood boys are harder to recruit than All-America quarterbacks at Carolina. Last summer, I spotted a young fellow leaning on a shovel by a small pile of dirt in a North Raleigh yard. I pulled over and asked if he were for hire. He was. At $7.50 an hour. And leaning.

Recently a likely looking lad selling grapefruit came to our door.

"Are you ever available for yard work?" I asked tentatively, as my wife wrote the check.

"Oh no," he said quickly. "I have band practice on Saturdays."

I've always been a loner when it comes to leaves. When my daughters were growing up, I could never find a leaf rake that fitted their sensitive hands. They meant well, but after 10 minutes of leaf raking, they would be stricken with excruciating headaches, prolonged spasms of coughing or severe low back pain. Apparently, my oaks were highly toxic.

Not long ago, the eldest, home on a visit, looked out the window at the falling leaves and sighed nostalgically, "Daddy, remember the time we helped you rake the leaves?"

Ah yes, I remember. But I did not realize until now what a traumatic, scarring experience that one day's brief exposure to manual labor must have been for my children. I apologize.

Do you wonder where the neighborhood boy has gone? I can tell you. He's going door-to-door selling cheese spread, pecan rolls and Christmas wrapping paper for the PTA. Or grapefruit for the band's trip to Switzerland or some such place.

He is far too busy and programmed for other things to become the neighborhood boy.

I have nothing against these kids. I admire their spunk and their willingness to aid their schools. But they and their parents are victims of the shameful system that puts children on the streets peddling junk food to purchase school supplies and equipment our state and local taxes should be buying.

And, ah, the irony. You can meet a neighbor's kid walking home from school and say, "Hi there, Tommy," and Tommy will look right through you without speaking. He's been taught to beware of "strangers" for fear of being molested or kidnapped.

Yet our schools — and some parents — have no reservations about sending these youngsters out to ring strangers' doorbells at night, trying to coax them into buying candy and popcorn and wrapping paper they don't really want..

I have just about had it with these PTA sale-athons. At this moment the residents of our street have bought enough cheese spread to constipate an elephant. Unless my wife, a girl who just can't say no, beats me to the door, we are not buying any more cheese spread or pecan logs. Instead, I plan to offer a check made out to the school PTA. Sure, I'll be knocking the candy company and the middle-man promo firm out of their 60 percent cut of the sales. But so what?

Please, no more candy, or magazine subscriptions or cheese spread, or any of the stuff most of us neither need nor want. Why not instead organize small work parties of kids who will go from house to house offering to do odd jobs, such as leaf-raking or wood stacking? For pay.

They will be welcomed with open arms. What they earn for their school won't have to be shared with anybody. And we homeowners will no longer mourn the long-absent neighborhood boy.

*November 19, 1988*

# Heartbreak and Hallelujah Time

September again.

For many of you, September's song is sadder than usual. Many of you are undergoing that first-time experience of a son or daughter gone away to college.

The house is stiller. In the lonely room that once vibrated with amplified sound, the silence is now deafening. There is one less load to launder, one less egg to fry.

For many of you, this is both heartache and hallelujah time. One moment you feel "Free at last!"

You have brought your birdling to the edge of the nest and it has fluttered away on uncertain wings. The next moment, you feel your life has been drained of drive and purpose.

You still sleep with one ear straining for the crunch of tires on the driveway, the click of the key in the lock. You always will, but not as desperately as you do now.

Believe me. The hurt becomes quite bearable. Many of you will suddenly turn around and say hello again to a husband or wife you've been too busy to notice for the past 18 years.

You'll rediscover each other. And feel guilty for enjoying again the togetherness you thought was gone forever.

My Carolina daughter and her friends are back from Nantucket, the Massachusetts island where the young go in summer to get rich waiting tables and cleaning bathrooms. It was, as we skeptical parents now admit, "a learning experience."

Here is a child who always had trouble getting her plate from the dining room table to the dishwasher, serving from the left and removing from the right at a high-class restaurant called Raffles, a place where 10 hours on your feet can on a good night earn tips up to $150.

Susan Duerson, whose daughter Beth also signed on for the Nantucket summer called me one night to gloat:

"When my Beth left home she didn't know a fitted sheet from the shroud of Turin. Now I want you to know she has been promoted to assistant head chambermaid in the most exclusive hotel on Nantucket."

You would have thought her child had been named Sweetheart of Sigma Chi or first vice president of NCNB's Texas division.

During a brief break from table waiting and the mop detail, the Nantucket girls had a whirlwind weekend in New York.

As we all know, the first visit to Gotham is an Alice-in-Wonderland trip through the looking glass. The cast of characters is the same, including the White Rabbit and the Mad Hatter. Only the costumes and the dialects have been changed.

Our daughter called late one night from New York, having just arrived in the pouring rain after a rough flight from Boston to Newark and a bus ride across the river to Grand Central Station.

Outside the station, the Nantucket trio was approached by a big, fast-talking fellow with a black umbrella who asked if they needed a taxi.

They did, to the Omni Hotel, a few blocks away.

"Well, get your money ready. The fare will be $7.50 per person," he said as he handed the girls his battered umbrella and rushed off to whistle for a taxi.

As the cab pulled over to the curb, the "Good Samaritan" collected $7.50 from two of the girls and $20 from my daughter who had no smaller bills. The man then just sauntered off through the crowd with their money, leaving the victims standing stunned and forlorn under a leaking umbrella.

"Daddy, I worked awfully hard for that $20," my daughter wailed into the hotel lobby telephone.

"That's one of the cheapest lessons you'll ever get for $20," I soothed. "Remember two things: Never pay for the product until it's delivered, and don't trust anybody in New York."

"Why you sound like our cab driver — the one we finally got," Katherine said. "He told us, 'It's a good thing I came along. Another five minutes and you girls would have given that thief your VISA card and written him a personal check to boot.'" The accidental tourist then described the harrowing ride to the hotel:

"We must have been going 70 miles an hour, missing cars and people by just inches. A poor man in a wheelchair was trying desperately to cross the street and our cabbie actually tried to run him down. I thought the guy was a goner.

"But somehow we missed him. Our driver just laughed like a wild man. He glanced back at the guy and shaking his fist, he yelled, 'I'll get you the next time, you so and so!'"

But the trio did all the wonderful things that kids do their first time in New York after they have waited tables and made beds and cleaned commodes for nine long weeks.

They had breakfast at Tiffany's. Lunch at Tavern on the Green. My daughter saw her first Broadway show: "M. Butterfly."

And now it's September, a time of new beginnings. The things they did last summer, they'll remember all winter long, perhaps for the rest of their lives.

But another word to those parents who serve and wait: The nest may be empty now but the birdlings are never far out of range.

Soon the telephone will ring and someone's daughter will say, "Guess what, Mom. I met the greatest guy in my psychology class. His name is Don, I think. Anyway, he's taking me to the game Saturday."

Or someone's son will call: "Hey, Dad, you won't believe this, but that stupid bank has screwed up its records and says I'm overdrawn. Could you maybe spare a . . . "

*September 3, 1988*

# About Death and Dancing

The four of us sat in a back booth at the Mecca, out of the way of the biting cold that slipped in every time the front door opened. Over clam chowder and pecan pie we relaxed, chuckling over the latest antics of our unpredictable children. Parents might as well laugh as cry. After all, as James Thurber wisely said, humor is emotional chaos remembered in tranquility.

Somebody's son had a speeding ticket coming up in court. Another's recently married son was soon shoving off for two weeks of tough endurance with Outward Bound. That's youth: taking a vacation from a honeymoon to rough it on the frozen slopes of Montana.

The news from our house had to do with the death of my daughter's one-year-old goldfish. I was still smarting from having been roused out of bed to go out and bury the thing during a freezing rain.

"What's wrong now?" I later asked my wife as she tossed restlessly in bed. She replied that we would have to re-bury the goldfish because "you know that metal box it's buried in is not biodegradable."

"We should have flushed it down the commode," I reasoned and went back to sleep.

As we were leaving the Mecca, the voice on the radio behind the cash register shifted into a new tone of intensity. Something was said about a "blackout." Then sentence by sentence, the terrible news of the Challenger's explosion after launch came tumbling out.

In the newspaper business, tragedy tends to become commonplace. It comes in not on little cat's feet, as Carl Sandburg said of fog. It comes on quiet, murmuring computers with little fanfare except the almost prissy tinkling of the bulletin bell on the printer in the corner of the newsroom. The news is read and reacted to quietly by people whose faces rarely reflect the inner emotion many feel. They edit the copy, write the headlines and re-make the front page as impassively as a mortician ministers to the body of a friend.

One tends to compare tragedy with tragedy. There was that black November Friday 22 years ago. Most of the staff had gone to lunch when the louder bulletin bell on the old Teletype machine clanged loudly, insistently. Like some human thing struggling vainly to communicate the horror, the Teletype clacked out the details in short bursts. At first a shooting along the president's parade route in Dallas, then that John F. Kennedy had been shot, and finally, that he was dead.

I was younger then, more vulnerable. So was our country, unprepared for tragedy of such gigantic proportion. The President murdered? Incredible! And not just any president, but the prince of Camelot. No wonder our hands trembled and we avoided each other's misting eyes as we worked over the type, getting out the special edition.

When my wife and I went out later that November afternoon, a shocked Raleigh talked in hushed tones about the national loss. But by nightfall the big question for many was whether the Duke-Carolina game would be played on schedule the next day or postponed.

This time was no different. A reporter who had heard the Challenger news on his car radio during a call-in show was astounded that the news was followed so swiftly by a caller asking, "Would you please repeat that pumpkin pie recipe for me?"

Someone else who had stopped at the Post Office was infuriated because a woman ahead of her in line had complained to the postal clerk that she was tired of hearing about "that explosion," and was disappointed that her afternoon "programs" had been canceled.

How long do we grieve? For a goldfish, a few moments perhaps, if the goldfish is lucky. For a friend or family member, perhaps forever. There are no good guidelines for grieving. As we leave the cemetery and return to the empty house, to the cakes and pies, the fried chicken and casseroles neighbors and friends have brought, what do we do next?

It is an awkward time, that time when the heart wants only to cry, whether it is for the forever gone parent, husband, wife or child or for a Christa McAuliffe whom we had adopted only a few weeks before. When do we start living again? Laughing again?

The answer may lie in a bumper sticker I read on a recent foggy morning as I pulled up behind a pickup truck at the Five Points stoplight. "Life's too short to dance with ugly women," it said.

Peering into the truck at the somewhat homely, rugged-looking trio, I concluded that if women felt the same way about ugly men, those guys won't be doing much dancing.

But the bumper sticker also said to me that life's too short to spend in endless grief. We have to pick up the pieces, get on with the pumpkin pie recipe and the dancing with ugly women. It's the only way a person or a nation can survive tragedy.

*February 8, 1986*

# Lead On, O Kinky Turtle

One of the things I enjoy on visits back to the foothills is the relaxed conversation, with its local color, the ebb and flow of words that is sort of hill-country poetry.

It is poetic to the point that you rarely want to correct it, even if you dared. For these are people who do not take kindly to criticism from outsiders — especially people from Raleigh.

But when I heard a relative refer to the discomfort she was experiencing because of her "hyena hernia," I felt obliged to intercede, even at the risk of offending.

"*Hiatal* hernia," I corrected.

"Oh, just listen to the family doctor," the victim remarked to another relative.

I explained that I hadn't meant to be critical, only helpful. We are all learners, I reminded her. I recalled that it was not until I was out of college that, thanks to a caring friend, I cleaned up my mispronunciation of "picture" as opposed to "pitcher."

There I was, a college grad, talking about hanging "pitchers" on the wall.

"I only mentioned hiatal because I didn't want you to be embarrassed in public," I explained to the afflicted Dorothy. "Someone hearing you refer to your 'hyena hernia,' might assume you've had an organ transplant from an animal."

It's uncanny how pronunciation suffers when, never having seen a word in print, we resort to word sounds that have been passed down to us, sometimes by previous generations.

I hate to think how our TV-addicted kids are going to talk years from now, having read little and listened a lot.

My mother-in-law says she grew up singing the familiar Methodist hymn, "Brighten the Corner Where You Are," all the while wondering why the bride was in the corner in the first place.

And quite a few of us sang, "Gladly the Cross I'd Bear," at a loss as to how a cross-eyed bear got involved with religion in the first place.

And surely I am not the only person who has a youngster who sang that old Christmas favorite, "Silent Night, Holy Night" wondering who "Round John Virgin" was.

A man down the hall tells me that throughout his childhood he sang the last line from a favorite hymn, "And take us all at last to Heaven" as "take a saw and last to Heaven."

Of course you would have to know that a "last" is a metal form shaped like a human foot on which a shoe is repaired.

And Bill Dupre, one of our editors, mentioned only this week that his

4-year-old came home from kindergarten distressed because her best friend was at home sick "with chicken pot pie."

In the American Scene section of a recent issue of Time, writer Gregory Jaynes, who admits he rarely went to church, recalled attending a service in a little Methodist church in the Blue Ridge mountains.

Jaynes and the rest of the congregation were somewhat startled when the minister announced from the pulpit, "Now let's turn to Page 508 in our hymnbook and sing 'Lead On, O Kinky Turtle.'"

The pastor blushed crimson, apologized and admitted the strange title for "Lead On, O King Eternal" had stuck in his mind because his own child called it that.

Jaynes said that over the years, "Lead On, O Kinky Turtle" has served as a kind of incantation. Whenever he feels frustrated, stifled and put upon by outside forces, he finds himself muttering, "Lead on, o kinky turtle," gritting his teeth and pushing his way past whatever obstacle he is confronting at the moment.

In the overall scheme of things, these are not serious crimes against the language. Instead, they provide a light touch to a difficult tongue that often seems without reasonable pattern.

All we need to do is welcome constructive criticism that helps us improve. I know that I am grateful for Grammie Robinson, the Burlington doctor's wife and true friend, who set me straight on "pitchers" and "pictures."

The last time I went back to the hills, I noticed the cousin who was afflicted with "hyena hernia" rarely brought up disease. This is partly because she has lost 24 pounds on a new diet and is not subject to as many attacks.

But, arching her eyebrows in my direction, she made a point of saying, "Since I have lost weight I am not having nearly as much trouble with my *hiatal* hernia."

Now if I can only muster the courage to approach a dear Raleigh friend who keeps raving about the "lovely African" that her sister in St. Louis sent her for Christmas.

*October 10, 1987*

# Free Advice From an Attorney

When I was younger, spring break was the time of year when my older brothers stayed out of school for a few days to plow the land that eventually would bring forth the crops that would feed and clothe us for a year.

For those young men, even a temporary respite from the drowsy drudgery of the classroom was a welcome one. There has always been something irresistible about the siren song of spring that revives us after a long, hard winter.

Back then, there was something exciting, almost sacred, in the ritual of the unfolding season: the plunging plow furrowing new life into the barren field, the clear high notes of the thrush from a dogwood-sprinkled woodland, a speculative crow cawing encouragement from the top of a lonesome pine, and the softer whisper of the river rushing past.

What was then a necessity for survival is now a national holiday for the young, an orgy of excess. It is so firmly entrenched in our school curriculum that well-meaning school boards meekly fold their tents in the face of kid-parent pressure and shut down school for a full week so students can go on cruises and beach parties.

As thousands of high school youngsters head out this weekend for the annual spring rite, we hope it's not too late to pass along some tips on how to survive high school spring break.

I take my text from a lecture that Ted Brown gave his daughter Lucy the night before she embarked for the beach a year or so ago.

Ted first had to dispose of the primary spring break issue that all father's face: "Dad, can I take the car?"

This question is usually resolved just after Mom has received her own assignment: two dozen chocolate brownies and a cheese-chicken casserole big enough to serve 20.

Next comes the matter of who is going to chaperone the girls.

Usually, it is someone from another planet vaguely identified as "Tommy Sue's second cousin from just outside Baltimore, Maryland."

She is exceptionally qualified because her step-father used to be a Methodist minister before he went to work for IBM.

"Yes, I'm going to let you take the car," Ted said. "But first nobody is going to drive the car but you. If you let a friend drive the car, he will in turn let a friend of his drive the car. Somebody will get picked up for speeding or driving drunk. And there goes the car. My car."

"Second: Beware the boys. They will come to your place for a visit. The first thing you know, they will be in your refrigerator and going through your food like a plague of locusts in a wheat field. Boys at the beach are the purest form of parasite. They have neither food nor a place to sleep."

"Third: "When the police knock on the door, as they surely will, you head out the back door as fast as you can and walk on the beach for an hour and a half."

Ted's daughter came back with new respect for her old man.

"Dad, how did you *know*? It all happened just like you said."

"One of the girls *did* let her boyfriend borrow her car. He *was* arrested for driving drunk and put in jail. And Susie had to call her parents, and they had to come down to get their car out of police custody."

"And the boys *did* eat almost everything we had in the house. They said they had just dropped by to say 'Hi,' but within 15 minutes they had cleaned out the fridge. And when I went back to the bedroom, one was taking a shower in our shower.

"Bad Dad, you were wrong about one thing."

"What's that?"

"When the police came, I went out the back door like you told me to do. I walked for an hour and a half on the beach. But when I got back the police were still there. I should have stayed gone two hours. They didn't charge me with anything. They just thought I was a casual visitor who had dropped by.

I could add a few pages to Ted's advice. So could most of you fathers.

One thing spring-break parents need to mention to their youngsters, especially their girls, is the necessity for putting gas and oil in the car and occasionally checking the tires.

I once had a call from Morehead City that went something like this:

"Daddy, I need money for a new tire."

"What happened?"

"Well, we were driving along U.S. 70 and a highway patrolman pulled us over. Scared us half to death! Thank goodness he only wanted to tell us we had a flat tire."

"Didn't you *know* you had a flat tire?"

"Not really. We had been hearing this awful flapping noise for some time, but we didn't pay much attention to it. And now we're at the Amoco station and the man is saying something about a rim being ruined. . . . Could I just put him on the phone?"

Good luck parents. When school board election comes around again you may want to back a candidate whose major campaign promise is "No spring break!"

*March 25, 1989*

# A Time When the Lilac Dies

In my mind, I keep seeing the little dog.

A small mixture of poodle and Pekinese who goes by the apt name of "Scuffy," she is just a fluff of a thing, and she lived only for my brother-in-law who died recently of a heart attack while on vacation.

Because nobody has found a way of telling the dog, she is wasting away waiting for her master to come home.

The funeral service in what would pass for the "little church in the wildwood" was typical of what you will find in most foothills farming communities.

Many of the friends and neighbors appeared in shirt sleeves, appropriate for a steamy, summer day. Through the windows, the sleepy sound of insects could be heard across the green fields of corn. The eternal mountains stretched blue in the distance.

While the choir sang "Amazing Grace," I reminisced over my years of association with this unusual man lying in the coffin at the front of the church.

I remember that he was probably the handsomest guy in the county when he first came courting my sister. But from the beginning, Leo marched to a different drummer.

A full-of-life extrovert, the boy in him burned brightly all his life. Perhaps that is why that, during my own boyhood, I was drawn to him.

Leo taught me nature's secrets: that the moss grew on the north side of the tree. Where to find the wild azalea. How to follow a honeybee through the woods to its hive and the rich lode of sweetness in a hollow tree. How to hold a crawdad without getting pinched.

When my daughter was 3, he piggy-backed her up Snow Creek to where the beaver built its dam, a trip she has never forgotten.

He always had a way with kids. Boy and girls alike, they came to him with broken bikes or broken hearts. He mended both, for he was gifted in that way. He offered time and understanding that many of these youngsters' parents were too busy or insensitive to provide.

His shortcomings—and he had his fair share—were magnified in the small community where everybody knows everybody else's business. It is a place where not going to church regularly and occasionally "taking a drank" rank as serious sins that can go a long way toward tarnishing a man's reputation.

But I think that in every man there is a sermon of some kind. My brother-in-law was not without his.

As for his church, I often think of four lines from Emily Dickinson, whom he never knew but whose work he would have appreciated had I taken time to point it out.

*Some keep the Sabbath going to church.*
*I keep it staying at home*
*With a bobolink for a chorister*
*And an orchard for a dome.*

Leo had a "live and let live" compact with God's creatures, leaving the windows and doors of his tool shop open so the wrens and robins could nest in its corners. Rabbits and squirrels played around his door.

On his path to the shop he had to duck his head to dodge a hornet's nest. "We have an agreement," he once told me. "If they won't bother me, I won't bother them."

On a later visit, I noticed the big, round papier-mache nest was missing.

"Those hornets got out of line," he explained. "For no reason at all, a couple of 'em took off after me one day. I burned them out that night."

The last time I visited him he told me about a new bird that had come to his yard.

"It's bound to be a nightingale," he said. "Prettiest sound I've ever heard out of a bird." He did not know that nightingales are not native to Surry County.

His nightingale was a wood thrush. Two grown men, together we traced its path to a low-growing sourwood tree where it had fashioned a nest in a wild grapevine that climbed the tree.

A few weeks later, he sent me a message: "The cat has eaten your bird."

When he heard I wanted to try to grow in Raleigh the lilac that flourishes so freely in the foothills, he begged one from a neighbor, rooted it and coaxed it through the winter and gave it to me. It survived for a year. Raleigh's summers are too abrasive for lilacs.

I can understand and accept the loss of the lilac, for I do not need the shrub to stir within me pleasant recollections of my departed friend. But it is different with the dog.

Every time a man comes to my sister's house, the little dog runs out to sniff his trousers' leg. Searching. Hoping. But she quickly turns and slinks away, her big, sad eyes brimming with the pain of longing.

The joy has gone out of her once sharp, teasing bark. The spirit is missing in the little body that once leaped and danced with joy when my brother-in-law appeared, whether after a brief trip down the road to the country store or an overnight fishing trip to the beach with his brothers.

How do you tell a dog that the person she loves most and lives for is never coming home again? How do you help her forget? How do you help her forget or realize that, yes, time will help, although never completely heal.

You can't explain to an animal that there always comes a summer when the lilac dies.

*September 12, 1987*

# An Encounter With Miss Brill

We arrived at our destination late and when we went in for dinner, the hotel dining room was almost empty. So I don't know why the hostess seated my wife within such easy earshot of the man and woman at the next table.

Dog-tired and bone-weary, neither of us was in a mood for conversation. But we made heroic attempts at small talk so as not to eavesdrop. Still, glancing words and phrases from the next table punctuated our pauses, teasing our imaginations.

He looked a little older than she, but handsome enough with thin, graying hair, a patrician face. She was slight, small-boned and soft-voiced, almost but not quite mousy. She reminded me of Katherine Mansfield's classic Miss Brill.

I fancied they were old friends, having a dinner rendezvous after a long separation. Her husband had died, apparently within the year. And, among other things, the man was advising her on how to get on with her life, how to cope with her loneliness.

They spoke of lawnmowers and lawns, subjects for friends, not lovers.

"I've mowed my lawn one time, just to see how long it takes," he said. "It took five hours. So I contract the job. I tell 'em it's a five-hour job andI'll pay for five hours' work. They can take as long as they want. But it's a five-hour job."

"My lawn is a two-hour job," she said simply, almost wistfully.

The waiter came with our prime rib. By the time he had refilled the water glasses and poured the coffee, the conversation at the next table had become more personal.

"Did you know Charlie's retired?" "Yeah, he's 65. I'm only 60. But I had planned to retire early and take some nice long trips, see the country. Then I developed this prostate problem and my doctor told me I couldn't sit in a car all day and drive. So I've given up the idea of traveling for the time being."

As the waiter brought our dessert, the man at the next table shifted in his chair. "We can go somewhere else or just sit here and talk," he said. They had long since finished their dinner.

"Oh, this is fine," said my Miss Brill, folding her napkin methodically. After a long silence, she said sadly, "You know I feel that my whole life has amounted to absolutely nothing."

There was total resignation and regret in her voice. And I wondered if the death of her husband alone had robbed her of life's purpose or if her spirit had been crushed years ago, perhaps by some childhood experience, or maybe her marriage or perhaps the all too common difficulty of shifting her life to fit the modern model of assertive womanhood.

After all, Miss Brill, who had had so little, was happy enough until the day when a chance encounter with cruelty snuffed out the light in the safe, separate little world she had created for herself.

A spinster with little income and no real friends, Miss Brill went to the park every Sunday afternoon to hear the band, wearing her "dear little fur" about her neck. She liked to eavesdrop on the people around her, creating imaginary lives for them.

Today she was especially thrilled when a young couple came over and sat nearby.

"The hero and the heroine, of course. Just arrived from his father's yacht," she fantasized to herself in Miss Mansfield's story.

The boy pressed the girl to him. "No, not here. Not here I can't!" she had hissed.

"But why? Because of that stupid old thing at the end there? . . . Why doesn't she keep her silly old mug at home?"

"It's her fu-fur which is so funny," giggled the girl. "It's exactly like a fried whiting."

On the way home, Miss Brill usually stopped at the bakery for a slice of honey-cake. Sometimes there was an almond in her slice. It made a difference. And she could hardly wait to get home to make tea.

"But today she passed the baker's by, climbed the stairs, went into the little dark room — her room like a cupboard — and sat down on her bed. The box that the fur came out of was on the bed." Miss Brill laid the poor little fur inside.

" . . . But when she put the lid on, she thought she heard something crying."

Wherever you go, you'll find Miss Brill, alone, as fragile as blown glass, vulnerable to the world's careless, cruel hurts. Be kind to her.

*October 31, 1987*